W9-BPS-492

May 9, 1938

Dear Captain Duvan,

Thank you so much

for the lovely bouquet of

flowers you gave me.

Love,

Chief Shirley Temple.

series edited and designed by Ian Cameron

ALLAN DWAN

the last pioneer

PETER BOGDANOVICH

PRAEGER

BOOKS THAT MATTER

Published in the United States of America in 1971
by Praeger Publishers, Inc.
111 Fourth Avenue, New York, N.Y. 10003

Library of Congress Catalog Card Number:
70-129772

Produced by November Books Limited for
Movie Magazine Limited, London

Printed in Great Britain

Acknowledgements:
My thanks go to Mae Woods, who transcribed
the interview, compiled the filmography and typed
the manuscript; to Polly Platt, who helped in the
editing of the interview; to Timothy J. Lyons, for
his research into Dwan's earliest films; 20th
Century-Fox, for running all their Dwan productions; Joseph Small, for enabling me to see the
pictures Dwan directed for Edward Small Productions; David Shepard and James R. Silke of
the American Film Institute, William K. Everson,
Don Malkames, and Maurice Cohen for arranging
to screen several rare Dwans; and Lee Atwell of
the National Film Catalog for supplying information on Dwan's films of the 'twenties. Many of
the stills appear through the courtesy of Milton
Luboviski, owner of the Larry Edmunds Bookshop
in Hollywood, the respository of thousands of
priceless movie books and memorabilia; other
photos came through the kindness, again, of
Mr Small and Mr Silke, and of Mary Loos,
Clark Wilkinson, Ernest Kirkpatrick of National
Telefilm Associates, Frank Roderiguez of 20th
Century-Fox, David Chierichetti, and Allan
Dwan, whose patience, cooperation, and general
good cheer in the preparation of this book can
never be properly acknowledged.   P.B.

A Louis B. Mayer American Oral History
Project prepared under the direction of
The American Film Institute.

For my Mother

CONTENTS

The Last Pioneer

INTRODUCTION

There will never again be a movie career like Allan Dwan's. Over fifty years, he directed at least 400 pictures, and produced, wrote or supervised as many more. Film history being the mess it is, his exact total is not likely to be known, but certainly two-thirds of that opus – almost the whole silent period – is virtually lost forever. The few examples that remain from those more carefree times make it clear that the years before 1929 – when he had the most independence – were his most creative, valuable and successful.

This is not necessarily to diminish his talkies, but after the coming of sound the assignments were so often unworthy of him and the restrictions such that it is amazing he was able to produce as many good films as he did. Through it all, his professionalism, humour and enjoyment in the actual job of picture-making never lessened. The movies have been his vocation, and he has been true to that calling.

To follow Dwan's career is to watch the evolution of an art. He came into pictures in 1909, less than a year after Griffith made his first film. Sixteen months later, he was directing. *Three Million Dollars* (1911), shot in his fifth month as a director (and already close to his fortieth one-reeler), reflects the primitive beginnings. The technique is still not much different from Edwin S. Porter's *The Great Train Robbery* (1903): the camera records the entire action of each scene from one set-up – usually a medium long-shot – without cutting it up. Though the pacing of actors is pretty fast (they are generally natural, too), and the locations all look real, Dwan obviously had not yet been exposed to Griffith's work, by which he admits being profoundly influenced.

A year and a half – and almost two hundred shorts – later, *Calamity Anne's Trust* (1913) reveals that impact. The camera is much closer to the action now, there is cutting within scenes, greater flexibility, the compositions are no longer merely functional, and the acting has some charm. While the film remains of purely historical interest, the speed of Dwan's development is significant; it would be invaluable to see the scores of films that followed in those mercurial first years. We know he continued to experiment – making from Gray's 'Elegy' a film (*The Restless Spirit*, 1913) with twenty-five dissolves – unheard of at that time – sharpening his craft, discovering one super-star (Lon Chaney), guiding another (Marguerite Clark) at the start of her career and bringing into

6

the movies such talents as Marshall Neilan, Victor Fleming, Wallace Reid and the Rosson boys – Harold, Arthur and Richard. For *David Harum* (1915), released the same month as *The Birth of a Nation*, Dwan invented the dolly shot – trucking the camera in front of (and later behind) the title character as he walks the main street of his small country town. The material is stagebound, but Dwan gives it as much air as he can, with some lovely pastoral photography of a completely unselfconscious kind – one of Dwan's trademarks throughout his career. (Worth noting is the frequency with which Dwan went to actual locations – something many silent directors did – contrary to the popular notion that the current trend towards location shooting is something new.)

Since he had been educated as an engineer and helped to develop several devices in lighting and electronics, it isn't surprising that a primary characteristic of Dwan is his ability to solve technical problems. When presented with an insurmountable technical puzzle in making *Intolerance* (1916), it was to Dwan that Griffith went for help. There seemed to be nothing he couldn't figure out – how in 1915 to shoot two people in a moving 'plane, or how in 1917 to give an impression of sumptuous sets with only lighting, or how in 1921 to create lightning without a special effects department, or how in 1929 to dolly with a microphone when everyone said you couldn't. This particular talent of his is also reflected in the common sense of his attitudes, his down-to-earth nature and ability to deal with even the most discouraging material. He is a practical man.

In 1916, having directed Lillian Gish, Mary Pickford, and Dorothy Gish in some successful vehicles, Dwan began a relationship with Douglas Fairbanks that was to produce eleven pictures, among them some of the best work of either man. *Manhattan Madness*, made that first year – and already their fourth together – is a good example, and also the earliest Dwan film I've seen that needs no excuses today. Fast paced (and not only because of the rapid cutting), cleverly written, even boisterously witty in its look at western and eastern life-styles (a cowboy comes to New York to sell his cattle), it is evocatively photographed on location in the city, features unusual and impressive lighting and confirms beyond question that by this time Dwan already had complete mastery of his medium. Fairbanks's open all-American nature and boyish athleticism were particularly well matched with Dwan's similar temperament; both also had a prankish sense of humour. Their early collaborations need to be revived (they are known to exist), because it is more than likely that *The Habit of Happiness, The*

Still: Lillian Gish in An Innocent Magdalene, *a Dwan film from 1916.*

Photograph: Dwan in the mid-'twenties.

Good Bad Man, The Half-Breed (all 1916), *A Modern Musketeer* (1917), *Mr. Fix-It, Bound in Morocco* and *He Comes Up Smiling* (all 1918) are among Dwan's most important movies.

Certainly *Robin Hood* (1922) is. Having directed Norma Talmadge and Erich von Stroheim in *Panthea* (1917) to great critical praise, guided Marion Davies through two of her earliest vehicles and filmed a rousing version of Richard Harding Davis's *Soldiers of Fortune* (1919) together with ten other features, Dwan joined Fairbanks again for what was to become (at a million dollars) the most expensive movie made to that time, featuring a giant castle that was also the largest set ever built. When *Robin Hood* opened in New York, it was the height of Fairbanks's popularity and Robert E. Sherwood wrote (in the Herald): 'It represents the high-water mark of film production – the farthest step that the silent drama has ever taken along the high road to art.' And 'Photoplay' said: 'Director Allan Dwan must be given great credit for his masterly handling . . . The spectacle is his triumph.'

In Dwan's own estimate, it has remained that; you sense that he agrees with Kevin Brownlow who wrote (in 'The Parade's Gone By . . . '), 'Nobody connected with it ever achieved anything quite like it again.' Dwan has only two framed photographs hanging in his home – both are from *Robin Hood*. Without question it is his most elaborate and physically impressive work – the recreation of the period is vivid, imaginative, often awe-inspiring – there is much grace and high spirits, but the film is nonetheless weighted down at times by its very size, and both Dwan and Fairbanks seem occasionally held back from their customary exuberance. Still, it is in every way a beautiful picture, a splendid work of silent moviemaking at its best.

The following year (1923), Dwan made *Big Brother*, a small-scale human interest story that was very popular and which he numbers among his best; it has disappeared. At the same time, he began an association with Gloria Swanson, one of the silent screen's greatest actresses, which resulted in eight films, several of them among her most successful. Most are inaccessible, but if *Manhandled* (1924) is any indication of their quality, we are missing a lot. Among Dwan's personal favourites, it is a comedy-romance with a superb Swanson performance as a poor New York working girl who has a fling with three high-society men before ending up happily with her inventor boyfriend. Filmed with great authenticity on actual locations, the picture has an ingratiating and bubbly charm that is irresistible.

With two exceptions, the rest of Dwan's silent career remains a question mark. Continuing as a respected and well-publicised filmmaker, he brought Marie Dressler back to pictures (*The Joy Girl*, 1927), directed such top stars as Jack Holt, Rod La Rocque, Bebe Daniels, Ricardo Cortez, George O'Brien, William Powell, Madge Bellamy, Thomas Meighan, Lois Moran, Neil Hamilton, Renée Adorée, was one of the first to try colour (*Stage Struck*, 1925), night photography with available light (*Night Life in New York*, 1925) and sound (a 1927 newsreel). *East Side, West Side* (1927), a bread-and-butter picture from those days, is a sprightly if unremarkable rags-to-riches story with some fine New York photography. But Dwan closed the silent era with great flair directing Douglas Fairbanks's last really successful movie, *The Iron Mask* (1929), an exceedingly likable swashbuckler, and certainly the liveliest of Fairbanks's later costume pictures. Its romanticism and innocent buoyancy went out of style with the arrival of sound, and Dwan's vigorous direction gives those better days a grand exit. He himself feels that the art of the movies as a uniquely visual form of expression died when the talkies took over.

Nevertheless, though he was never to achieve the freedom or success he had in the 'twenties, Dwan swept into the sound era without breaking his stride; besides *The Iron Mask*, four of his films (part- and all-talking) were released in 1929. Unhappy with the new 'gimmick', he still couldn't resist experimenting with it right away, and in 1930 was reunited with Gloria Swanson to direct one of her few successful talkies (*What a Widow!*). *Man to Man*, made the same year, is a weakly acted, static potboiler, but he followed it in rapid succession with three modest pictures, each in its way remarkable. *Wicked* (1931) has a pretty far-fetched and not uncomplicated plot, but Dwan with his usual quick pace and economy of gesture manages to cram what it would take most directors an hour and a half to tell into a tightly-packed 55 minutes. A man attempts a

robbery, is caught in the act and chased home, where he shoots it out and is killed; his pregnant wife, dazed, comes out with her gun in her hand, is arrested for shielding a fugitive and sentenced to several years in prison – all that happens in the first reel! There are some memorably disturbing scenes in a women's prison and only the picture's tacked-on happy ending prevents it from being a minor classic in the genre.

In *Chances* (1931), Dwan comes full circle and directs Doug Fairbanks's son (Doug, Jr.) in an effective World War I drama, distinguished by a fine sense of British atmosphere and several gripping battle sequences, most of them shot at night. But *While Paris Sleeps* (1932) is probably his best early talkie, and is one of his most interesting films. Taking another improbable plot (a condemned Frenchman escapes to Paris to see his daughter and ends up sacrificing himself for her), Dwan turns it into an expressive, moody vision of life among the down-and-out in Paris, evoked with the skill of a master silent director – for, though a talkie, it has much more of the silent touch than any film he was to make. Among its curious and striking aspects is its gloomy, dank and shadowy atmosphere, so similar to the films Marcel Carné made with Jean Gabin (*Quai des Brumes*, etc.) much later in the 'thirties. And, of course, Dwan's was shot not in Paris, but on the Fox lot.

Dwan went to England for a couple of years, made three pictures that have not been seen since, and came back to Hollywood in 1934 to find himself forgotten. The town had changed in his absence. After a tacky patch-job on MGM's all-star disaster, *Hollywood Party* (1934), Dwan got his foot back in the door with a little shipboard comedy-romance he wrote and directed called *Black Sheep* (1935). Even at its most familiar, the film retains an air of freshness, and is played with snappy charm by Edmund Lowe, Claire Trevor, and Eugene Pallette (whom Dwan had started out in pictures twenty years before as a slim heavy).

Unhappily, *Black Sheep* was to be his last satisfying movie for three years. Having signed with Fox and been relegated to their B-unit, he was assigned a series of scripts that would have made a lesser man throw in the towel. Somehow, Dwan managed to keep himself going through a period including weak ladies'-magazine fiction (*Navy Wife*, 1935), a grim backstage musical (*Song and Dance Man*, 1936), mawkish social melodrama (*One Mile from Heaven, That I May Live*, both 1937), relentlessly silly romantic comedy (*Woman-Wise*, 1937; *Josette*, 1938), routine crime melodrama (*High Tension, 15 Maiden Lane, Human Cargo*, all 1936) – these last are by far the best of the lot, even likable, because of Dwan's light and energetic handling – and, finally, Shirley Temple (*Heidi*, 1937; *Rebecca of Sunnybrook Farm*, 1938).

His direction of the first Temple picture is notable for its often wryly tongue-in-cheek treatment of the material – a Dwan attitude that was to be applied on several equally outrageous projects in later years. Even at the film's most tearful moments, you have the feeling that Dwan is sending Heidi up. Little Shirley loses her pants and gets butted so often that Dwan's intentions must have been less than chivalrous; the treatment is often quite funny, and makes tolerable what would otherwise be a cloying and syrupy vehicle. (The second Temple movie has not this redeeming feature, though it, too, is nothing if not unpretentious.)

The two Temples were a success and Dwan was rewarded with his first big budget in the sound era (something he was only to receive one other time). Fox assigned him to *Suez* (1938), a strongly fictionalised version of Ferdinand de Lesseps's adventures in building the Suez Canal. A spectacular typhoon sequence and the recreation of the physical construction of the passageway outweighs the personal story, but it is nonetheless an engrossing, and

entertaining period piece, among Dwan's most respectable pictures.

Finishing out the decade with three movies, Dwan did an amusing if deeply frivolous musical take-off on *The Three Musketeers* (1939), featuring Don Ameche as D'Artagnan and the not very palatable Ritz Brothers comedy team; Dwan managed to make them better than they had ever been (or were again), but could do nothing to salvage their next vehicle, to which he was also assigned (*The Gorilla*, 1939). His last thirties picture and first sound western, *Frontier Marshal* (1939), is tough and to-the-point. Loosely based on the same material from which John Ford made *My Darling Clementine* (1946), it is interesting to compare the two; if Ford's is poetry, Dwan's is good prose.

The Fox contract ended with three indifferent comedy assignments (*Sailor's Lady, Young People*, both 1940; *Rise and Shine*, 1941); his only outside film of 1940 is by far the best: *Trail of the Vigilantes* was originally planned by Universal as a straight drama, but Dwan saw its inherent ridiculousness – no doubt Franchot Tone, Broderick Crawford and Andy Devine as the unlikely trio of good guys, with assistance from Mischa Auer, gave him further incentive – and turned it into a deadpan comedy western that is fast and funny.

After three mild comedies starring various radio personalities and a talky adaptation of a World War I play (*Friendly Enemies*, 1942), Dwan began to hit his stride again with a series of four breathless farces, all starring Dennis O'Keefe. *Up in Mabel's Room* (1944) and *Getting Gertie's Garter* (1945) were both vintage stage hits that had been filmed in the 'twenties, but Dwan and his cast brought new life to them with hilarious business, wild dream sequences and an unflagging pace. In essence both have the same plot (in one, O'Keefe is trying to conceal from his wife a slip he bought a former girlfriend; in the other, it's a garter), but they

Photograph: Dwan and Annabella on Suez.

are different enough to make delightful companion pieces, featuring many of the same actors. The first half of *Getting Gertie's Garter* has more uproarious Dwan bits than the whole of *Up in Mabel's Room*, but the second half drops slightly, so that as a sustained work, *Up in Mabel's Room* has the edge. *Abroad with Two Yanks* (1944), in which O'Keefe and William Bendix spend half the film in drag, never achieves the level of the other two, but the best of the group is *Brewster's Millions*

(1945), which had previously been filmed four times; in fact, the story is irresistible: a soldier, just back from the war, is told that a distant relative has left him seven million dollars – *if* he can spend an additional million and have nothing left to show for it before his 30th birthday – in two months! The reversal of all our frugal instincts – not 'that's too expensive', but 'that's too *cheap*' – makes for a marvellous comic situation, which Dwan embroiders and exploits brilliantly.

In 1945, Dwan signed a long-term contract with Republic, where he remained for eight years, turning out 14 pictures that ranged from an odd educational comedy (*The Inside Story*, 1948) to frothy, expendable little musicals (*Calendar Girl*, 1947; *I Dream of Jeanie*, 1952), uneven western melodramas starring those impossible Republic regulars, Vera Hruba Ralston and John Carroll (*Angel in Exile*, 1948; *Surrender*, 1950); and war films of widely differing quality from poor (*Flight Nurse*, 1954) to good (*The Wild Blue Yonder*, 1951) to what is certainly his most famous and expensive sound picture (and perhaps his best), *Sands of Iwo Jima* (1949). Between these poles were two memorable minor works: *Rendezvous with Annie* (1946) stars Eddie Albert in an ingratiating comedy about a soldier who goes AWOL for one night – returning from London to his New Jersey hometown without anyone but his wife knowing it – then nine months later, finds himself a father with nobody believing the baby is his. Though far-fetched, Dwan handles it all with great charm and conviction. *Driftwood* (1947) is an affectionate and touching little fable about an orphan girl and her effect on several people in a small town; sensitively directed, the acting of Walter Brennan, Dean Jagger, Natalie Wood and Charlotte Greenwood is exceptional.

Customarily, when the material struck him as ludicrous enough, Dwan resorted to his own

11

brand of subtle satire, which even the actors were rarely, if ever, aware of. One or two shots of open-mouthed Nelson Eddy singing jovially as he rides through *Northwest Outpost* (1947) are sufficient to destroy him forever, and the Joan Leslie–Audrey Totter confrontations in *Woman They Almost Lynched* (1953) are equally devastating. Consciously and only to amuse himself, Dwan was creating camp twenty years ahead of its time – which he did again in one of his last pictures, *The Restless Breed* (1957), a western made for what looks like a $100 budget, in which everyone in the entire film spends their time peeking at everybody else from behind walls, through windows and round corners. Appropriately, Dwan staged curtain calls for the cast which he shot through a window!

Even the director's most pedestrian project at Republic, however, is occasionally enlivened by his instinctive, relaxed camera style or sense of atmosphere. The musical numbers in a badly acted bit of fodder like *Sweethearts on Parade* (1953) impress with their flow and rhythm, and the dark, moody look of *Belle Le Grand* (1951) manages to steal the attention away from the hopeless posturing of Carroll and Ralston. The feeling persists that Dwan could effectively do *something* with anything.

Obviously, therefore, when presented with the challenge of *Sands of Iwo Jima*, Dwan comes fully alive, guiding John Wayne through one of his best performances (he was nominated for an Oscar for the first time). Very much a war film in the old style – patriotic, affirmative, stirring – it was made at a time when Americans still believed in the fight they had won. The story is almost ritualistic in the genre: a tough Marine sergeant takes a group of green and rebellious recruits through a rigorous training; their hate for him turns to respect and finally grows to love as they follow him into battle. There have been many imitations since – and this was not the first of its kind – but *Sands of*

Still: Natalie Wood and Walter Brennan in Driftwood.

Iwo Jima remains the most affecting and vigorous.

After leaving Republic, Dwan finished his last decade as a director (he retired at the end of the 'fifties) with six westerns, three exotic adventure stories, a war picture, a science-fiction film, and a couple of crime melodramas, all low-budget affairs. Only three, perhaps, have real merit, but most of them have their compensations. *Escape to Burma* (1955) has Barbara Stanwyck, Robert Ryan and little else, *Montana Belle* (1952) and *Cattle Queen of Montana* (1954) have Stanwyck and Jane Russell dominating what is properly a masculine genre, *Hold Back the Night* (1956) is a lightweight Korean War story; but while *Slightly Scarlet* (1956) is compromised James M. Cain and *Enchanted Island* (1958) compromised and miscast Melville, Dwan manages to provide some provocative passages: in the latter, a certain tragi-romantic mood is cast over the piece that could only come from Dwan – just as surely the source of the appropriately cheap, grimy atmosphere that pervades *Slightly Scarlet*.

On the other hand, two John Payne westerns, *Silver Lode* (1954) and *Tennessee's Partner* (1955), need no alibis. The first, though conventional in plot, is a nonetheless compelling genre movie – excitingly directed and well acted, especially by Dan Duryea as the heavy. The second is among Dwan's best sound films. Inspired by the Bret Harte story about an innocent cowboy and a gambler, and how each influences the other, the film is beautifully photographed and Dwan has given it a melancholy glow that is most affecting and memorable. (Some people, however, will have to get over their political prejudices in order to appreciate it – Ronald Reagan is co-starred.) Certainly Dwan's most personal and sensitive work of the fifties, *Tennessee's Partner* is also, significantly, the only project from this period the director himself initiated.

The River's Edge (1957), the last really challenging piece of material Dwan was given, is a savage chase picture that follows the adventures of two men and a woman as they try to escape over the Mexican border with a million dollars; the main tensions that exist are from within the group, and their often fascinating, ambiguous relationships are presented with a kind of bitter humour and a ruthless detachment. Filled with unheralded violence, it has a properly vulgar, dirty quality, the colour scheme consisting mainly of varying shades of red – from the Mexican mud to Debra Paget's artificial-looking hair. She is weak in a pivotal part, but Ray Milland and Anthony Quinn are unusually good compensations.

If there is no unifying theme nor imposing visual style to Dwan's work, it is certainly not devoid of personality and character. His approach to material has always been pragmatic, and his camerawork expressive but unadorned, in the most classical American tradition. The mischievous, occasionally even wicked, humour that runs through many of his films is that of a man amused by the pomposity and pretentions of the world, though he is equally tolerant of our most frivolous behaviour; never one to judge his characters, he still cannot resist deflating them. Yet, throughout his career, the lives of simple people have most often inspired his finest movies, from the open enthusiasm of Doug Fairbanks to the uncomplicated cowboys of his last films.

Only a man of inherent modesty – he claims that 'a team' makes a movie, not one person – could have survived with such good spirit and without cynicism his years of inferior projects and crippling limitations. It has been his curse, as well as his peculiar glory, that he would prefer to shoot almost any old thing that came up rather than wait for just the right project; it was more fun that way, and since he has never had any pretensions, he would rather exercise his craft than not be out there at all.

Sixty years ago he began and now, at a lively 86, he has seen more than 800 of his films come and go – and many have come back again – been a part of the whole history of the movies, and forgotten more about film-making than any of us can ever hope to learn. For he was among the first – and is certainly one of the last survivors – of that lucky breed who stumbled into an occupation for which no one had been trained, and to which no one could have aspired because it did not exist: unexplored territory, with no rules, no limits, no guidelines. Miraculously, and despite all odds, the occupation became an art. Dwan was there when it happened.

Galloping Tintypes

INTERVIEW

[The following is an edited version of an interview with Mr Dwan, tape recorded at his home in Van Nuys, California, over a period of nine days in the Winter of 1968 and the Fall of 1969.]

Before you got involved in movies what had you planned to do?

I planned to be an electrical engineer. I'd studied for it, graduated from the university and was busy at it long before I thought of pictures.

As a kid hadn't you thought about getting into the theatre?

Well, at school I was in the dramatic society and acted, in fact, played 'King Lear' and 'Richelieu' and other little roles. Mostly Shakespeare. I was quite a ham on the campus between football seasons.

You were a football star.

In a small way.

Had you seen any films at all? Did they have any impact on you?

Well, they only had little things in stores – imitation of a railroad train moving – things of that sort. It was some time before moving pictures as we know them came. There were nickelodeons. The price to get in was five cents. And they were pretty horrible. I seldom went to them. I was only interested in the scientific aspects. Anything mechanical interested me.

Photograph: Dwan in the 1880's.

14

Well then, how did you finally get involved in movies?

Well, it was a sheer accident. Even before graduating from Notre Dame, I had begun working with a great genius in electrical engineering – a man named Steinmetz who was with Westinghouse. I was one of his assistants, and it was through him that I got into illuminating engineering – he arranged for me to get to the Peter Cooper Hewitt Company in Chicago where I worked on the mercury vapour arc, which was the great-grandfather of the neon light. We made up the tubes and put them in the Chicago Post Office for sorting mail; they're very fine on the eyes, and the mail-sorters could work many hours more a day without eye-strain.

Didn't they make you look awful though?

Well, they made you look mortified because they lacked red rays. But the red ray was the eye-irritating one and we were glad to get rid of it. Anyway, a man named Spoor came in and asked if these tubes would be any good for photography. I told him I thought they should be since the negative in those days didn't like the red ray either. The actors wouldn't look pretty when you saw them with your eyes, but photographically it was perfect. So Spoor asked if he could experiment with them at his film studio, which was on the north side of Chicago. His company was called Essanay–Spoor and Anderson.

That was Billy Anderson, the cowboy star?

Yes, Bronco Billy. But he was off in California some place making his westerns. The studio up on Argyle Street was only used for domestic dramas. They had a glass studio and worked with sunlight – it looked exactly like a hothouse – and on bad days they were handicapped – not enough light. They also had a lot of scrims, curtains, that they pulled across to control the sunlight – black ones, light ones, all with different degrees of texture. They finally came

Photograph: G. M. 'Bronco Billy' Anderson, the A of Essanay.

up with what they called a 'broad' or open arc – a Klieg light. These emitted carbon dust – burned carbon – which ruined the eyes. People used to get what was called 'Klieg eyes'. So they were very expensive to use because they tied the actors up – many of them were at the eye doctor's instead of the studio most of the

15

time. Anyway, I designed some lights for this experiment, had the factory make them, and then stayed to see that they operated properly. And so in the process of supervising the lights, I watched these movies being made. It was the first time I'd come in contact with anything of this sort. All us great actors sneered at motion pictures – no legitimate actor from the theatre would go near them. So only the lower grade of stock company actors were used, together with types that were picked up and turned into actors – reluctantly. And if you were really short, it was customary to use every member of your family: just 'Come on over to the studio – you're working today . . .'

But I watched these things, and I finally said, 'Where do you get these stories you're doing?'. And they told me they bought them from any source possible – paid as much as $25 for a story. Now that intrigued me. I had written a lot of short stories for the scholastic newspaper at Notre Dame, so I brought a load of them over. And they bought about thirteen or fourteen of them from me at $25 each, and were so impressed with me as a writer that they asked me if I'd be their scenario editor. Not knowing what that was, of course, I said, 'What do you pay?' And they named a figure – not a big one – around three hundred a week – but *much* more than a young engineer fooling around with electricity could earn in those days unless he owned the company. So I said, 'Well, perhaps I could do both – I'll be a scenario editor and still supervise these mercury vapour arcs.' They said, 'All right', and I went along reading scripts that were sent in, selecting them now and then, probably buying a few. And in about two weeks, three or four executives of this company asked if I'd like to leave Essanay and join them as scenario editor in another company they were forming – The American Film Company. I said, 'What will you pay me?' And they doubled my salary. (Their trick of getting

everybody was to double salaries in those days because they weren't very high.) Well, that was terrific. I said good-bye to engineering right then. The mercury vapour arc went out the window, and I became a motion picture scenario editor.

By the way, did the mercury vapour light work?
Oh, yes, it worked, and every studio in the world bought them and used them for years. They were all over the place – in the ceilings and on the floors. I guess the company made millions of dollars out of it. They were quite successful for years and years until the neon came along.

Neon is a gas and therefore quickly illuminated, whereas mercury had to be tilted until a stream of it connected and blew. Sometimes it took three or four times before you'd get a contact, but then it would immediately becomes gaseous and luminous. Had terrific value. It was great in the picture business for film projection – made possible the long throw in the theatre – because the old carbon arc was too hot – and too dangerous – there was a flame there – whereas the mercury vapour arc was luminous without any flame.

And how did you become a director?
In the summer of 1909, I was sent out to Arizona by the American Film Company to work with Frank Beal, who was a very good stock company director they had got from the theatre and sent out to make pictures in Tucson, Arizona. I went as a sort of unit manager – handled the money, took care of the payroll – and did work with him on stories. If he saw something he wanted to get into a story, I'd write it in for him. In those days Tucson had a main street that was very, very 'old West', with lots of saloons and cowboys and things. We were luxuriously situated in a hotel that had just been built – the Santa Rita I think it was – right next door to a natural western street and great looking backgrounds. It was the perfect

place to make westerns. And then something happened, because the Chicago office sent word for us to stop operating, discharge everybody on the spot and come back to Chicago. Well, that didn't sit well with me because these people had been brought out from Chicago and how would they ever get back? So, against orders, I arranged for everyone to get back, and the company got very sore about it because they thought they were going to save that fare money – a couple of hundred dollars or so. Of course, in those days, a big picture cost five or ten thousand dollars top. Not even that much, because some of the ones I made much later in New York for Triangle with pretty good people only cost from fifteen to eighteen thousand. Anyway, they got sore and I got fired. But they changed managements right about then and a fellow named A. M. Kennedy hired me back. I was to go out West again, because in the meantime they'd sent Beal back out with a company. Now all of these things happened within a relatively few months. They said, 'How'd you like to go out to California and see what's going on out there with Beal? They claim they have no stories.' I said, 'It sounds fine.'

I went out – not to Hollywood, because there were no studios in Hollywood – Selig had one on Glendale Boulevard and Griffith was down in a car barn on Georgia Street with the Biograph Company. And after a long search, I finally found our company at San Juan Capistrano in a little hotel. There were about eight actors, a lot of cowboys, some horses, and everyone was sitting there doing nothing. I said, 'Why aren't you working?' They said, 'Well, our director has been away on a binge for two weeks in Los Angeles, and we don't see him very often, so we haven't made any pictures.' It looked like a pretty sad situation and I wired the Chicago office, 'I suggest you disband the company. You have no director.' They wired

back, 'You direct.' So I got the actors together and said, 'Now, either I'm a director or you're out of work.' And they said, 'You're the best damn director we ever saw. You're great.' I said, 'What do I do? What does a director do?' So they took me out and showed me. And it worked.

What did they show you?

Well, it's hard to remember exactly. I know the first thing they did was give me a chair and say, 'You sit here.' And they gave me a megaphone and said, 'You yell through this.' And I said, 'What do I yell?' 'You yell "Come on" or yell "Action". When you say that, the cameraman will start turning the camera, and just say "Cut" when you want him to quit. And then you wave a flag or something and we'll ride over the hill, or we'll walk in and do our scene.' Now, for instance, fights. I knew nothing about film fights. I'd seen these fellows swing haymakers at each other and miss by three feet, and I'd say, 'Come on. Can't you reach him? Get in closer. You're too far away from him.' And they'd laugh at me and say, 'Sure, we better be or you won't have any actors.' I couldn't get used to the faking. Finally I learned, but I thought it was all for real up to that time.

Then you actually learned about directing as you were making the pictures?

Yes. I knew nothing about directing. I found it was a good idea to let the actors have a lot of free play. I learned that in the beginning and I never got over it. I don't believe in telling an actor every move to make. Sometimes you find them so dull or so frozen or so frightened that you have to pet them and help them, but *not* try to teach them to act. A director's job shouldn't be to teach acting. That's another kind of a profession. Your job is to sort of keep everything going together, as a coach does with a lot of fine athletes. Keep them coordinated, keep them doing their job, and not let them run away from the rest or be too slow so they can't catch up. And see that the story is getting its full value – that's the director's job. But a lot of directors make the mistake of trying to teach the actor every move or gesture he makes. Sometimes he can do that with the little girls who are beginning, or boys willing to take advice – providing he *knows* – but very few directors know acting. As a matter of fact, most directors are terrified of the camera. If by accident they get caught out there when the slate is being shot, they almost faint when they turn around and see that thing is *going* and they're in front of it. To get up and *perform* in front of it is out of the question. Ninety-nine directors out of a hundred would faint if they did one scene.

RATTLESNAKES AND GUNPOWDER (1911)

Anyway, we all got along pretty well and the first story I conceived of was called *Rattlesnakes and Gunpowder*. I asked the cowboys if they could get me a rattlesnake, so they went out, caught one and pulled out its poison sacs as was their custom – but they didn't tell *me* that. I had to have it for some close-ups because it was the heavy in my story, so I picked it up by the back of its head. I was blowing at it and it was sticking its tongue out at me, when suddenly it stretched – I didn't know it could stretch – and snapped my nose. I pulled it away quickly, but the nose was cut and bleeding. The cowboys said immediately, 'Oh boy, you've been bitten by a rattlesnake. We got to fix you up.' They got a pint of whiskey and I said, 'What's that for?' They said, 'Well, that'll cure it – it'll keep you from dying.' I thought they were going to pour it on the wound, but they made me drink it – and I'd never had a drink in my life! Well, we were out pretty far from town in the sagebrush with our horses and things and I began to feel terrible. It was the

liquor, not the snake, but I didn't know that. I thought, 'Well, this is it. I'm going fast so I better make something while I can see my way.' I told them, 'Let's get some scenes.' So we started chasing. Well, I made so many chases that the horses dropped exhausted, and finally so did I. Out like a light. They took me in and pumped me out – and when I came out of it I realised I was stone drunk and not hurt by the rattlesnake. So we finished the movie and that was the beginning of my career as a picture director.

At what point did you begin to feel you really knew what you were doing?

Well, I think shortly after the cowboys gave me that drink of liquor and I recovered, I said to myself, 'I think I know what I'm doing now.'

Now, that was the first picture I put together and it was sort of tongue-in-cheek because my attitude toward the whole thing was rather light. We kept it fluffy and never took ourselves too seriously. I started to make it in San Juan Capistrano, but moved out of there because of its proximity to the railroad – a convenience for the Patents' Company men to get at us. I wanted to go some place a little more remote where we could protect ourselves. Someone steered me to Lakeside, which is above La Mesa and where there was a pretty good hotel and lots of nice background, and I moved them all up there.

Why did you have to protect yourselves from the Patents' Company men?

All the big companies of that day – Vitagraph, Biograph, Kalem, Selig, probably Essanay and many others – had grouped together and called themselves The Patents Company. And they claimed they had exclusive use of the camera due to the fact that when you threaded the film in the camera a loop was necessary. It was called the Latham Loop, after the man who figured it out, and the Patents Company claimed the loop was their patent. It was silly, but they said it was theirs exclusively and we were not entitled to use it. They couldn't stop us by law – nobody could get an injunction against us – and the camera itself was not exclusive because we bought it from the makers. But these people tried to prevent us from using their loop, and without the loop you couldn't run the film through the camera.

You still can't.

No. The whole thing was thrown out of court eventually. The idea of boycotting was restraint of free trade, and the fact that they banded together was a government violation too. It was just ridiculous – like selling an automobile and not letting anybody else drive it because you have a patent on putting your foot on the pedal. So that's what we were up against. Now, to prevent us from operating, they employed roughnecks and hard-arm people and gangsters to destroy us. At one time, they raided the Universal facilities in New York – almost burned them down. Two or three people were shot. That was a hoodlum attack – probably a number of gangsters there – and the police were in on it. Big headlines. But in addition to that kind of violence, they sent snipers out with long-range rifles.

Did anybody ever get killed?

They always shot at the cameras. Their instructions were to destroy the cameras, since they were expensive and hard to get. Most companies only had one. So a lot of companies had to run for it and many went out of business on account of them. We'd always be working in hills and they'd get up in back of a tree or up on a mound above you and wait for their time. Sometimes they'd wait until a fellow was cleaning the camera – we didn't have any studio for our headquarters – and take a shot at it. Anything to destroy it. That was their job.

Nobody ever really got hurt then?

Nobody ever got hit that we knew of. Of course you never know where a bullet will ricochet, but we never had any wounds in our outfit. But if our boys had caught one of those guys they'd have shot him – in the foot or in the rear end – they'd have let him know he wasn't welcome. We were forced, therefore, to go into remote spots to work and also to arm our cowboys and ourselves – we all wore sidearms. Our cowboys had loaded rifles and they stood sentry duty and watched for snipers while we worked. But even with that caution, sometimes our cameras were hit. Mine never got shot. One day in La Mesa a rough-looking character got off the train and looked me up. He said he was sent out to make sure me and my company got out of there and quit making pictures. Well, we took a walk up the road to talk it over. I hadn't been out of college for too long and was in good physical shape. So I wanted to get him far enough out of town to see if I couldn't beat his brains out. We stopped at a bridge over an *arroyo* where people had thrown some tin cans. There was a bright one sitting out there, so to impress me he whipped a gun out of his shoulder holster and shot at the can and missed it by about five yards. I pulled out my gun and hit the can twice, and that afternoon he left town. Also he was accompanied to the depot by my well-armed cowboys. From that time on we were never molested. But that was the reason we went to remote spots. We got as far away from New York as we could.

So you not only had to learn how to make a picture, you had to be fast on the draw.

Yes, indeed – had to fight your way through – it was a rough business.

How did the company get around in those days?

We used horses and rigs at Lakeside. I'd pile everyone into two buckboards, a ranch wagon for our equipment, the cowboys on their horses – the actors too if they were riding in the picture – and off we went out into the country to make a picture. On the way out, I'd try to contrive something to do. I'd see a cliff or

something or the sort. I had a heavy named Jack Richardson, so we'd send J. Warren Kerrigan, the leading man, up there to struggle with Richardson and throw him off the cliff. Now, having made the last scene of the picture, I had to go backwards and try to figure out why all this happened.

THE POISONED FLUME (1911)

Once we were out looking around and I saw a flume. It carried water from one ranch to another in the air like a great bridge – came from a reservoir up the hills. It fascinated me,

Still: Jack Richardson, j. Warren Kerrigan in At the Halfbreed's Mercy (*1913*), *not by Dwan.*

so I immediately said, 'We've got to use that for a picture.' And I wrote something called *The Poisoned Flume*. Jack Richardson was putting poison in the flume and the water was killing J. Warren Kerrigan's cattle so that's why he threw Richardson off the cliff. That was the typical way of making pictures in those days. All off the cuff.

They were all one-reelers?

Yes. And we developed our own negatives. I

20

rented a couple of stores. One was for offices, the other was for the development process, the lab. Our cameraman had to be able to develop film in those days.

What was your shooting schedule then?

We would work, say, Monday, Tuesday and Wednesday shooting and make two pictures. Then on Thursday and Friday I'd develop and cut them and take Saturday and Sunday off – go down to San Diego or Los Angeles for the weekend. Beal was a slow worker. If he did one one-reeler a week it was considered pretty good. During the rest of the week, he'd get ready and prepare. He shipped the negative back to Chicago – until I decided it would be better to develop the negative ourselves and know what we had – not leave it to them to send us word about our 'mistakes'. But Beal

Photograph: La Mesa,California, in 1911.

let them develop it and cut it and print it – do the works – he had nothing to do with editing. We wouldn't ship them until we had maybe six, and then they'd release them in their own order. We kept that up until we kind of outgrew Lakeside, and wanted to get a little different background and a little closer to people. We couldn't get enough extras there so we came down to La Mesa which was not too far from San Diego and stayed there awhile. I lived in a minister's house. His wife, a wonderful cook, asked me what I wanted for breakfast. 'An egg, boiled on one side and fried on the other', I said. And damned if I didn't get it. She soft-boiled an egg, then broke one end and let a part of it flow into a hot frying-pan. One side boiled, the other fried. She topped Christopher Columbus with that one. And it taught me nothing is impossible. Whenever I hit a tough problem, I think of that egg.

And it was in La Mesa I decided to buy an automobile for transportation. It was brought to me by a young fellow from the auto company who had to stay to teach me how to drive it. And I got to like him. His name was Marshall Neilan. I said to him, 'Would you like to be an actor in the pictures?' He said, 'Sure. What's it pay?' I told him – pretty good pay. I needed a character to play Kerrigan's weak brother, so Neilan was elected and played that in the next fifty films we made. He was a Californian and he knew everything around there, loved to roam around – he was a poetic kind of a guy – very romantic. One weekend he wanted to go back to Los Angeles and I said, 'Why don't you go a little further and find me a place where I can have the ocean and the mountains and ranches and everything we need to make pictures?' He said, 'Well, I'll look for a place.' So a few days later I got a phone call from Santa Barbara, and

he said, 'I've found exactly what you want down here.' So I packed up the outfit, put them on their horses and their wagons and off we went from La Mesa all the way to Santa Barbara [1912]. It took us about two or three days to get there. But we went like gypsies. Now we needed a central location, so up on State Street was an ostrich farm that wasn't working – there were only a couple of ostriches left – so I rented the place, gave the gate to the ostriches, built a stage and put up some posts and curtains, and when we wanted an interior, we did it there. We didn't have very many.

Photographs: Dwan 1912, in his Mitchell Six, the car brought him by Marshall Neilan. Opposite – at the ostrich farm in Santa Barbara; top – publicity shot and personal souvenir with annotation (captioned 'A Tough Nut'); the director on the Flying A stage for interiors.

Didn't you bring Victor Fleming into films?

Yes. We developed some sort of engine trouble in that car we bought and all the mechanics in Santa Barbara didn't seem to be able to fix it. And Neilan said, 'There's a fellow works as chauffeur for a wealthy family in Montecito – if I can find him, he knows more about engines than any guy I ever met.' So we drove around looking for this fellow, and at one of these estates there was a tall, young boy shooting a .22 (with a Maxim silencer) at a target in the garage. Mickey said, 'There he is now', and we drove up behind him. Without even looking at us, he said, 'One of your tappet valves is stuck.' Anyway, while he was fixing the car, I looked around the garage and saw over in the corner a bunch of photographic equipment – still cameras. So I said to him, 'Are you interested in photography?' He says, 'You bet I am – I like it very much.' And he showed me some stuff – very pretty things he was doing. So when he got through with the car, I said, 'How'd you like to go into the moving pictures business and be a photographer?' He said, 'Well, that sounds pretty good, but I've got to eat – do you pay for it?' I said, 'Yes', so he joined us, and became a very good friend of mine – we really had some grand times together. He learned the camera very quickly and became an excellent cameraman. And then a fine director later.

Did you ever have any contact with your bosses?

We'd hear from them, but we never contacted them much. We'd just send the negatives in and they'd print them and write back their congratulations. They didn't make any comment except 'Fine, keep them coming'. By now, we were making three of these single-reel stories every week and taking the weekend off.

You cut your own pictures?

I cut the negative – never saw a print – and put it together the way I wanted the picture to run. They'd simply print it that way when it got to Chicago, and that's the way it stayed.

What about the titles?

We put the titles on it. But ours were usually crude, just scratched on the negative with a pin. Then there was a specialist who would print and photograph them, and they'd cut them in where I had indicated. And they sent the money every week and that was it. I never asked anybody's permission for anything.

Did you physically cut the footage yourself?

Yes, we didn't have cutters. And we didn't have any instruments or machines – we did it by hand. I would take the reels and run them through in front of a light. I could read the negative. Wherever I wanted to end a scene, I'd just cut it with a pair of scissors and that'd be a scene. Then I'd get the next scene I wanted and we'd glue it together. When I'd have a thousand feet – one reel – I'd roll it up and send it to Chicago.

How much footage did you have to shoot to get 1,000 feet for a film?

We never shot over two thousand feet. I was very sparing with film – all of us were. Very often, if I had gone out and hired twenty extra horses and men for a chase, I'd make two or three extra chases since I was paying these men for a certain period of time, and so I accumulated a library. Having a stock company, and being careful not to let their costumes change too much, I could use any scenes I wanted to in any picture I wanted to – like a ride-through or a stagecoach arriving, those kind of things. The same one over and over and over again if I wanted. That was economical and saved us from doing it over and over. Today we wouldn't be able to do that. You've got to pay everyone each time you use the shot. But in those days we had no rules, no unions, nothing. It was just what you wanted to do.

The superiority of a picture you made in 1913 called Calamity Anne's Trust *to* Three Million Dollars *made just over a year before is extraordinary. How did you develop so fast?*

Photograph: Eugene Pallette, a mean heavy.

Yes, not by choice, but just because we had to. There was no organisation for writing. We would buy a story if we could get one. Living in Santa Barbara was a well-known novelist named Stuart Edward White. I had an idea for a story called *Oil on Troubled Waters*, using the oil wells in the ocean off Carpenteria. Now I wanted to make it sound important, so I arranged to pay Stuart Edward White for the use of his name on this story. I told it to him and he said, 'Let's do it better than that. Let me

have that story.' So he took the idea, wrote it and sold it to the Saturday Evening Post who published it, and then I made it. And it got us a lot of money. This was the first time anything as big as a Saturday Evening Post story hit the screen. Of course, some of the things Griffith did were famous and in public domain, but this was like having Hemingway, you know – White was a top writer. The stunt was so successful that I used it frequently. I had three or four other good writers and some of them would say 'Go ahead' not even hearing or reading the story. They didn't care – they just wanted the dough.

How did you keep supplied with stories for so many films?

Well, if I saw a Griffith picture I liked, I'd give it a few little twists and put my cast in it and that made it different – different actors made it a different story. And we'd buy them. People would come around with a basic idea, even members of the cast, and I encouraged that. I said, 'If any of you come in with a decent synopsis for a story, I'll buy it from you.' And I did.

Then, of course, I put a second company to work. We were having such a good time making these things and they wanted all the films they could get, so I made one of my property men a star. (We'd always *star* them immediately.) That was Wallace Reid. And I'd have Eugene Pallette for a heavy – he wasn't a big fat fellow then – he was the mean heavy. And that was my second company.

Did you direct both companies?

No, I'd direct the J. Warren Kerrigan company and first I gave Mickey Neilan a break in the second company. And everybody helped everybody. The formula was there. We had a system of making them and they rolled out. But Kerrigan didn't like the second unit idea, he didn't like Wallace Reid being a star. Kerrigan was pretty fond of himself at the time so he put

27

a knock into the company by letter saying *I* was getting out of hand and that unless I was replaced, he was going to leave the company. So out came Hutchinson – the head of the studio – and the first executive we ever had come to us. He talked to Kerrigan and he talked to me and I told him very frankly, 'Things are going to be just the way I want them or else they're not going to be at all, as far as I'm concerned.' So he left a note on my desk and when I came in from work one day, I found it: 'As of now', it said, 'you are no longer with the company'. It was quite a shock. It was terrifying – never having been with any other company – to suddenly find myself out of work.

Neilan had left me about two weeks before – he was stuck on a girl in Los Angeles – so I got on the phone to him, and he said, 'Don't make a move till you talk to me. Meet me at the Van Nuys Hotel as soon as you can and we'll do something.' So I drove to Los Angeles, and met Neilan, who had two men with him from Universal. They asked me what I wanted and Neilan wouldn't let me answer. He said, 'Wait a minute. Let's not get to that yet. Let's find out first whether he wants to work for you. You know, he runs his own company and he doesn't want a lot of bosses around.' They understood that and they liked my pictures. I didn't know our pictures were popular, you see, I had no way of knowing we were right up there with Griffith. You can't tell when you're out alone like that how you're doing. At any rate, they finally made me an offer – it was twice as much as I'd been getting at Santa Barbara. Neilan jumped on them and said, 'Look, I didn't bring you here to insult him. If you're going to make an offer, make an offer.' So they went a little higher, and I accepted around $1500 a week – it was a fabulous price which was out of line then and everybody was amazed at it.

But it entailed a lot of work, as it developed.

They asked me to go to New York and talk to Carl Laemmle, who was the head of the company, and he asked me if I could get any of the people that had been working with me at American and he'd pay them twice as much as they'd been paying. So I sent word back and strangely enough the person I contacted to represent me down there was J. Warren Kerrigan's brother, Wallace Kerrigan, a nice guy who thought his brother was an awful ham.

Photographs: Wallace Reid and Marshall Neilan (right), directors on Dwan's second company.

And he went around for me and hired *everybody* there – including J. Warren Kerrigan – and the whole crowd came with me to Universal. I had two companies, so I put Wallace Reid and Mickey Neilan in charge of the other one – they'd alternate as director.

Didn't Neilan become a very good director?

Yes, he had a light comedy touch – human comedy. He had the Irish point of view and there was always a little humour to everything – he himself was a victim of it. I remember one time a few years later, in Paris, he was wooing Gloria Swanson and she had given him a gold-headed cane as a present. He used to go out in the afternoon and do a little tom-catting, and one day he left his cane some place and was halfway home before he realised it; now, Gloria was a pretty shrewd girl and he knew she would miss it, so he went into a store and bought one he thought was identical and when he got back, she said, 'Where have you been?' And he had the usual blarney. 'Where'd you get that cane?' 'That's the one you gave me.' 'It is *not*.' The argument began. Finally he says, 'Well, the hell with it', and he picked it up and smashed it over his knee. But instead of the cane breaking, his kneecap did, so we had to put him in the American hospital in a cast for about two weeks while the rest of us took care of Gloria.

He had a sad end, didn't he?

Yes. Well, he ruined himself with liquor and indifference and bitterness. He became a humorous cynic. But liquor did it.

Howard Hawks, who admired him greatly, told me the studio heads had it in for him because he was so insulting to them.

That's right, Mayer especially. But you can't say he didn't earn that treatment – he antagonised them and they'd always get back at you any way they could. They threw him out.

What was the difference for you between American and Universal?

Well, mainly company – I was alone till then. Now I could look around and see another director at work, talk to him, see that there was somebody else going through the same thing I was going through. We had open air studios at the corner of Gower and Sunset, and we used to divide them by laying flats of scenery on their sides, covering them up and mapping off the parts we were in with our sets. So the only thing that separated me, for instance, from Bob Leonard on the next stage, was some thin little stuff six feet high that anybody six feet tall could look over. There was no sound, but if somebody was playing a difficult death scene over there, and I was doing a ho-down dance right next to him. I'd be polite and halt my racket until he got his scene made. That's the way we cooperated.

I remember we had a supervisor – he wasn't very big, but he was a vicious little guy – and he was one of the first butt-in-skies I ever knew. He used to come down on the set to talk to you about something in yesterday's rushes while you were trying to make some scenes. I'd say, 'Look, get out of here – I don't want to talk to you – I'll see you later in the office.' He annoyed me so much one day coming in there that I picked him up and threw him over the separating wall into Bob Leonard's set. And Bob Leonard threw him back!

THE RESTLESS SPIRIT (1913)

I made a rash statement once. I said, 'You can make a motion picture out of anything.' So somebody wanting to stop me, said, 'You can't make one out of Gray's "Elegy",' because that *would* be pretty difficult – in the first place, it's a long poem. But I said, 'Well, I'll read it again and see.' So I studied it a little bit and began to dream about it, and more or less as a challenge, on a bet, I made it. It had twenty-four dissolves in it. Now, in those days a dissolve had to be done in the camera – there was no laboratory process. You'd reach the point you wanted to dissolve and you'd take eight counts to get out, then you'd wind back the film and take the eight counts again on the next scene, which would be on another set with another crowd of people. But with twenty-four of these on one roll of film, it was quite a risk. If one shot was wrong and the cameraman made a mistake in the counts, the whole thing was gone. And it drove him out of his mind. Poor fellow, he had to go to the hospital on account of it.

How did you cast the early pictures?

Well, there was a new breed that grew up in the business. As I told you, no self-respecting actor would come near us at first. No theatrical actor would even use his own name when he came into a picture – he'd be disgraced. I remember the first actor I ever knew was a fellow named King Baggott. He was a good movie actor in his day – a very third-rate actor in the theatre – but thoroughly ashamed of being in pictures. Yet he was a star and making good money. Finally he relaxed and said, 'I guess this is my forte', and he stayed in.

But our actors came from anywhere – we picked them up and trained them. They'd come to your gate in the morning to see if there was any work, and you'd bring them in. You'd ask one to do a little bit of business and he'd do it pretty well, and first thing you know there's a fellow who's intelligent, so you'd keep him in mind. He might turn into quite an actor. Girls were a natural. Children are great actors because they're always making-believe. As a rule women could make-believe more readily than men. A man gets embarrassed. But they learn and if there's money in it, they'll try. And, of course, our cowboys *were* cowboys, and they were very natural, very real. Nearly 90 per cent of the western actors in all pictures are fellows who at one time or another were associated with cattle.

Now, in Griffith's case, many of his people were completely inexperienced when he got them. He rehearsed them thoroughly - that was a trick not very many of us ever used. He rehearsed long enough to get them familiar with the story and what they were doing. They didn't use scripts. He built the scene as he rehearsed it, then went out and shot it, and if he didn't like it, shot it again. Or he'd shoot a close-up and things of that sort – to gradually mould and build a scene. And these people all got trained and soon became his type of actress or actor.

Now, for instance, I picked up a new property man at Universal who was quite a nice guy. He used to come around with funny teeth in his mouth and weird make-ups. I guess he was hinting – nobody goes around with a putty nose on unless he wants to be noticed. But he loved make-up. Finally, I said to him, 'What the hell is this? Do you want to get in front of the lens?' He said, yes, he'd tried acting once in a stock company and had liked it. He was a property man because he had to make a living. So I put him to work as a couple of weird

Still: Lon Chaney (as the man) in Nomads of the North (*director, David Hartford, 1921*).

characters and he caught on – people began to notice him – and I took the tip right away and said, I'll feature him. And that was the start of Lon Chaney.

What was he like to work with?

Oh, great. Just a joy. In pictures, personalities are it, you know. It isn't acting *per se* as it's known in the theatre. It's sheer personality. What were you photographing? What was there? You'd bring some kid in who just blazed off the screen – a girl or a fellow would hit you instantly. Just astonishing people. That's what we looked for – some photographic quality,

some mysterious hidden thing certain people have. And you still can't define it. What makes a star?

Did John Ford work for you at Universal?

His brother Francis was working for me as an actor, and he asked me to give Jack a job. Jack was cutting his teeth in those days, just starting, and he became my property man. I remember him as a good, efficient one too. We always needed unusual things, and he was always able to dig them up. Prop men were very important, you know, because you didn't have a big prop house. They had to go all over the place to find things, and he was practically a set-dresser. The art directors and set decorators didn't exist then – they gradually came into the business.

In those days, weren't films becoming more popular daily?

Yes, after I got to Universal, I began to see that pictures were sweeping the world, becoming a big business. And there was no competition then, no television, nothing to stop us. I didn't know that in Santa Barbara – it was still nickelodeons to me. Then we began to expand, make four- and five-reelers, and I started to realise it was a serious business. We had to make better things to hold for that running time, and they cost more money. And so I felt a responsibility. I began to go to theatres and look at pictures and realise that we were obliged to give the people their money's worth and also reward the investor who was taking quite a risk letting us spend his money. He should have a profit. So from that time on I became what is still known as a commercial director. I've never attempted deliberately to be a so-called artistic director. I was a practical person. As a matter of fact, the extravagance of ninety-nine per cent of us caused the introduction of supervisors and producers, men who were sent out to watch the budget, see where the money went. Because a lot of directors were taking sixteen and seventeen weeks to make a picture that I'd make in

seventeen days.

But your films have a great deal of artistry.

Well, that's a natural taste. It's like being a painter – you paint well or you don't. And you paint quickly or you don't. And the good painters learn what *not* to put on canvas. And economy of line is the essence of art. Extreme simplicity. And working the way I did, the supervisors would respect me enough to say, 'Let him have his way.'

Anyway, along came an outfit I thought would make a mark called Famous Players. They were going to bring big theatre stars to the films. That intrigued me. Having always had a little inkling for the theatre, having once been a great actor myself, I thought, 'Well, that's a step up – now *my* class of actor is coming in.' So when Famous Players made me an offer I was very happy to accept. But the theatre actors were terrible. They couldn't work our way. They'd come in and say, 'What do I do? Let me read the script.' But if there *was* a script, they didn't know what they were reading because it's nothing like a play. Because we'd just say, 'You come in and say so-and-so,' and they'd come in and couldn't remember what it was – *or* you couldn't stop them. They'd start to talk and say all the lines from all the plays they'd ever been in. But, you see, it was a different technique altogether. Today, with talking pictures, they have an advantage because they can deliver lines. A good actor can make a dull scene sound pretty good with his ability to speak, and if he has some pretty good lines, it's interesting. But the great movie stars learned the technique and a few mannerisms and a few moves and became sort of public idols. They couldn't do anything wrong – if you liked them – no matter what they did – it wasn't what they played. A fellow like John Wayne is the same in every picture, but you like him because it's Wayne. And you like to see that strange walk of his and you're satisfied. He can

Photograph: Marguerite Clark as she appeared in The Goose Girl *(1915) – not by Dwan.*

play certain scenes very well, his way, and you accept them his way. And if there are scenes he can't play well, he just won't do them.

WILDFLOWER (1914)

When I started for Famous Players, I went to New York, up to the third floor of a loft building that they'd converted into a studio of sorts on West 23rd Street. And they assigned me a young actress they'd signed up named Marguerite Clark. She was quite a hit in some play in the theatre, and they thought she was going to become a rival of Mary Pickford. They *had* Mary Pickford, but I guess they wanted to cover their bet and keep anybody else from having this girl who might become Mary's rival. They gave us a script called *Wildflower*. I cast successful picture actors around her, and

we went out and made the picture. And Adolph Zukor, the studio head, and his clique looked at it and they were heart-broken. They were going to scrap it – thought it was a complete loss of money – but they couldn't afford that – they didn't have too much money – so they *had* to get it out. They put it into the theatres and it was a smash hit. The girl really clicked in a big way. A new personality. And she had that photogenic quality – she was a good personality on the screen. Well, they had pretty good success with her for quite a while, but I never saw her again.

DAVID HARUM (1915)

It was a well-known play, and William H. Crane had starred in it on the stage, so it was regarded as a good package from Famous Players' point of view. From the picture point of view it had no meaning, since we were appealing to audiences all over the country and all over the world, and they'd never heard of *David Harum* or William H. Crane. But in New York, it sounded good. That picture was the first time we moved the camera. And we didn't get very much praise for it either – nothing but abuse. The scene required David Harum to walk down the street talking to people as he went, to show that he was well-acquainted with everybody; he was a horse-trader, quite a foxy old man, and very gay. He'd greet one person and stop to chat with another as he moved down the street. Well, I thought, if you set the camera at one end of the street and start him at the other end, you wouldn't see anything; you'd see a fly speck approaching and finally when he got away down near the camera you'd say, 'Oh, that's David Harum', but all the rest would have been wasted. So all this atmosphere would have to be made as a series of short scenes: let him walk this far, now put the camera down, let him walk that far – and so on. Well, instead of setting the camera backwards each time, it occurred to me, wouldn't it be nice if we could just *move* it backward with him. I said to the cameraman, 'How can we move it back?' And he laughed at me. Because in those days cameras were anchored or chained down on tripods so there'd be no vibration. He said, 'You could pick it up and carry it' – you know, that big heavy thing. So I said, 'No, but we can put it on wheels. Now what wheels can we put it on?' Well, the only thing we could think of was the Ford car. And the cameraman said, 'That sounds good, but won't it jiggle too much?' Well, we got a farm scraper and we scraped the street flat, got all the bumps out. And then we softened the tyres so they wouldn't joggle, we locked the springs and fastened the camera on securely with a few two-by-fours, got it well wired down so it wasn't bobbley, and it worked great. As he walked down and met the people, we'd stop if he stopped and moved when he did, and we made this long shot – it ran around seven hundred feet. Now, later, when we cut it, if there was an important point to make, we'd put a title in. Anyway, the scene was effective, except that when we put it in theatres the movement – according to theatre managers – disturbed the audience. They said it made them feel dizzy. Some of them grabbed their chairs and hung on because they thought *they* were moving. They'd never seen it happen. So instead of praises, we got reprimands. But we perfected it and used it often.

The same thing had happened when Griffith invented the close-up. Like all the rest, Griffith had started out being conventional – he used full figures. Then he probably looked at some of Rembrandt's paintings (as I did later for lighting effects) of heads and said, 'Look at that magnificent face. I'm going to take the camera and get faces on the screen.' Now he would show the full- or three-quarter figure and then cut into the close-up and it was as though you were talking to a person and suddenly lunged forward at him so that his head was right in front of you. It was a funny effect. It wasn't smooth. The camera didn't move in – it jumped and gave you a shock – just as you get today with the hysterical cutting that's back in. Bang-bang-bang – senseless cutting. But Griffith was doing it artistically. And they didn't object to the heads, but when they turned around or moved across to another spot, they roared and raised the devil about it. They said, 'What's this idea of people running around with no legs? Heads walking around the screen. It's ridiculous. You've got to see their feet if they're going to move.' But when I started doing that, instead of jumping into the close-up, I dissolved to it, or I moved into it. I put the camera on wheels and got the cameraman to learn how to change his focus while I moved the camera in.
You had to have scripts at Famous Players?
Yes, it was the custom to have scripts there because they had an executive staff that had to go over them and budget them. So they gave us one and sometimes we used it and sometimes we didn't. We had to manufacture a lot of scenes. You can't put it on paper. A script is a lead sheet – something you can work from – but you've got to ad lib. a great deal. With the best of scripts, you have to introduce things, and sometimes things that are right on the spur of the moment are the best. You had to improvise constantly, take advantage of accidents.

A GIRL OF YESTERDAY (1915)
I was assigned to Mary Pickford and she was assigned to me. And we both wanted to come to California, so we came back and established a little studio over on Santa Monica Boulevard and made a couple of pictures. On *A Girl of Yesterday*, we had a scene in which the heavy had to take Mary up in an airplane and we had a hard time getting Mary's mother to agree to let her go up. We had a great flier, Glenn Martin,

who'd built his own 'plane (he later made the Martin Bombers) and finally she agreed if we promised not to go over one hundred feet high. Now it's ten times more dangerous at one hundred feet than ten thousand feet, but we said fine, she won't be over a hundred feet from ground at any time. I said 'ground' not '*the* ground' because my scene was a peculiar one. She had to ride in the back with the heavy, with Glenn Martin up front at the controls. It was an open 'plane, double wings, the old ginny. And we were driving right along beside them on a road along the top of the Griffith Park mountains; they flew parallel to us and that's how we were able to photograph them. Followed them right along the contour of the mountain for miles. We had to go like hell to keep up with it, really give it the gun, but we did. It was a great shot. They were within twenty feet of us at all times – very close. Now the fellow who was playing the heavy was frightened to death up in the 'plane, and Martin wanted to show him how easily it was controlled, so he turned around and said, 'Look, I don't even have to hold on.' And this fellow fainted dead-away. We could see him flop right over – with Mary trying to support him and shaking him, trying to get him back. Finally I signalled Martin and he went down to the landing field. But I had kept my word to Mary's mother. She was never over 100 feet from us on the mountain – so she was close to ground!

Why did you move to Triangle in 1915?
Well, one of the reasons was my disappointment in the legitimate actors emphasised at Famous Players. Mary was terrific and one or two others came through pretty well, but most of them suffered and disappeared back to the theatre. So I was glad to accept Triangle's offer and I liked joining Griffith – Triangle was Griffith and Ince and Sennett – but I didn't stay out here very long with him. They gave me the studios up in Yonkers, New York, and I had

three companies working there. I made directors out of Al Parker and Dick Rosson, and did my own pictures there with Doug Fairbanks.
How did Griffith's supervision manifest itself at first?
Only in a pleasant way. When we were going to make a picture, we'd all go into a room with two or three of the actors assigned and the script we were going to do – or a synopsis of it – and we'd go over it. Sometimes we'd play a scene, discuss this and that. And he was just seeing that I wasn't going to do the same thing one of the other fellows was doing. Or seeing if maybe I should use Lillian Gish instead of Mae Marsh, or someone else out of his stock company. After that we got whatever we wanted and were completely independent.
Didn't you help Griffith on Intolerance?
Oh, just a mechanical thing, yes, on camera-movement – because I was an engineer – I suggested something that was adopted. But it was not important. If someone says to you, 'How do you get downtown – would you take a bus or a train?' and you answer, 'The bus is convenient, take the bus', you can't say you're responsible for what happens when he goes downtown. Now, we didn't know what he was doing over there with that gigantic set growing up across the street. And we weren't allowed to know – it was clothed in secrecy. We used to look at that thing looming above the fence and wonder, 'How did they get those plaster elephants up on those poles?' Well, Griffith's problem was how to photograph the big set with a moving camera – because there was no such thing as a boom. The camera platform had to be steady and it had to carry the director and the cameraman and it had to have a very steady flow of movement from a gigantic long-shot down to a real intimate close-up of some people. The question was how do you produce a parabolic movement with a lens.
And you figured out how to do it?

Sure. Put an elevator on a railroad track. Go backwards and upwards at the same time. And there was the parabolic movement.

Did Griffith's actors have certain fixed ways of working which you had to follow?

Oh, we never attempted to change them – they were so perfect we just left them alone. I wish we had more like them now. They had learned economy of gesture, which I love. They projected their personalities and didn't try to cram

Still: the Babylonian set for Intolerance.

them down your throat. They let your mind work. That's the great trick in any enterprise that looks for public acceptance – make the public work. If you do all the work for them, they sit there bored to death. Their imagination must be stimulated. When you can make an actor sit dead still and think of something and have the audience know what he's thinking, you've got a hit. If an actor can do that, he's a great actor, and that's what Griffith's girls learned to do. These little movements they made and the silences that followed – you knew what they were thinking, what their problem was, and your heart went out to them. Lillian Gish, for example. She was a queen – very fine, very gentle. And her sister, Dorothy, was a

Still: the Gish sisters in 1916 Dwan films –
Dorothy in Betty of Greystone *with George*
Fawcett, Kate Bruce and Owen Moore; Lillian in
An Innocent Magdalene, *with Mary Alden.*

clown, a little hoyden. She was a lot of fun, too. They were both great – on different ends of the scale.

Did you talk the actors through close-ups?

I talked as little as possible. We had to call people in or tell them to speed up their tempo or move over not to destroy the composition, but never about their emotional movements. I left that to them. We rehearsed and then let them play it.

Did you discuss the character's feelings in a scene?

Very often. Sometimes they'd ask for an interpretation if they were a little uncertain. Other times I'd watch them rehearse, correct little things or suggest changes. The usual job of a director. But the megaphone director who constantly talked to them about their emotions, it seems to me, would have been very disturbing. If I'd been an actor it would have annoyed me because I'd be listening instead of giving out.

Still: Lillian Gish in An Innocent Magdalene.

Did you have music on the set?

Sure, on the sidelines – always. Keep them pepped up. A little combo. We played for the mood of the scene, or sometimes we played what an actor enjoyed or would respond to.

But Griffith used to talk his actors through emotional close-ups.

Well, he was a hypnotist with his girls. He had them so wrapped up and they believed so devoutly in him that whatever he asked them for, they'd do. And he himself was quite a ham, you know – he had that big Southern voice – he could have been a Shakespearean actor. He was a delightful guy, but very lonely, I think.

Even then?

Yes, he was always pleasant, always a little reticent – I never saw him in an angry mood – and he had a good sense of humour. Fairbanks and I were sitting in front of our bungalow one

38

day discussing a picture we were going to do, and I was scratching in the sand, illustrating something, when suddenly I was aware that somebody was with us, and I looked up right into the face of the biggest lion I ever saw. When Doug was aware that I'd stopped, he looked up and saw the lion and there we were – this big lion looking right square at us as if to say, 'Who the hell are you and what are you doing?' We just froze – didn't dare get up and run – didn't know what to do. And suddenly along came Griffith. He walked up, took the lion by the mane, and said, 'Come, little pussycat', and he walked away with it. He had done that as a gag – but we never sat on those steps again!

Did you see him in his later years when he couldn't get a job?

No, nobody ever saw much of him. As a matter of fact, I didn't know whether he didn't want to make any more pictures or what was happening. Only recently, I heard about some of the problems he had. I don't think there is any other business more brutal in the world – unless it's politics. The manner in which they discard people in our business, the cruelty with which they wipe them out and forget them is beyond excuse. I have nothing but the greatest contempt for the higher echelon of management in this business for allowing it to happen. And they're all guilty. They're all heartless and ruthless and I hope they rot in hell for it – and they will. The things they've done to people. And he's an example. But there's lots of others. Too many. And there'll be more.

Why does it happen?

Partly money. And mainly superb egotism and jealousy. The average producer is so jealous of his star or his top director that as soon as he can, he'll chop him down. They conspire to chop him down. They don't want them big – *they* want to be big.

Is that what you meant when you once said, 'When you get your head above the mob, they try to knock it off. If you stay down, you last forever?'

Yes. Let the other fellow get the kudos if he wants it. You have the pleasure of doing your job and making it last a long time, until you're ready to stop. That's why I say don't get too big. They wanted to control Griffith, and when he became too independent, they just let him go. They didn't sell him any more. Francis X. Bushman had his head chopped off. And there are two kinds of stars, I think. One is the public's star – the one they made. The other is the producer's, or company's, star – built up by sheer publicity, by constant repetition of the name. When the public made a star, they were pretty loyal. But sometimes the stars were forced to make pictures they didn't want to make, which they knew were bad for them – and when a star does several bad pictures in a row he'll lose his following. They begin to think it's his fault. So your life at the top is very brief. It can last forever at the bottom – or in the middle – but you get to the top and you're doomed.

Did you try to keep the number of titles down in your pictures?

Well, titles frequently had nothing to do with what we were shooting. They were very often the afterthought of somebody who had nothing to do with the picture, but just happened to see it and say, 'I think it'd be funny if they said such and such at that point' – and somebody who had the authority said, 'Go ahead.' We'd be astonished when we went to a theatre and saw some of them. In fact, the whole aspect of a picture was frequently changed by the titles.

I think many people today are put off by the poor titles in some pictures and it colours their opinions of silent movies.

Well, a breed of title-writers came in and I guess turned into scenario writers. Where they came from God knows. Some titles were cryptic and short, but not many. We once thought the ideal picture would be the one with no titles, but that was an exaggeration because sometimes a good title would help for changes of environment or mood. For instance, after a fadeout or a night scene, we'd put in something like Griffith's 'Came the Dawn', and then come up on a daylight scene. Now a title like that was helpful because without it you'd have been shocked when we cut straight from night to day. But when a man said to a girl in a title, 'I love you', it was ridiculous if it was already obvious in the scene that he was saying 'I love you' to her. Many pictures were ruined by titles, and that's largely because they had such ignorant bums working around the office. They'd say, 'Nobody'll understand it, but I'll fix it.' Insulting the intelligence of *all* the audiences. They used to say the audiences were composed of immigrants and ignorant people who had come over here in steerage and they wouldn't understand. Well, if they wouldn't understand the scene, they wouldn't be able to read the semblance of English in the titles!

How were cameras in those days?

The camera is no better today than it was then except it's mechanised now. We *had* motors for the cameras, but everybody preferred to crank them, because we could control the speed of movement better. The cameraman turned the crank at a count of '101, 101, 101, 101', which made the actors move at normal speed. If he slowed down and got fewer exposures, the actors moved faster. If he speeded up, the actor floated. Of course, we used to have a lot of fun with the hams. They'd strut around and make gorgeous exits – it would take them ten minutes to get off the set. So we simply tipped the cameraman off and he slowed down the crank and they *jumped* off! In comedy we always cranked slower to make it faster, which is how those very funny effects were done in the Sennett pictures. But we were doing a drama once and the producer came on to the set and told the cameraman, 'Crank slower, you're using too much film . . .'

JORDAN IS A HARD ROAD (1915)

Frank Campeau had to play an Evangelist, so I got a fellow named Billy Sunday who was a well-known Evangelist, like today's Billy Graham, and used him as my technical adviser. We put up a huge tent over in Hollywood across from the studio and filled it full of extras – not professional ones – just people off the streets. Now, in the story, Campeau is supposed to harangue them about religion and make them come to God, but I got Billy Sunday up there and he let them have one of his best hot lectures, and I had about three cameras filming only the audience. And pretty soon these people began to feel it, and the first thing you know, they were crawling up the aisles on their knees, coming up to Billy Sunday to be saved, hollering 'Hallelujah' and going into hysteria. A terrific scene. No bunch of million-dollar actors could have done it. You could see the frenzy in their faces. And after we cut, he actually went on with a religious revival right there. Then I was able to put Campeau up there and let him go through the gestures of talking, cutting back all the time to these people I'd already shot. The effect was astonishing.

THE HABIT OF HAPPINESS (1916)

In this picture Doug Fairbanks's character had the idea that any ailment at all could be cured with laughter – make people laugh and they'll laugh their troubles away. He tried it out on a millionaire to good effect, but he wanted to work it on the lower echelon so he went down to skid row and into a flophouse to see what he could do about brightening the lives of those fellows. We built a set over in our New Jersey studio and went down with some buses and brought back these bums from the real flophouses. They didn't know where they were going – half of them didn't have any mentality – they were all booze-soaked old winos. We put them in our flophouse set and Doug went to work trying to get them to laugh. He told some funny stories, and not a smile – the place looked like a flophouse and they all wanted to sleep. It got pretty discouraging. So I said to him, 'Try a little off-colour story – see if that'll work.' It was a silent picture so anything he said couldn't be heard. Well, he tried an off-colour thing and

one guy got a slight quirk on the side of his face – very small – it wouldn't even photograph. I said, 'Well, let's go a little further', and we tried a real seamy one and got several grins and some teeth – or lack of teeth – appeared now. Open mouths. So we came up with jokes as raw as we could find and finally we got so low-down that they really were roaring, and we had what we wanted. When we cut it, the title would say simple humorous things and then howls of laughter would come. But when we released the picture, I began to get letters by the hundreds and finally censorship appeared

Photograph: Dwan with Douglas Fairbanks.

in the form of a couple of executives who said, 'You've got to do something about that picture.' They were scared stiff because all the deaf-and-dumb people all over the place had read Doug's lips and were horrified at the awful things he was saying to these fellows to get them to laugh! We had to call the picture back and make different shots of Doug. And that's how I learned to be very careful about what actors said even in silent pictures.

Did you have an influence in moulding Fairbanks's screen personality?

Well, Doug came out of the theatre – he'd been a star and fairly good – but he learned picture technique very rapidly. We talked and told him our experience – which effects were good and which weren't. A lot of things. And he was very athletic and active, liked movement and space, so he enjoyed every minute. Pictures were made for him. The theatre was too little.

But did you have anything to do with establishing that all-American character he played?

I probably did, in a sense, because I was a little bit like that myself when I was young – a restless, atheletic type. So I'd move *with* Doug – work with him and surround him with athletes. He worked with speed and, basically, with grace. Stunts *per se* were of no interest to him or to me. The only thing that could possibly interest either one of us was a swift, graceful move – the thing a kid visualises in his hero.

He did all his own stunts?

Yes, he did it all himself and everything was gauged for him – we never made him strain. If he was to leap on a table to fight a duel, we'd cut the legs of that table so it would be just the leap he ought to make. He never had to reach an extra inch for anything. Otherwise, it wouldn't be graceful – it wouldn't be him and it wouldn't be right. He was a good, strong athlete but he never strained. Stunt men have tried to imitate him and it always looks like a stunt when they do it. With him, it always

looked very natural. Graceful.

What was he like to work with?

Oh, great, because he was very creative and on-the-ball all the time. He wasn't doing you a favour in coming to work. It was a real privilege to work with him.

THE HALF-BREED (1916)

That was a story from Bret Harte, but Doug's wife, a charming woman, wasn't sure he ought to do it. She had quite a lot to do with what he did and didn't make. She said, 'Why, a half-breed's such a dirty, filthy character and so greasy – I just don't see Doug running around that way.' So I said, 'We'll fix that.' And in the first scene we had the half-breed, wearing practically nothing, dive into a river and swim across. Then he got out and dried himself off with leaves, came out smelling like a rose, put on his clothes and went on with the picture. That made her happy. We had proved that he took a bath.

MANHATTAN MADNESS (1916)

Fairbanks and I wanted to work in New York, and they wanted him to be a western character, so we said, 'All right, we'll do a western in New York.' How do you do that? Well, you bring a westerner to New York and have him buck the New York racket. And we paced the film fast – which was done in the camera, not in the cutting room.

PANTHEA (1917)

'Panthea' was a known story, and I wanted to make it, so Norma Talmadge and Joe Schenck and I formed a company and we did it. She was a very good worker, never late, but one morning she didn't show up at 9:00 when we were supposed to start. At 10:00 she finally came in, and I was a bit concerned – thought maybe she'd been ill or something. I went to her dressing room and she was crying. 'What's another director, because I'll go up against any kind of opposition in this business, but I'm damned if I'm going to buck pillow talk. You two people would have me tied to the mast.' So I left.

Erich von Stroheim was your assistant on Panthea?

Yes, and also an actor. He was very military in his attitude, very superior, very much of a dandy – or tried to be. But he was all right. To me, he was an actor above everything else, and so I made him a Russian officer with a Prussian attitude and a whip. We had some tough-looking White Russians we'd picked up – he played their officer and he was very commanding, cracking his whip at them. He made the mistake of socking them with it a couple of times and finally they started to beat hell out of him. I had to pull him out from under a lot of Cossacks, and I didn't dare put him back in again, so after that, he was just my assistant. And he was very, very good, particularly in this instance because I asked him to dig up a lot of authentic Russian information for me and he did.

I got a good lighting effect in that picture. I wanted to show Panthea playing a piano for three connoisseurs who were judging her talent while her old music master nervously stood waiting in the doorway. We had no set provided for this and no money to make one, so I made a set out of nothing – and it was one of the best scenes in the picture. I put a window-frame way up high and shone a very powerful light from it right down onto her at the piano. And I sprinkled aluminium dust in the light so you could see the beam coming down – it was a terrific effect – and I threw a very faint light on these three men's faces listening, and in the doorway (which was also just a frame) was her professor. And it became a big set – all of it in one shot. Anyway, this effect intrigued everybody who saw it, and my reason for doing it

Still: The Half-Breed *with Sam De Grasse and* Jewel Carmen.

the matter?' I said, 'What's happened to you?' She said, 'I'm married.' I said, 'What!?' She said, 'I'm married to Joe Schenck.' I said, 'That's fine. When?' She said, 'This morning.' That's why she was late. Well, *Panthea* was very successful and we were supposed to make another picture, but I said to Joe, 'You get was to save money. The old economical angle. Art is economical. Whoever invented spending millions of dollars has absolutely ruined the picture business. And I used that trick again for a big banquet sequence in the same film. I had fellows up on the rafters just sprinkling aluminium dust like snow where the light would hit – it was a nice stunt. Everyone was covered with aluminium dust, but that was O.K.

THE FIGHTING ODDS (1917)

That was for the Goldwyn Company. When I first met Sam Goldwyn, his name was Goldfish. He was a glove salesman and had dug up some money and got ahold of a theatrical producer named Arch Selwyn and formed a company with him. When I was engaged to make a picture with them, they still hadn't arrived at a name for their company, but they finally decided to take the 'Gold' from Goldfish and 'wyn' from Selwyn and call it 'Gold-wyn'. And I said, 'Why not take the other two syllables and call it "Sel-fish" '. But Goldwyn won out.

Were producers like Goldwyn difficult in those days?

They never came around. They would discuss the project, talk about the casting, things of that kind, but the rest of it was all yours. Our objection was to the incompetent people they sent out to represent them – either relatives or someone they had to take care of – so they sent them out to see where the money was going. Those fellows used to get out of hand. Instead of being nice and sitting down and doing their job, they'd try to come in and assert themselves. And they were objectionable – they were the ones who started the trouble. At first they called them supervisors and then associate producers. They were carbuncles.

A MODERN MUSKETEER (1917)

That whole picture was an accident. Doug was wooing Mary Pickford at the time she was married to Owen Moore, who lost his patience and began making threats of some kind or another. I was coming back from New York to make a picture with Doug and I got on the train and was riding toward Los Angeles when I got a telegram from him saying, 'Imperative. Meet me in Salina, Kansas and we will return to New York.' So I got off at Salina and Doug arrived on the next Chief and while we rode back to New York, he told me why he

Still, above – Douglas Fairbanks in A Modern Musketeer. *Photograph (opposite): Dwan and Fairbanks on location in the Grand Canyon.*

had to get away from Los Angeles and that embarrassing situation. But we still had to make a picture, so between Salina and New York, we cooked up the idea of *A Modern Musketeer*. I asked him if he'd ever been to the Grand Canyon because I thought it'd be an interesting place to work, and he said, 'No', so that was one location. And I'd never seen Canyon de Chelley over in the Navajo country near

45

Albuquerque, so we decided to work out there too. We made up a story of an imaginative young fellow who's very restless in his little Kansas hometown. He dreams of riding out like D'Artagnan on a horse. To show how restless he was we had him run through the town and onto the church and up the steeple. Well, finally, he rides out in a little yellow Model T Ford – that's his steed – and he gets into a series of adventures we invented as we went along. And it was a comedy, but with plenty of melodrama. We had our heavy and we had to throw him off a cliff. Whenever I see a cliff, I've got to throw someone off it.

You seemed to be spoofing the melodrama in the Fairbanks pictures?

Oh, yes. We did it to keep the audience from doing it – because nobody takes those things seriously. We had plenty of suspense, but we were playing from the humorous side. These dangers were all real to him, though, and the

Photographs: making A Modern Musketeer. *The Model T on rails – Dwan talking to Fairbanks; Marjorie Daw in front seat. Right – in the Canyon de Chelley.*

audience enjoyed his discomfort. We had a lot of funny things in that one.

I remember I rode in a race from Los Angeles to Phoenix with a friend of mine. Quite a long, tough road race – a hundred cars would start and only one or two would get there. And this friend contrived an idea: on the way, he took the tyres off his car, mounted flanges instead and put the car on the Southern Pacific railroad tracks and we drove all the way to Phoenix on them and got in hours ahead of everybody in the race. There was nothing in the rules that said you couldn't do that. So in *Modern Musketeer*, we put Doug's little Ford on the railroad tracks into the Grand Canyon. Later, at Canyon de Chelley, we camped under

this magnificent sandstone cliff that sloped outward and had these great old cliff dwellings you could only reach by high ladders. We had our tents pitched directly under this cliff, and none of the Indians would come near us. They were way across the canyon on the other side, and they kept saying, 'No, we don't want to be there.' Finally the trading post man came over and said, 'They're trying to tell you you're in danger there – the place is haunted.' We thought it was a silly Indian superstition, but to please them and get them to work, we took our tents and moved them over. And that night the whole damn side of that cliff fell down right where our tents had been.

Did Fairbanks contribute to the stories?

Oh, a lot. He didn't do any directing *per se*, but he did a lot of creating, a lot of the stories, the movements, the gags. We all did. Vic Fleming was our cameraman and he used to come up with ideas too. Sometimes we'd invent them on the spur of the moment. It was a team at work, and I always insisted on that, so I can never recall which member of the team was responsible for any definite thing. Everybody contributed.

BOUND IN MOROCCO (1918)

Doug was in an automobile being chased by a motor-cycle cop in the sand dunes. I had them build a long plank road under the sand leading up to a cliff, so we were able to run the car rapidly over the sand. People wondered how we did it. We tipped Doug off to cut fast to the right when he got to the end; he did and the fellow on the motor-cycle sailed merrily through the air off this big dune and onto the sand below. It was a great shot and a wonderful stunt, and fortunately he didn't get hurt because the sand was so soft. The motor-cycle disappeared completely into the sand – only thing sticking out was this fellow's head – looking in amazement. He didn't know he was going

Photographs. Above: Fairbanks and Dwan during the making of A Modern Musketeer *(top); Fairbanks in* Bound in Morocco. *Opposite – Clara Kimball Young and Jack Holt in* Cheating Cheaters.

to do that – because if we'd told him, he'd have been scared to do it or wouldn't have done it well. But this way he was completely surprised, and we paid him for the stunt and he was happy.

The only other thing I remember about the picture was that at the end, after Doug and the girl embraced, we cut to a title, '90 Years Later',

48

see the fellow suddenly lunge back toward the camera where he belonged. After that they quit upstaging each other, but I kept them all on ropes for safety.

THE DARK STAR (1919)

Marion Davies was lots of fun. She stuttered and stammered and it was a little difficult for her to speak at times, but she was fine. As an actress, I can only say that she was very pretty, but no great shakes – never tried to be – and nobody ever tried to make her very much of an actress. But she had a sense of humour and if you gave her anything funny to do, she'd do it funny. She had a great smile. Half the time they didn't pick stories for her with enough humour in them.

Was Hearst actually involved with the picture?

He was involved in the sense that he was very interested in her and he'd come around and see how things were going, invite us all to lunch and take too much time – the whole afternoon would be gone before we'd get back to work – which didn't bother him much. It was a toy – not his business – and he didn't care much. He'd just pour in the dough and that was it. He could buy it, and he did. He was a nice guy.

and then showed two tombstones leaning together. Fade out.

CHEATING CHEATERS (1919)

I had a very good cast, but there's a thing called 'upstaging', a tendency of actors to move up-stage so the other guy has to turn his back to the camera, and I had about four or five of those kind of people in this. I couldn't get them to stop it until I contrived a way. I tied ropes on their ankles – which was below the camera line. I sat in my chair, and anytime one of them moved upstage I gave the rope a jerk and you'd

SOLDIERS OF FORTUNE (1919)

I liked the way that picture worked out. It was very good, and one of the reasons was because I fell heir to some great backgrounds. I went down and used the fairgrounds in San Diego which were perfect for a small Latin republic. They were kind of magnificent too – all in plaster. And I got practically all the people in San Diego working in the picture. There were no unions in those days, so I put an ad in the paper inviting the populace to bring their lunches and come out to Balboa Park to see a picture being made. And they came in droves. I put straw hats on them, and when I brought my actors by, I said, 'Wave those straw hats', and they all waved them. Thousands of people in the picture, all having a good time, eating their lunch and waving straw hats and getting no money, being allowed to see a picture being made.

That was made for a company called Mayflower. Boston money. They gave me *carte blanche*. I just did as I pleased. I found the story, made the movie and they distributed it, and that's all. I made several pictures under that banner and liked all of them, I think.

Did you have censorship in the early days?

Oh, yes, from the beginning. And then organisations were formed. We couldn't open a picture anywhere without passing four or five groups of censors. We'd have the town police first, and then individual groups. They'd all be in our hair. And every little teeny thing was censorable. It was like a Sunday school business in those days. But I think it stimulated us into inventing something that would get by and be decent. We made cleaner pictures, but better pictures. I don't know anything sexier than the stuff Valentino used to do, and yet it was done with a suggestiveness that wasn't dirty.

What was Hollywood like in those days?

It was a pleasant, intimate place – everybody knew everybody. We had little clubs where we'd gather together – Photoplay Club, things of that kind – and we'd go to parties and everybody'd be there. It hadn't divided up into cliques yet, or become snobbish. It might be compared to a circus lot – everybody got along. And we were closer together. The studios hadn't spread out quite so much. Very few of us lived in Hollywood – I lived at the Athletic Club, downtown. And we'd take streetcars out to Hollywood to work. Some people had automobiles, not too many. As I recall, it was a pleasant gang of gypsy-like people, getting away and making a living doing galloping tintypes – that's what we called the pictures. Even

the weather was better and more accommodating. Very often it'd be raining on one side of the street and brilliantly sun-lit on the other. In fact, we'd go across the street and make a rain scene, then come back to the other side and make a sun scene – same day, same time. And it was rural – hardly any traffic to speak of – orange groves and lemon groves everywhere; not many houses and no big buildings. It was just a small town, I'd say.

Was the air of extravagance there?

Not quite yet. The Bel Air set didn't begin to appear until around 1922. Bel Air began to draw people and they started building houses – the ones who had some money. Very few people had gotten into the big money yet, but it was to begin around that time. Then practically everybody had to have a mansion. And, of course, we worked constantly. We had to. We hadn't reached that leisurely method of picture-making – many, many weeks to do one.

You were still making three or four features a year?

Oh, sure, and still having lots of time to go travelling and see the world. We all travelled a great deal.

Did the foreign films have any influence on you or others?

Well, we admired them or got a giggle out of some of them. A thing called *The Cabinet of Dr. Caligari* [1919] interested us because it had some effects we liked. They had some very good technical things we enjoyed, and some pretty good comedians. And, of course, we liked their backgrounds – they were different from ours – and that intrigued us. But outside of that there wasn't too much we got from them – except the people who made them – we got *them*, all of them. The minute a fellow would make a picture somebody would send for them right away. 'He's too good – get him away from Germany or France – get him over here.' Mary Pickford brought Lubitsch over and got a

Photograph: The Luck of the Irish.

headache – they didn't get along at all. But we liked him. And Murnau, I remember. But the 'influence' was on our executives, not us. They'd bring all these people over – and most of the time they were disappointing. And some of them were good.

THE LUCK OF THE IRISH (1920)
I cooked up a way to introduce characters. This fellow had some kind of mechanical shop in a New York basement, in which there were some windows level with the sidewalk. He could see feet going by, and he'd study them and know who they were or what they were – their character. And a very beautiful pair of legs walked by that struck him because later on he sees them – remembers them – and they belong to the girl – and that became the love-story. It was a nice stunt and attracted a lot of attention.

A PERFECT CRIME (1921)
I saw a kid playing baseball on the street with some other kids. (It was next door to a friend

of mine who was a Paramount executive.) She was a cute-looking little tomboy – about twelve – a hoyden, out there knocking hell out of the other kids, playing better baseball than they were. And I needed someone of her type for this picture. She'd never acted, so we talked to her parents and they let her do it and she was very good. Her name was Jane Peters and she later changed it to Carole Lombard.

Was it a big part?

Oh, sure, and she ate it up. Of course, it was silent. If we'd given her lines to remember, she'd probably have been terrified, but we always made kids feel they were playing and not working. When you give them words to learn, it becomes an ordeal.

THE SCOFFER (1921)

We had a very important scene to do in which a bolt of lightning had to strike a tree and set it aflame – a kind of miracle that affected the leading character. Now it was easy to *write* that, but in those days we had no technical tricks – no laboratories to double print onto a negative, no step printers. So engineering presented itself. I fixed the location of the cabin and put beside it a large, almost dead tree, leaving a lot of sky space around which we filtered down for night effect. We got the explosion and the fire with a magnesium bomb in the top of the tree which we'd soaked with gasoline. But how could I make a bolt of lightning come out of the sky and *cause* that explosion? Today I wouldn't have any problem. I'd shoot some static electricity and turn the two pieces of film over to special effects and they'd deliver it very quickly, going through the laboratories. Well, after scratching my small-sized dome for awhile, I came up with this: I took a sharp push-pin and, starting backwards from the explosion, I scratched the emulsion a little bit on one frame – maybe an eighth of an inch in the dark sky above the tree. And I went on scratching

through a series of frames simulating the lightning that way through the dark sky. We made a dupe negative from the print I'd used and from that we were able to make our prints. And I made some other lightning going through the sky ahead of the one that hit the tree so that I could cut it in occasionally to prepare you. Scratched that on too – there was no other way. The moral is when you're stuck for something, work it out, never quit. Of course, today it's pretty hard to get stuck. Still, I've made lightning since with static machines, but it's not as effective. It was such a startling effect and it brought a lot of questions, a lot of letters, a lot of kudos. Most people thought we waited for a bolt of lightning to hit a tree. In the industry, they all tried to find out what we did, but we kept it a big secret.

Still: The Forbidden Thing, *a 1920 Dwan film.*

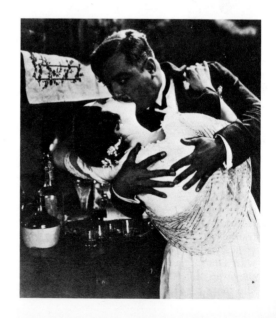

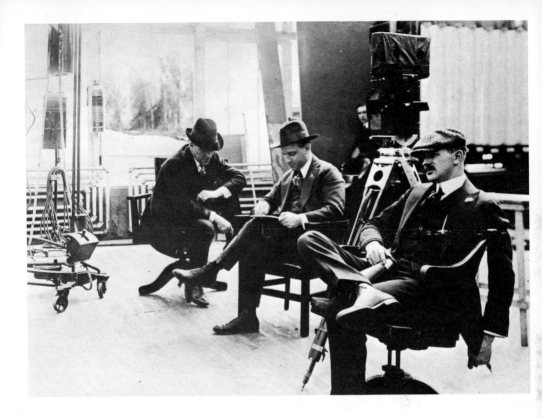

ROBIN HOOD (1922)

Somebody proposed the story to Doug, and he said he wasn't interested. 'I don't want to play a flat-footed Englishman walking through the woods', is the way he put it. He had just finished *The Three Musketeers* and had a studio right across from where I was. There was a fellow on our lot I used a good deal, and who was training there – Jack Dempsey – and we used to go across the street and throw a football around with Doug. One day, Bob Fairbanks told me they were trying to get Doug to do *Robin Hood* and that he didn't want to. 'Well', I said, 'Get

Photograph: Dwan (centre) in the early 'twenties with a writer and Arthur Rosson (right) who directed films supervised or produced by him. On the left, a mercury vapour lamp.

some bows and arrows out here and a target.' And the first thing you know Doug got crazy about shooting these arrows. We got an expert to come up and teach him everything correctly, and it fascinated him so much that it sowed the seeds of *Robin Hood*. He decided to make it *if* we could come up with some kind of a continuity, a story. So everybody began to dig,

and pretty soon the story grew, and I was invited to come and make it. So it's on its way – it's in production.

Now, about that time, Doug and Mary went to New York to do some business. And while he was gone, Bob Fairbanks and I began to oversee the building of the sets. They bought some property on Santa Monica where another company had a one-barn studio. (It's where United Artists is now.) No houses – all open country – and excellent for our purposes. Wilfred Buckland and some other artists had drawn gorgeous pictures we wanted reproduced – especially the big castle. Bob and I were both engineers and we contrived a method of building these massive 90-foot high walls. We had a gate and a moat and the interior hall was 450 feet long, which was an amazing length for pictures. The whole thing was massive – even little corners looked gigantic. But when Doug came back from New York, he saw these sets and ran right out of the studio. 'I can't compete with those,' he said. 'That's not me. What can I do in those big sets?' And he was really ready to call it off.

Well, there was a big balcony up high, and on its rail I hung a great big magnificent sweeping drape, made of burlap, but hand-painted to look like a piece of tapestry. I got Doug back to the studio and I said, 'Now, look, Doug, you get into a fight down here with some of these knights that are after you, and you fight your way all the way up those stairs round that curve, and finally you get up onto the balcony. Men come out the other door and now you're stuck in the middle, fighting knights over here and knights over there.' I paused a minute. He said, 'Then?' I said, 'Then you jump up on the rail.' And I did it for him – so I'm now 50 feet off the stone

Stills: Robin Hood – *Douglas Fairbanks and the set of the castle hall.*

floor. 'You're fighting them on the rail, but they're too much for you – they're crowding you.' He said, 'So?' I said, 'So you *jump* into the curtain', and I jumped into the curtain – under which I had put a scoop that kids use to slide down – and I went swoosh to the ground, struck one of his poses, and said, 'You run out here under the arch and get away.' Well, he went up and jumped in the curtain, came down, and then got everybody he knew to come over

56

Still: Douglas Fairbanks in Robin Hood.

and see him do the trick! Then he looked up at those high windows, and I told him, 'You suddenly appear in that window up there.' He said, 'How the hell do I get in that window? A fireman couldn't get me up there.' I said, 'Why, outside – you go up the wall by climbing the vines.' 'How do I get onto the vines – swim the moat in my armour, or what?' I said, 'No.' There was a little wall down in the foreground and I had a trampoline on the end of it. 'You hit the trampoline and it will throw you onto the vines.' So he tried it, and boom! – again everybody had to come in and see him do that. Up he crawled and appeared in the window, and that was it – he was sold – we were into *Robin Hood*. Now he was no longer the flat-footed Englishman walking through the woods – he was agile, a bird in flight – and, of course, in addition to that there was the splendour and magnitude of these gorgeous reproductions of medieval days. All in all, he was very pleased once he got into it and loved the things we did in the woods – the whole gang dropping out of the trees – he loved to invent them and fall for them.

Then you had a great deal to do with the script?
Well, if you could call it a script, yes – we were all in on it – we used to have conferences in Doug's dressing room. Incidentally, he was a great practical joker and one of his favourite stunts was to give you electric shocks. He had a rubbing table in his dressing-room and also a barber chair he sat in to make up. So you'd go in and jump up on the rubbing table to talk to him, he'd press a button, and we'd all get an electric shock and fly to the ceiling, hollering. He was looking for suckers all the time. So I got a little fed up with it, sneaked in early one day and switched things on him. Being an electrician, I knew my way around, wired the barber chair and put the button over where the table was. So when he reached over to push, I let him have it, and he flew. Well, he didn't think that was a bit funny. From then on that electrical thing was dead – he was scared to sit down any place in his own dressing-room. But Doug was like a kid – he wanted to play all the time.

I remember when we were all done Chaplin pulled a gag. He told Doug he wanted to use the castle set and he said, 'I'll show you what I want to do with it.' So here we are all standing and looking at the great huge thing; the drawbridge slowly comes down, and Chaplin – this little tiny figure – walks out, puts out the cat and takes in a milk bottle, turns and goes back in – and up goes the drawbridge again.

Generally, how closely did Fairbanks work on the preparation of the films he produced?
Well, he *was* the film. He was everything – the writer, the casting director, supervisor. Until he felt he knew all the moves, he didn't even attempt to have his own company. So at Triangle, he was studying the business finding his errors, watching what was being done, choosing what he thought was good, eliminating what wasn't and planning for the future. Dreaming up things he ought to do. But, when he got his own company, I don't think there was ever anybody more successful, both financially and artistically. And he was daring – he did fairy tales – he was a dreamer. He tried not to stay with a stodgy, ordinary story and went into the exotic – like *Thief of Bagdad* and *The Iron Mask* and *Robin Hood*.

Were you concerned with historical accuracy on Robin Hood*?*
Well, we were accurate as far as the period of the story is concerned, the costuming and so on. We had experts come in and work on that. And the story of Prince John's perfidy was true – the Sheriff of Nottingham *was* in cahoots with him. And there may have been a Robin Hood – nobody knows. If there was, he was probably 'a flat-footed Englishman walking through the woods' as Doug said. Certainly there was no band – we took complete liberties with the spirit of Robin Hood and his crowd, and naturally the love-story was more or less invented. But Doug was always insistent on historical accuracy, though I doubt there was ever a castle as big as ours. But, you see, most castles are disappointing – they're so little, There are some big ones in Germany, and a few in the Alps are fine, but most of them are

squatty things, and *all* the English castles are unimpressive. Even if I were going to do Windsor Castle, I'd make it bigger and more elaborate.

There are elements of comedy all the way through Robin Hood.

Well, that's just using Fairbanks as he should be used. He may be fighting a lot of men and life and death is at stake as he's rescuing a girl, but he just doesn't do it as a serious actor would. He does it with a touch of humorous bravado.

The sets were even bigger than in Intolerance *?*

Yes, physically bigger. In fact, nobody had yet had a picture that big. Not only did we have this ninety-foot wall, but on top of it were parapets and platforms. And we shot it with double-exposures. We'd put five thousand people on the ground for the first exposure – which went halfway up on the film – and then moved the same five thousand people up on the walls for the second exposure, which got the top half of the film. We had to be very careful not to let the people on top drop anything, because if they did, of course, it would disappear halfway down. So we tied their napkins or handkerchiefs to their wrists and took everything loose away from them. But it was a terrific effect – when you looked at the sets on the screen, they were bigger than they really were. And we did the same thing for the interiors. They were big enough for anybody, but we still put tops on them with glass shots. That was the most fascinating thing we ever did in films – the old glass shot – it's gone now. We'd have a set of a certain height and then right in front of the camera we put a big plate glass and an artist would paint on it – in exact proportion to our camera's perspective – the top part of the set – the ceiling, the chandeliers, whatever you wanted there. When you photographed the real thing and the painting, they were lit so they'd tie together. And it made very great effects; nearly every picture of any importance had glass shots in it. And you couldn't tell the difference because it was done so artistically and lit very, very carefully.

Of course, *Robin Hood* was all lit with tin reflectors because we didn't have lamps. We had

Stills: Robin Hood – *Fairbanks and a scene in the castle hall, lit mainly by daylight.*

a little floor light for certain effects, but not to matter. All those big light effects were done with huge reflectors we had to build – some of them 12 feet high and 8 feet wide. They'd blast the sun back into those big sets, keeping corners dark, but hitting certain spots. And then we had blacks up and above and whites – we'd pull the blacks and let some light through and balance it up and paint – paint with the light. Arthur Edeson was the cameraman on that, and he was a very good cameraman.

Glass shots would be impossible in colour, wouldn't they?

Well, yes, because colour changes so fast that the paintings couldn't change with them. Light changes a little bit and colour changes. With great pains, it *could* work in colour, but it would be too much of a job.

Did you use tints for Robin Hood?

We always used tinted film for different periods of the day. If we wanted to make it look like dawn, we'd use a pinkish effect – sometimes we'd put a little yellow in – and night was blue. We couldn't actually shoot at night yet, so we had to fake it. Shoot 'day for night' and put filters on to hold the light down and then tint it blue. That was done two ways – either it was printed on coloured film stock or it was dipped in a solution afterwards. Putting it through a tint bath was generally more satisfactory than trying to put it on Eastman stock.

Didn't you invent the crane shot for Robin Hood?

Well, I just used an ordinary construction boom – the kind they use even today to get steel beams and things to the tops of buildings – to lift and move the camera; it was long before today's camera-boom was invented.

What gave you the idea for it?

Well, I don't like static cameras – something ought to move in a moving picture. What I really wanted to do was go from the ground up to a balcony where some people were watching whatever was happening on the ground. I wanted to *move* up, not to cut up because that wouldn't reveal where they were – you wouldn't be sure. And I wanted that feeling of taking your eyes up to the balcony and then going in close to the people. So I said, 'Well, let's make the camera go up there.' Well, how are we going to do that? We can't throw it up or put it on a balloon. So I said we'll just do what they do with a building – get a crane out here and put it up. There was a certain amount of vibration at first, but when we got through constructing a cradle that would always stay on a level, it stayed steady as a rock. And it couldn't be like the thing I thought up for Griffith – we couldn't build a track and an elevator where we were – it had to be done a simpler way, and the crane was also the cheapest way, because they don't cost anything to hire. Of course, today's motion picture crane is very expensive; there's a large crew and it costs a lot of money to rent.

Didn't Robin Hood *have a score especially composed for it?*

Yes, Victor Schertzinger wrote the music after the picture was finished; the love theme was very good and very popular. We opened the picture with a full orchestra in the theatre. And the music went out with it. Of course, *Robin Hood* wasn't just distributed for quite a while – it had only special runs. And it was carefully staged. All the effects we wanted were cued in – they'd have to rehearse a picture in those days. Cue on everything, and they came in right on the beat – the conductor had to really watch it.

Did the director generally have anything to do with the music that was played?

No, he suggested themes that would fit, and very often used them on the set when the actors were working and then passed them along. It

Still: Robin Hood – *Douglas Fairbanks and Enid Bennett as the Earl of Huntingdon and Lady Marian Fitzwalter.*

was usually up to the musical director himself to put them in or not.

So it wasn't often that a score was composed specifically for a film, as it was for Robin Hood*?*
No, because there weren't that many *Robin Hoods*. It was only done now and then for an important picture – though finally it got to a point where every picture that came to big theatres had to have a score. And very often these were prepared at the studio by the music department and the whole thing was sent out with the picture so that other theatres could have it. Now you go back to *The Birth of a Nation* – Griffith had a score with that. He had some beautiful little love themes that went right out with the picture, and wherever it played, you heard them. But the average picture just relied on the theatre, where the piano or the organ ad libbed.

So no film was actually shown silent?
Oh, no – half the effects were done with the piano and the organ. Even the nickelodeon had the piano going.

How did you handle the crowd scenes in Robin Hood*?*
Well, those crowds were extras picked up on the street – we had no guilds of any kind, so we got crowds where we could. We went downtown with buses, let them fill with people and brought them up. Many of them came up not knowing what they were supposed to do. And then we'd take them into the dressing rooms and let them put on the equipment. But I had a telephone exchange on my platform connected with all the departments. I put a lieutenant with every twenty people and I'd call him by name and tell him what I wanted his group to do. If there were a hundred of them, I'd call five groups at the same time and tell them to move on the cue. 'Numbers one and seventeen – move forward twenty paces . . .'

Like being a quarter-back again.
That's right – it was exactly the same.

The film was a big success, wasn't it?
Oh, yes. But it was made at a time when there was a complete lull in the business – no other studio was working. Therefore a lot of those people in the crowds were some of the best actors, writers and technicians in the business; they all came over to get a meal ticket. It was one of those times when all of a sudden the box office fell apart – the public deserted the picture business. The only answer to it is that the pictures we were turning out were lousy. So Doug put his own money into *Robin Hood* because he couldn't get financed. It opened Grauman's Egyptian Theatre, which had just been built, and was a terrific success. Then Doug and I took the picture to New York where it was a smash too. People came back to the theatres and it made an awful lot of money.

We stayed at the Ritz Hotel in New York, had the press come in for lunch and went up to the roof for photographs. Somebody brought a bow and some target arrows in and Doug obligingly posed as Robin Hood. He pulled this gigantic bow back as only he could, and, on some impulse, he let it go, and off this arrow whizzed eastward. Now we come to a title: 'Doug shot an arrow in the air – it fell to earth but I know where.' And you cut to a five-storey loft building on the East Side. This is a true story. Sitting on a window sill in a sweat-shop is a little Hungarian sewing button-holes – when an arrow swooshes down and sticks him in the rumbleseat. He turns around, sees the arrow and immediately he knows he's being attacked by Indians – those fearful redskins he's read about. Howling, he runs down through the building, out onto Third Avenue and into the arms of a cop – who sees the arrow sticking in the fellow's rear end and takes him to Bellevue Hospital. That evening out came the papers emblazoned with Doug's picture pulling a bow, and next to it is the story of a little fellow who's been shot in the rear end by an arrow. Well, it cost Doug five thousand dollars to square it. And the fellow put himself in business and became a rich man. Now, even to this day, they tell me that if you go over on the East Side, you can see some people sitting in windows praying for an arrow to come along and put them in business.

Robin Hood *begins with a Charles Kingsley poem, 'So fleet the works of men,/Back to their*

earth again:/ Ancient and holy things/ Fade like a dream.' That recalls Gray's 'Elegy' which you filmed as* The Restless Spirit. *Is that sense of the impermanence of human work something that concerns you?*

Well, it's passed away now. I still like the philosophy of it, but I don't give it very much

Photograph: shooting Robin Hood – *at the megaphone Fairbanks and Dwan (in topee).*

thought. It seemed important when I was younger. Lots of things that seemed terribly important then are just of no importance at all anymore. They're just thoughts, and so many other thoughts come in and crowd them out.

ZAZA (1923)

That was the first one I did with Gloria Swanson. She was out here working for Paramount and they kind of had a grudge against her for some reason and weren't handling her well. And I was having a problem with them myself. They had put a fellow named B. P. Schulberg in charge and he'd elevated some

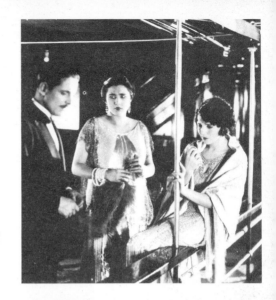

Pictures: 1923. Stills – Nita Naldi in Lawful Larceny *(left); David Powell, Nita Naldi and Bebe Daniels in* The Glimpses of the Moon. *Below – Dwan and cameraman Hal Rosson with Hope Hampton making* Lawful Larceny.

relatives to supervisors; one of them kept coming down on my set and bothering me and I threw him off and told him not to come back. Anyway, I finally said, 'Look, let me work at the New York studio.' It was idle. They wanted everything out here under one head, but I guess I stood pretty well with them and they finally let me come East. I chose *Zaza* as one of the stories. Now Mickey Neilan was interested in Gloria and he asked me to get her out of this bad environment too, so I brought her over and put her in *Zaza*. My agreement with the studio was that if I met the budget I'd receive a bonus on each picture, so of course I was interested in keeping the budget down, and did. Gloria worked well, *Zaza* was a smash hit, and that was the start of the new Swanson. She wanted to stay in New York so I made several pictures with her, as well as others in between.

BIG BROTHER (1923)

That was at the beginning of the Big Brother Organisation, which still exists, and the idea of which is that it's a good idea for any man who has the time and the ability to take over some kid with no guidance and help him – become a foster brother. The character Tom Moore played became attached to a tough young East Side kid who was neglected – put in detention homes and so on because he was obstreperous; and Moore – who was a rough guy himself – befriended him, and they got into all kinds of trouble. It was that type of story. The basic thing was that we worked in real environments – we went to the toughest part we could find on the East Side and worked among those people. We didn't build sets and worked outside as much as possible. There were two gangs who were bitter enemies – the Hudson Dusters and the Gas House Gang – and, through diplomacy and some money, we got them both to bring their girls and come up to a big famous dance hall at the edge of Harlem, just across the street from the Polo Grounds. And we laid it on the line with the two gang leaders, and asked them, since they were being paid, to do exactly what we asked and nothing else. No trouble. If we gave an order from my platform, they were to obey that order and no other. And they agreed – shook hands on it – that they'd be peaceful all through the picture. But the police department – just in case – sent up their famous hard-arm squad – the toughest gang of policemen we'll ever know. They were standing by. But the gangs were very obedient, did whatever we said: 'Stop dancing. Go over and sit down. Move over.' Now to light this big hall, we were using the old Klieg lights I told you about, which we called 'broads', and to soften the

Stills. Left – Dwan's first film with Gloria Swanson, Zaza. *Right –* Big Brother; *Tom Moore with the boy, Mickey Bennett, and Edith Roberts.*

light, we'd hang silk scrims over them, which were known as 'silks'. We had our cameras up on a balcony shooting down at the dance floor – these lights were all around – and just as we were ready to start a big dance number my cameraman decided he needed more light so to his electricians and grips he called out loudly, 'Take the silks off the broads.' Well, in gangland, 'silks' are dresses and 'broads' are girls, so they heard this command come from my platform, thought it was an order – 'Take the silks off the broads' – and started to take the silks off their broads. Well, the girls revolted and ran for their lives, and for some reason or other, the guys got tangled up with each other and the fight was on. Somebody blew the whistle and the hard-arm squad came in and started to lay their clubs down. Well, it lasted for ten minutes or so and we photographed it all. Nearly took all the police ambulances in New York to take these guys away to get

patched up, and it cost us a little money to buy new dresses, but it was worth it. It was the most vivid gangfight I've ever seen. And I had to go back and write it into the picture.

But we got a very seedy, very authentic background for the picture and it was a real heartbreaker with fine characterisations, both from Tom Moore and from the kid, Mickey Bennett. He became quite popular on account of it. The scenes were good and they piled one on top of the other and turned into a very, very good picture – one of those that just jelled and meshed – everybody loved it. A nothing that turned into something big.

A SOCIETY SCANDAL (1924)

That was with Gloria too. And Ricardo Cortez, who got in our hair. We were working in the Astoria studios on a bedroom set. Cortez had to come in through the window and take a glass of brandy Gloria gave him and drink it. But I didn't like the way it was done time after time – and we were giving him real booze – so pretty soon these drinks got him, and he went out like a light. We all tucked him nicely into his bed and went home. At four in the morning, not a soul around, this poor bum wakes up in the bed in a dark, deserted studio – and he doesn't know where the hell he is. Can't remember anything. And when he did, he didn't know where to go without falling over something – and it was locked up anyway. So he had to stay there all night, until people came around to open up in the morning and found him. He said to me, 'What the hell'd you do that for?' And I said, 'Well, you were just so dumb you couldn't get the scene right. You *act* too much.' He said, 'But it was real booze, wasn't it? I thought they drank tea.' I said, 'No, not in a *good* picture.

Stills: Gloria Swanson. Left – with Ricardo Cortez in A Society Scandal. *Right – in* Manhandled, *Dwan's favourite Swanson film.*

very jolly – a clown if there ever was one. A little bit of a woman, yet she was the prize clothes-horse of the day. Astonishing. She was quite short, but perfectly put together I guess, carried herself like a queen and for that reason looked well in anything she did. Of course, in *Manhandled* she even did Charlie Chaplin. Came out one day dressed like Chaplin, did it for me and I put it in the picture. Which was quite a big hit. And also I used it in an interesting way. She was trying to make a terrific impression at a party and some girl who didn't like her induced her to do Chaplin knowing it would make her seem ridiculous. And she did the impersonation very effectively, but instead of her getting applause, she got ridiculed for being so silly and stupid. She should have come out more sexy, strutting, instead of being a clown, and every move she made was wrong in the picture – trying very hard to establish herself as something more important than just a very humble, hard-working little shop girl who worked at the bargain counter at Macy's or Bloomingdale's. And she just got kicked all over the place.

Now, Gloria had never worked in a store, and seldom even been near a bargain counter. I decided the best way to get her into the character was first to find her a job in a bargain counter and let her learn what it's like. So we got her a job at Macy's and she made herself as plain as possible – and got hell beaten out of her. She was back of a bargain table and these women would come down and press so hard against her – she was against the wall – they nearly squashed her in half. She had to be rescued. Then somebody from the studio came along, recognised her and yelled out her name, and there was pandemonium. She lost the job. Well, also in the course of this story, the character had to ride the subway to and from work – which was, of course, purgatory. She had a hat with grapes and birds and things on it which she

That's for kid stuff. This was the real thing. One take wouldn't hurt you, but you couldn't get it right – it was your own fault.' After that he was as good as he could be and did everything right the first time.

MANHANDLED (1924)

Which of the Swanson films do you like best?
Well, I like them all, but I think I might have liked *Manhandled* best for some reason – I can't remember why. She was always just perfect – a pleasure on, off and everywhere – just great. She was a wonderful worker to start with, and

Stills: Manhandled – *Gloria Swanson in society (with Ian Keith) and in the subway.*

loved very much, and in this scene it was supposed to be destroyed by these big lugs hanging on the straps and smashing her in between. Gloria had never been on a subway and couldn't understand what that would be like, so I dressed her up – with no make-up – in the funniest, most awful-looking outfit that looked no more like Gloria Swanson than my left ear – she *looked* like she'd been working all day long at a real bargain counter – and I took her over to what we called the Shuttle, which only runs back and forth from Grand Central to Times Square. Nobody paid any attention to her. I waited for a real pack, shoved her aboard, and left her in there. Well, she rode to Times Square and when she tried to get off, the crowd coming on shoved her back again – and she ended up going back and forth about ten times. She was a wreck – everything she had was ripped off. Finally she got out at Times Square, made her way to the street, went over to a taxicab, said, 'Take me to –' and he looked at her and said, 'Beat it, sister – beat it.' She said,

'You take me to my hotel.' He says, 'Go on – go away – don't try to pull anything cute.' She says, 'I'm Gloria Swanson and I want to go to my hotel.' And he said, 'Well, I'm Valentino, so get the hell out of here or I'll call a cop.' And finally he beckoned and a cop came over. 'What's the trouble?' 'Well, this dame tells me she's Gloria Swanson.' And the cop said, 'Look, sister, what are you pulling?' Well, she insisted and the cop wanted to be safe, so he said, 'Well, we'll ride over to your hotel and see, and if you're wrong I'm calling the wagon.' They came to the hotel, but I'd tipped off the doorman. 'When she comes along, you don't

Stills: Gloria Swanson. Left – as a shopgirl riding the New York subway in Manhandled. *Below – as a Balkan princess in* Her Love Story (*also 1924*), *with George Fawcett (Archduke), Echling Gayer (King), Mario Majeroni (Prime Minister).*

know her.' I really wanted her to get a dose of it. So when they drove up, she got out and said, 'You tell these people who I am', and he said, 'Well, who are you?' The cop took her into the lobby and nobody would recognise her. She grabbed a pen at the counter and signed her name and finally they called the manager and he said, 'Well, of course. That's her signature', so she was allowed to go up to her apartment. She never forgave us for it. She did everything she could to get back at me – more practical jokes – which were typical of her. But I had indoctrinated her, and when we did the subway scene it was terrific. She got howls of laughter. She knew what she was doing. Same as the bargain counter when we worked at it. She was

Stills: 1924. Top – Her Love Story; *Gloria Swanson and Ian Keith. Left* – Argentine Love; *Ricardo Cortez and Bebe Daniels. Right* – Wages of Virtue; *Gloria Swanson and Ben Lyon.*

no longer a high-society actress pretending to be a little working girl. She said, 'Don't tell me – I know what it's like.' And she did – she'd add and contribute a lot. And we practically had no scripts – we used to manufacture things as we went.

But Gloria was always full of hell, always pulling things. It was always fun with her – a game – it wasn't just a studio because we'd be playing tricks on each other all the time – terrible things. Once I had to go to France where Gloria was making *Madame Sans Gêne* to get her interested in *Coast of Folly* [1925]. She'd reached the end of her contract, and Paramount wanted to sign her again. Making big offers. Anyway, we found she had picked up a romance over there with the Marquis de la Falaise de Coudray, so when I arrived in Paris with my assistant Dick Rosson, she met me at the station in a big yellow car with two liveried men on it! I

drove with her over to my hotel – she had a house some place – where I was to see her for dinner – which she said would be formal. I had no white tie, and she thought that was too bad – couldn't I rent one? She wanted to rub it in, you know. Dick didn't have one either, so we said no, we'd come in black ties and if they didn't like it, to hell with them. Anyway, I discovered she'd suddenly gone social – oh boy, in a big way. This was going to be quite a thing – with royalty present and everything. So we went to this lovely house, where footmen took our hats and a butler in livery announced us, and we were introduced all around to Lord and Lady This, Prince That and Duke of This. Finally, a Hindu with ribbons on his chest and a big jewel on his turban arrived and everybody kowtowed to him. But Dick Rosson whispered to me, 'These bastards are all wearing make-up', and I began to look and saw this Hindu had a

phony beard and I began to smell a rat. Gloria was up to something. At dinner some kind of an argument began between the Hindu and another guy; they got into fisticuffs and finally the Hindu pulled out a gun and shot the other one down. Dick reached over with a glass of wine and poured it on the dead man's face, and the Hindu began to be abusive, so I swung on him. His beard went east and his feet went west – he was out cold. And that turned out to be the Marquis de la Falaise de Coudray. After that things were fine.

NIGHT LIFE OF NEW YORK (1925)

Jesse Lasky had agreed that Edgar Selwyn (an actor who had become a writer and was a good friend of mine) would write a story called *Night Life of New York* and that certain people would be in it. One day the three of us had lunch and talked about the general idea. Edgar was going to Europe, so the agreement was that while he was away, he'd work on it and soon after he got back, deliver it. Three or four weeks. I had something else scheduled, but something happened – I had to drop what I was doing and Lasky had made some contracts – and for some reason *Night Life* had to be done now. But Edgar Selwyn's gone and all I've got is the little conversation we had at lunch – and Rod La Rocque and Dorothy Gish. At any rate, I began it on a Monday night – and within five days – not over that – I had the whole picture shot. And I had it cut and printed and ready – titles and all – before Edgar Selwyn got back from Europe. When he arrived, he called me and said, 'Gee, I don't know how to apologise, but I haven't got a goddamn thing on paper.' I said, 'The hell you haven't – you've got the film finished.' And his name is on it as the author. Well, he was so astonished – everybody was – but it was just one of those things that rolled together. And a very good picture. But the point was it showed the world how New York operated at night – all the scenes and places and people were real – and there was a little story running through. We went into real nightclubs and real theatres and real night exteriors – all with available light. That was the first time I used fast film and a wide shutter. Photographed people leaving a theatre at night – under the marquee – I had the cameras in a truck so nobody knew we were there – and it photographed brilliantly – with no additional light. Fast film. Eastman made it *that* day, got it down to us and we had to use it *that* night. It wouldn't have lasted overnight, it was so sensitive.

COAST OF FOLLY (1925)

It wasn't a blockbuster, but it was a good commercial picture. And at that time there was a feud on between Pola Negri and Gloria Swanson. Press agents started it – they always wanted feuds between actors because it at-

tracted the public's attention. We were all still working on open stages, and Negri was at one end of this big stage, we were on the other, and she used to make very important entrances. All things must cease. There'd be a hush and everybody would stand up as Pola Negri floated in to her onstage dressing-room. Well, of course, that amused me. So I had Gloria ride through the grounds in this Palm Beach wheel-chair pushed by one fellow, with another one holding

Stills: Coast of Folly. *Opposite – Robin Hood and Pollyanna (Antony Jowitt and Gloria Swanson); Above: Gloria Swanson and Dorothy Cumming.*

an umbrella over her. And when she'd arrive on the stage, we'd have a little orchestra play – which disturbed Pola Negri, who said she couldn't emote with our music. She'd walk huffily off her set to create trouble at the front office, and they'd come down and say to me,

'Can't you play the music softer or something?' I'd say, 'No. Miss Swanson has to be greeted, just as Negri has to be greeted'. So it got to the point where one of them had to go, and I thought, well, I'll put a quietus on this. I arranged for one of the big school bands to come – must have been seventy people in the damn thing, all in uniform – and when Gloria got in the wheel chair, this band appeared and 'Woom-ti-ti-dum-bam-boom-BOOM!' – they played 'The Trojan March' or something, and it pretty near shook the scenery down. That was the end of the feud – Negri gave up. Because I said, 'We're going to *keep* the band because the little orchestra isn't loud enough. There's so much noise over on Negri's set we can't hear the music and respond emotionally to the mood. So we're going to use the band.' That scared hell out of Negri's group, so we finally went back to our Tendler String Quartet, which was beautiful. I had them all through those years.

STAGE STRUCK (1925)

That was Gloria again. We went down to New Martinville, West Virginia, so we could get a real showboat – the Columbia River runs down through there. And I had a little guy who had been a busboy in the Paramount restaurant – and he was so pleasant and his eyes were so interesting – he could hardly speak English – that I finally pulled him out of there, first made him my call-boy and eventually something like a fifth assistant. I sent him down to New Martinville to keep track of what was going on and get certain things ready. His name was Joe Pasternak. That was his beginning. By then he was dressing up, looking pretty good and becoming very American – he'd learned four or five more words of English – all backwards, of course. Now, preparing a house for Gloria down there, he got eight or ten of the town's young society girls, dressed them up like French maids

from a musical, and when Gloria and the Marquis arrived, had them lined up in a row, and trained to act like the Duchess was arriving. They all bowed. Gloria said, 'Who are these people?' 'These are your attendants', said Joe. 'They'll take care of you.' In the meantime, the Marquis de la Falaise de Coudray was eyeing them – 'Oh, ho.' And Gloria said, 'Get them out of here.' Wham! they all got fired right there, and they dug up some plain-looking dame to come in to take care of her. She didn't want Henry fooling around with those little girls. But we had a grand time down there – riverboat, a lot of very good hokum and horse play, and Gloria did a fine job. It was a good comedy picture.

It was also the first time I can recall anyone using Technicolor. There was a dream sequence in which Gloria, playing a little punk who wants to be an actress, fancies herself a great person in the theatre – and it was a magnificent pageant – all in colour. But the sets, of course, were just ordinary, made for black and white and there wasn't much colour on the walls, so I said to the Technicolor man, 'Let's project some colour on the walls.' 'Oh, you can't do that.' 'Why? You do in the theatre. Put magenta in front on the lamps and change

Stills. Left – William Powell and Jack Holt in Sea Horses. *Above –* Stage Struck, *Gloria Swanson and plate of beans.*

everything from pink to blue. In fact, you can change it as you're shooting – ' 'Oh, it wouldn't work.' 'Well, can't we try it?' Finally, we did and, gee, the effect was immense – just perfect. Those colours came out just as well as the clothes, and it added to the dream effect. (I remember Nita Naldi was in that sequence dressed up like the Queen of Sheba or something.) But, you know, Technicolor would give

demonstrations of their stuff and nobody had much use for it. We would never dream of using it for a whole picture – but for a short sequence of that kind, I thought it might be effective.

SEA HORSES (1926)

We had a wonderful cyclone in that – a typhoon that came over the water and sucked it up. A terrific effect. It was done in reverse, of course, poured water down, then reversed the film. Wrapped a ship up in it somehow and got a good effect. The only other thing I can

79

remember about that picture is that Jack Holt had a little too much to drink one night and swallowed a bridge of about four teeth. We fixed him up with putty or make-up so he could work, but we had to wait for the bridge to go its course – and the question was, would it turn sideways and require an operation? Would we

Stills. Left – Louise Dresser and Charles Lane in Padlocked (*1926*). *Above – Renée Adorée and Thomas Meighan in* Tin Gods. *Photograph, right: on location for* Tin Gods *with* Meighan (*front row, left*) *and Dwan* (*seated*).

lose him? Because it's pretty serious to have that damn thing going down through you. He had to be X-rayed every day and it went further and further, into his intestine, and fortunately didn't turn around. Some among us published the fact that Jack was pregnant and little Brigitte was waiting to be born – it had come through all right. And everybody'd say to him, 'How's little Brigitte?' 'Aw, get out of here!'

THE JOY GIRL (1927)

Marie Dressler was in that – she was a big musical star in the theatre – but she'd had a slump. Now, I was in New York looking for some people for this picture, and I went to lunch with my studio manager at the Ritz Hotel. While we were eating, I looked over and I saw a woman sitting alone at a little table, and I said, 'Isn't that Marie Dressler, the actress?' We called the head waiter and he said, 'Yes, it is'. I said, 'Is she here at the hotel?' He said, 'Yes, she's in residence here.' So I wrote her a note to this effect: 'Dear Miss Dressler, I'm an admirer of your work in the theatre. I'm a director of motion pictures and I'm interested whether you would care to play in a picture of

mine which is to start immediately.' The head waiter handed her the note just as she was turning to go up some steps that led onto the main floor – and she read it and started to stagger and grabbed the stair rail. The head waiter rushed over and helped her go out. Well, I thought, she's either had a drink too many or she isn't well. Then a bell-boy came to me and said, 'Miss Dressler would like to know if you'd see her before you go – she's in her room.' So when I was finished, I asked for her room and was directed to a floor that consisted of rooms used only for the servants of guests at the hotel. And in one of these little rooms was Marie Dressler. She said, 'Did you mean what's in this note?' I said, 'Yes.' 'Well', she said, 'you've saved my life, son.' I said, 'What?' She said, 'I just had my last meal downstairs and I was going to go out that window. I'd reached the end of my strength. The world was through with me and I was through with the world. But this looks like new hope.' Now there were other reasons for this dementia which I'll tell you in a minute, but I took her out to Palm Beach and she was a riot with society there – they all knew her – she was very famous with them and every estate opened to our use because she was with us. Really, she was the queen of Palm Beach, and had the time of her life. Everybody entertained her, had dinners and lunches for her. We both came back to New York and I didn't have anything for her so I said, 'You did so well in my picture – and New York theatre seems dead for you – why don't you go out to California and get into pictures?' She had played in a Chaplin picture, *Tillie's Punctured Romance* [1914], but hadn't really been established because she went back to the theatre. So I wrote some letters of introduction, got ahold of a good agent, paid her way out here and took care of her. And pretty soon she was hired by MGM, caught on and became famous. But a cancer she had even at that time finally killed

her about six years later. She knew she had it in New York though she didn't tell me that. So I didn't realise when she told me she was going out the window that it was because she knew she was doomed anyway. It was a slow thing and it finally got her. But she never forgot – every time she was interviewed, she always told them I was responsible for her career in pictures. Which I wasn't – it was just that *moment*.

THE IRON MASK (1929)
Did you work on the script?
Well, such as it was, yes, we all did. The credit went to Elton Thomas and Lotta Woods. Lotta was the one who put it on paper – the big secretary. 'Elton Thomas' was twenty people. It was everybody who said, 'Let's do this,' and 'Wouldn't it be great if we did that.' We had an exchange of ideas. We'd bring Tom Gerrity and other writers Doug knew well, and they'd all contribute suggestions and then we'd put them together.

Doug brought Lawrence Irving, Henry Irving's son, over from England to design the sets, and they were very imaginative. He'd draw the pictures and then William Cameron Menzies would have to build it, reproduce it. And Maurice Leloir who was the famous illustrator of the Dumas books – he came over to do the costumes. Doug went to all that trouble – which cost money too – but he wanted it right.

Just at that time, sound had been introduced to the picture business, and in those days it was ridiculous. The cameras were locked up in padded, sound-proof cells like telephone booths with the cameraman looking through a sound-proof window and suffocating. When Fox built their new sound stages, they had engineers come out and put up huge, thick, padded walls. The camera was shooting through windows in sound-proof rooms built up on balconies. That was how they built the stages,

Still: The Iron Mask.

forgetting that sets were going to be put up and the camera wouldn't be able to see the action from up there because the sets would be in the way. It was all a bust. In fact, those rooms are still standing over there now in complete disuse. Anyway, I saw this ridiculous thing in the booth and I said to Doug, 'You know, we're just under the wire with this picture because sound is coming in, and I think we'd better beat them to the punch.' So we made a prologue in which Doug made a speech as

D'Artagnan – some poetical thing we wrote – 'In days of old when knights were bold' and so forth – and then the picture unfolded. And at the end we made an epilogue in which the older D'Artagnan said farewell. Certain theatres didn't have sound equipment yet, but since this was a roadshow picture we were able to do it. And it did have a wonderful effect on the picture itself – made it very up-to-date. Otherwise they might just have said, you know, 'last of the big silents'.

That was my first experience with sound in a feature. But in 1926, before the Jolson picture, a friend of mine named De Forest had just perfected the tube that was going to make it possible to have sound pictures. And, at that time, Tom Meighan was the top man at the famous actors' club, the Lambs, which every year put on a show called the Lambs Gambol – and no woman had ever appeared in them (nor were they allowed in the clubhouse). This year the show was being held at the Metropolitan Opera House. So I took Tom Meighan and Gloria Swanson up to De Forest's sound laboratory and shot a scene with them. She came in and Tom said, 'You don't belong in here – this is the Lambs Gambol and no woman is allowed.' She said, 'Oh, well, I must have made a mistake, I'm sorry, but I just came in here to sing a song.' There was some more back and forth and she started to sing the club song until two or three people threw her out. That was it – and we showed that at the Lambs Gambol. So it was the first talking picture they'd ever seen, and also the first time a woman had ever been in the Lambs Gambol.

Around that same time, Fox had developed the sound wagon for the use of Movietone News, and I took one up to West Point and shot a troop review that set them all on their heels when they saw it.

For a newsreel?

Yes, with all the band music and sounds of the drill – it was extremely effective – and, naturally, I learned what the wagon could do – how simple it was. Of course, if there was some extraneous noise – a hammer dropping, a buckle clinking, we didn't stop everything and say, 'Take it again, you clicked', as they did in sound pictures, where the sound man was always yelling, 'Hold it! Hold it! Cut! Something dropped. I heard a bing.' As if it mattered. They drove us out of our minds. In an argument scene, we'd have an actor jump over the other fellow's line because that made it sound natural, and they'd stop the machine immedi-

Still: The Iron Mask – *Fairbanks in action.*

ately and say, 'You've got to cut there – he was talking over his lines.' I'd say, 'But I *want* it that way.' 'Well, you can't record it that way – you haven't got the mike right – the mike's aiming at him and the other guy's talking. You haven't got a balance.' So I'd say, 'Well, put two mikes on it – let them each have a mike.' 'Oh, no. You can't do that. You gotta work with one mike.' And in those days the mikes were hidden in bouquets, in back of chairs – they hadn't come around to the fish-pole mike yet. So we were up against a bunch of sound men who were green as grass, and whose only rule was, 'Every syllable must be heard.' That meant you had to wait before picking up your cue. You'd say, 'My mother's coming this afternoon', and before I could say, 'What time?' I'd have to pause one-two-three – 'What time?' They finally got over it because we just said, 'To hell with you, we're going to do it this way.' But at first the sound man took over.

And, in fact, we found ourselves really struggling for existence because the executives thought we were no longer needed – that silent picture makers didn't know anything about dialogue or sound. So they imported directors from the theatre to do the directing. Well, of course, they were like lost sheep. They came in and didn't know where to put the camera or what to do with it or how to direct the actors. They didn't understand that scenes had to be stopped and cut – they wanted the act to go all the way through. But we were practically out of work, and it took a long time for anybody to recognise the fact that we could handle dialogue and things with sound in it. They forgot that we'd been using dialogue since time began – you just weren't hearing it. Fortunately. Finally they made a concession with those of us who had contracts and couldn't be fired. They said, 'Well, you'll come and sit down with the theatre director, watch what he does and learn what you can from him.' That happened to me on *The Far Call* [1929] at Fox. And, of course, just the reverse occurred – he'd turn around and say, 'What do I do now?' And they became *our* assistants, the ones who lasted.

And, of course, when they put sound on the film, they stole a piece of the image and reduced our picture to almost a square which was ugly. It lost that nice oblong balance. Then later they widened it again by reducing its height and lengthening the sides – until now it's really out there – you play tennis when you look at a picture.

Why did Fairbanks decline in the talkies?
Well, you see, technically, sound was wrong in its pitch when it began – and for a long, long time – only recently it's beginning to be right. In other words, if your voice was high, sound made it higher – it became shrill. Now John Gilbert just didn't have the kind of a voice that

went with his personality, and Doug Fairbanks didn't either. Doug was a manly-looking young man, but he had a high voice. And Gilbert's was higher – manly, but high. They talked Irish tenor – so, of course, it didn't fit. Today that could be corrected. But then it just didn't go down. He tried a talkie with Mary – *The Taming of the Shrew* [1929] – and it didn't come off. Doug didn't have it.

What did you think about the potential of sound?
I thought it was the end of a fine art. I thought, 'That's it', and I kissed it off. Because I don't think talking pictures compare with silents. They're a different thing – an extension of the theatre – with more and bigger sets, more expanse, but otherwise the same, because everything's based on what you say or what's the sound. And I liked pictures as pictures in motion. We used words for titles, but we always got the best effect from *doing* something rather than saying something, and we said as little as possible.

But I think sound came at about the time silent pictures needed something stimulating. They were beginning to lose the audiences. People would rather stay home and listen to the radio than spend money to go to pictures. So talkies did stimulate the box office. It was one of the new gimmicks that brought people back, and they went along with that for quite a long time until television came along. And they've had to look for other gimmicks – colour and wide-screen. But they've never regained their big adult audience.

TIDE OF EMPIRE (1929)
It was a western, and we were shooting on the street at MGM one night when suddenly we heard a commotion and wham! a fellow came flying out the saloon doors. It wasn't part of the scene at all – I didn't expect it. And he did two or three somersaults – amazing flops – slid down the street, sat up and looked around. It

treadmill. The effect was all wrong. The lens also wasn't popular because it wasn't available and it was too costly. And it wasn't an attachment to the camera then – but a gigantic affair that hung out in front of the camera – about two yards long and bulky. I think it was just experimental, and later it got to be a practical thing that anybody could use. Though even today it doesn't have the effect of movement, but the effect of extension. It just seems to open up instead of move. Of course, even in dollying as a rule we find it's a good idea to *pass* things in order to get the effect of movement. We always noticed that if we dollied past a tree, it became solid and round, instead of flat. So we used to take buildings with pillars and get a wonderful effect dollying past.

FROZEN JUSTICE (1929)

They brought the cumbersome sound equipment down on the stage, and I objected because it cluttered us up. They said, 'What's your alternative?' I said, 'I want a wagon outside the studio door. Let the men sit in the wagons and record the sound out there. You just bring me the microphones in here and I'll put them where I want them.' And I made them put the microphone on a boom and move it around instead of hiding it in back of pictures and things. The reason I insisted was because, as I told you, I'd used the Fox news wagon up at West Point and I knew it'd be all right.

So I had a scene in a real tough Alaskan town in this picture, in which every second store was a dance-hall or a saloon. And I dollied the camera down the street, with the sound on a boom, and went into every one of those halls, one after the other, with camera and sound,

was Buster Keaton. He did the stunt to amuse the Talmadge girls (he was married to Natalie) who were on the set. And I kept it in. Bit of atmosphere – a bum who's thrown out of a saloon.

The picture was pretty good. It was the first time I used the zoomar lens, which had just been invented. We were on this western set looking off into the distance and up the hills from where a stage-coach is supposed to come toward us into town. So I got real brilliant. I said, 'Here's a great chance to use the zoomar lens. We'll bring the stage-coach right into town with it.' So we did. But it looked like the camera must have been on the horses' noses because it came right with them; they were always in close-up and the town finally appeared, but actually you didn't see them *approach* the town. In fact, the town must have approached the horses since it looked like the stage-coach stood still all the time. Or galloping on a

Still, above: Tide of Empire – *George Duryea and Renée Adorée. Photograph – Renée Adorée on location at the San Fernando Mission for* Tide of Empire.

86

without stopping the camera – no cuts. It terrified the sound people: 'You can't do it – impossible!' But we did. A girl would be singing in one saloon and you'd hear a portion of her song and pull away and she'd gradually die off as we'd go into another one where a dance was going on to guitars and so on through four or five of them before I stopped at a more remote spot to pick up some dialogue. There was a reason for the shot – somebody was going in and out of these places looking for someone. But the idea of moving the sound really staggered them. Well, the first time we did it, as we were coming out of one place, they raised the sound boom too high and it hit a high-tension wire and shorted. The whole thing went to pieces – fireworks in the air. So we had to go get another boom and rig it up again. But finally we got the shot and it worked fine. It limbered things up.

Around that time, I got in the habit of running my talking pictures with the sound turned off. I had to know whether or not we were still making motion pictures – if it was moving. Of course, when I was controlling the picture, I was able to correct things, but when I was making the picture for somebody who considered it finished, I'd still run it without the sound track and see if I liked it.

How did you fix it if you found a sequence that was too static?

Well, generally you shoot a scene two or three ways. I always made a master shot of the whole scene, sometimes running as much as thirteen pages of dialogue. Usually you shoot four or five pages a day, but I'd make one scene in thirteen or fifteen pages all at once. Just like an act on stage, with eight or ten actors sometimes, occasionally moving the camera too. Then I began to break it up. Get closer shots of the dialogue and so on. Now somebody cuts the picture and they use practically none of the master shot. They just sit them down at the desk to have their conversation. But in the master, maybe there was a place where one fellow got up while the other one was talking to get himself a drink. And they've taken all that movement out and just gone on with the dialogue. Well, to me, when those two people are talking – it's dead. It's no longer a motion picture. So I'll go back and at least get a movement while they're talking. And very often I'll cut out half the dialogue if I think it's uninteresting, cut to something else and come back to them. Anything to get that dead stuff out.

Did you generally cover a whole scene from many different angles?

Not necessarily. I'd sometimes deliberately not do that so they'd *have* to use the shots I wanted. Because very often if you shoot too much, they take advantage of you. The cutter or the executive says, 'Ah, I'm gonna use the close-ups here.' But if you don't give them any, they've got to use what you gave them. Often I'll just shoot the master shot and not bother with anything else. Then after we put it together, if it really needs an accent, I'll get the actor back and make it if we still have him on contract. But there are so many problems. These executives sit there and judge you in the projection room at night. And if they just saw a master shot, they'd say 'Where the hell are the close-ups?' And the order will come down to cover the scene. So you overshoot to please those guys, and it takes time and costs money. You're not trying to please yourself or do what you want to do – you're trying to do what they *might* want to do. And it stretches your schedule. It's just stupid, but we don't make pictures for ourselves any more. We make them for vague

Photograph: Louis Wolheim, Leonore Ulric and Dwan (1929). Still, opposite: Louis Wolheim in Frozen Justice.

people who might want something. And we shoot things we hope they'll never use, and invariably they use the things you don't want them to. Because when you're directing, you're working with a pair of scissors in your mind all the time. And you're aware – more than anybody in the world – of how you can fix something that broke down somewhere or isn't moving right. But there wasn't much you could do when you were making it for somebody else. It's the most annoying thing in the world – you're working with people, trying to build a scene and along comes an office boy who hands you a note from upstairs: 'We ran the dailies last night. We feel it's necessary to retake scene so-and-so and inject a so-and-so.' Here you are trying to go on and make some scenes and you've got this in your mind. 'Well, what the hell, now I've got to get all those actors back in that set', and so on. And your enthusiasm goes out of the stuff you're doing at the moment. All because this guy upstairs writes a note. Couldn't wait and talk about it sometime or maybe let you be there when he was running the stuff to see what he had in mind and argue. Because otherwise it's two cooks trying to cook the same dish in a different way, and it doesn't work.

Were you ever able to ignore the notes?

Always able. The kid would hand it to me and I'd say, 'Thank you', and crumple it up and throw it away. It didn't make them happy – or make you popular with them.

I'm surprised you survived.

Well, I'm sometimes surprised too.

WHAT A WIDOW! (1930)

When it was finished, we had no title. So I said to Joe Kennedy, who was the producer, 'Why don't you invite all the best writers in town to come over and look at it and offer a Cadillac to the fellow who thinks up the best title?' He thought that was a fine idea, and so they all

assembled and saw the picture. It was about a
very young widow, played by Gloria Swanson,
who got into a lot of trouble. And when it was
all over, there was a silence – they were all
rattling their brains – when a voice said – not as
a suggestion, but just as an exclamation – 'What
a widow!' And that title was chosen and the guy
got a Cadillac. I tell you that just in case you
think it's a sane business.

Was Swanson scared of sound?

No. But she and Kennedy were a little timid
because they'd just come out of an unfortunate
experience. They had made a picture with von

Stroheim called *Queen Kelly*, which they didn't
finish and couldn't release. A complete loss. So,
right after that, Gloria asked me to come over
and talk with her and Kennedy about *What A
Widow!* I made a few suggestions and decided
to do it, but to avoid uncertainty or another
trap, I suggested something that had never
been done, and may never be done again. I got
the nucleus of the cast together and went on
some standing sets and photographed the
entire picture in two days – every scene in
master shots, with all the dialogue – but without costumes or make-up or any extras, and
none of the action. It didn't cost much under
those conditions. We cut it together and that
way we could see and hear the flow of the story
– and were able to correct the parts that were
weak. And when we went out to make the
picture, everything went very rapidly and
smoothly because we had already been through
it. If it weren't for union problems today, it
would still be an excellent system – photograph
a picture, look at it and then make it.

You never did that again?

I never found any occasion where it was necessary or where anybody would stand for it. We
just used kitchen chairs for furniture, or sets,
as you do in rehearsal. You pretend a chair is a
door. But you learn the delivery of the lines,
the relationship of the characters, and you see
how to fix things. We had no retakes because
we'd done them in the beginning. And got ideas
for characterisation and lots of pieces of
business. And, later, watching the film, the
actors could say, 'Wouldn't it have been funnier
if I'd been in my pajamas in that scene –' or
whatever. It made a hell of a difference. And it
was a successful picture.

Why didn't Swanson have much success after that?

I would say choice of material. She had a good
voice, sings well, but was miscast. She chose –
or they chose for her – pictures that weren't as
good as the silent pictures had been. Gloria was

Stills: What a Widow! – *Gloria Swanson with Owen Moore (opposite) and Lew Cody (above).*

surrounded by sycophants – it was one of her troubles – she let herself get surrounded by people who weren't too good in advising her. When she left Paramount to go to United Artists, I told her I thought she'd made a mistake. But she said she wanted to make her own pictures, that she was sick of working for other people. Paramount asked me if I'd use all my influence to try to get her to stay. I said, 'No. I'll make her one offer for you and that's all.' And they authorised me to offer her a five-year contract, starting at $17,500 a week and ending at $22,500, with complete control over her story, cast and directors. In other words, she'd be as free as if she had her own company. And she turned it down. She said she could make a million dollars a picture making her own. And she never made a successful picture.

What was Joseph Kennedy like?

Oh, fine businessman – nice guy and shrewd as anybody could be – a really brilliant brain financially. I think he was just playing with this business – it was a toy – and he enjoyed it.

91

CHANCES (1931)

I liked a lot of that, particularly the World War I action – you don't very often see horses in modern war. But I had a difficulty with that picture. It's hardly noticeable, but there's one little scene in it that was made after I'd gone. In the story, the British retreated – there ,was a rout. And there was a squawk about it because they said the British market would be shot to hell – they wouldn't release it there if the British Army retreated. So they had to put in a scene between a couple of officers in which they decide to *pretend* to retreat. And then go on with what I'd shot – which was a retreat during which they'd turn around and resist – but the hell was knocked out of them – nobody had a victory. They didn't march through and grab the German flag – they were licked. But the only way they could release it was to change the retreat to a ruse.

Stills. Left – Chances; *Rose Hobart and Anthony Bushell. Above – Elissa Landi in* Wicked.

Then there was the fog, which in these days was made with vaporised castor oil. And since breathing it was like drinking castor oil, it had its usual effect over the entire cast and crew . . .
There's one shot you did with the camera mounted on the hood of a car shooting back at the driver, which everyone thinks is a new technique.
Well, somebody had to start it. But they're doing a lot of things now that were done. This business of three or four images on the screen at one time is very old.
I hate that.
We hated it so much, we quit it. In fact, we were invited to quit it real quick. Exhibitors said, 'Oh, nuts, don't do that to us.'

WICKED (1931)
I went down with the troop and did some

scenes in the women's section of San Quentin. And I was startled to see the girls' rooms – which they were allowed to fix up. Some of them had beautiful rooms, with little doilies they'd put around, lace and frills here and there, and on the barred windows they'd even put nice lace curtains. A few had painted little pictures and put them up. They were allowed to live decently if they were able to. Of course, others were just slobs and had sloppy rooms. But it cued me on the character I was doing with Elissa Landi. I allowed her to express herself that way and so she wasn't just dour and down.
The pace is terrific – there's an attempted robbery, the girl's husband is killed, she's arrested, we find out she's pregnant, and they've got her in front of the jury – all before the first reel is over.
I probably had a date and was in a hurry!
But that's typical of your work – tremendous economy.

Just impatience, I suppose. I don't like things dragged out. People catch on and it spoils the picture for them. It's better to get along with it. *The only thing wrong with the film is what looks like a tacked-on ending.*

Yeah, we had to compromise – put on what they called a happy ending. We had to do that a lot of times. We always resisted it, and I even tried to do both endings if I could and let you take your choice. I always hoped the exhibitor would end the picture earlier.

WHILE PARIS SLEEPS (1932)

When I saw that again recently, what I particularly liked about it was its economy of dialogue – all clipped and short – no long, drawn-out diatribes, no conversations of any great length. And I liked the story too. It was good melodrama.

Photographically, it had a gloomy, fatalistic quality – dark shadows and fog – very much like some French films made in later years.

Well, I saw a lot of France before I made the picture. And out-of-the-way places too. I avoided the big popular cafés and prowled down into the other sections of Paris. And it might be that some of that smokey atmosphere stuck. I understood that very well. But it was a design and an accident – it just worked out. A lot of pictures are accidental. No matter how hard you work on them, accidentally something good comes out of them – or sometimes something bad too.

HER FIRST AFFAIRE (1933)

I used to go to Carlsbad every year – we all did – take about three weeks or so in the springs, lose about 19 pounds and then come back and put it on again. On my way, I stopped off in London and somebody asked me if I was

Stills. Left – Victor McLaglen and Elissa Landi in Wicked. *Above – McLaglen in* While Paris Sleeps. *Right – Arnold Riches and Ida Lupino in* Her First Affaire.

available to make a picture. Nothing much was happening over here, and I thought it would be fun to try, so I did. And I liked it, and stayed to make three. The first was *Her First Affair.* I went up to an agent's office to get some actors. I wanted a girl about 14 years old who, in the story, was going to have her first affair. And the woman they brought in for that part was

around 35 years old, though still a girlish type. And she had her daughter with her, just because she didn't want to leave her home. And she and the agent went on with their spiel about why she'd be good in it, and I'm looking at the kid. I said, 'What about her – can she act?' 'Well, our family have been actors, but no, she's not an actress.' 'Well,' I said, 'that's who I want – I want her.' Well, they were shocked – *everybody* was when the word went out I was insisting on this girl whose mother had come for the job. Finally they bent over my way and I got her. She was Ida Lupino. And she was

Still: Ida Lupino in Her First Affaire. *Opposite – publicity photograph of Ida Lupino for the film.*

great. But it was unknown in England for a little girl to play a little girl. If you're a juvenile there, you're still a juvenile at 98. They've pegged you.

The sound men were still pretty nervous over there. On one occasion I had a fellow going up some stairs and it made a noise, bump-bump-bump. They stopped us. I said, 'What's the trouble?' 'Well, we can hear his feet on the steps.' I said, 'Fine, make a little

96

more noise the next time you go up. Now get it this time.' It was a good effect – sounded like a guy going upstairs! Every once in a while the sound man would say, 'I can hear something humming – I think it's the camera.' I said, 'No, it's me.' Because I used to go over close to the sound man and hum, just to keep him from hearing little, teeny sounds, like a pin dropping.
How did you like the English pictures as compared to the American?
Oh, I don't know, I enjoyed the change of working in England, not the pictures themselves – I hardly ever thought of a picture after I turned it in. Generally, I was on another one right away. And I don't remember ever paying any attention to how it did. All I know is I would have been fired long ago if they weren't doing all right. You just don't last if they don't. But I liked being in England. I stayed there during the worst part of the Depression over here – everybody was so gloomy because their nickels were flying away. I didn't have to rely on American money because I had English money. The trick was to figure out how to get it *out* of England because you weren't allowed to. And that's when I really got well acquainted with our ambassador – Joe Kennedy. I said, 'What do I do with it?' He suggested I let him handle the money for me. This is how it worked: his New York office sold cars and things to Argentina. Argentina sold beef to him in England. He paid Argentina in English pounds (my money). Argentina paid New York in pounds. New York sold pounds for a profit in dollars. Thus, my English pounds came back to me in dollars. When I left England, Kennedy gave me a letter to his New York office. My profit was more than 100%. He asked me if I wanted to gamble further with him, but I thought I'd better stick to pictures. He had a brilliant plan which he couldn't reveal at that time. Prohibition was on in this country, but Kennedy knew it would soon have to end. He

bought the export rights to nearly every good distillery in England and Scotland. At first he exported only for medicinal use. Perfectly legal. After Prohibition, he sold franchises all over the U.S.A. and at the same time retained an interest in the retail sale on each franchise. The deal has paid him over a quarter of a billion dollars. If I had accepted his offer, it would have netted me more than a million – perhaps two, because it isn't finished yet. Get it clear that there's no inference of anything illegal in this deal – it was just far-sighted financial genius.
Why did you decide to return to America?

Well, naturally, it was where I belonged. And things were calming down so I wanted to get back. And a very funny thing – having been out of the country three years, I was forgotten – they didn't remember me around here. They forget you quick in the picture business – overnight. People say, 'Yeah, that name's familiar.' 'Why, sure, he worked for you last week.' 'Oh, that guy, yeah. What about him?' 'Well, he wants a job.' 'What can he do?' You found everything changed. First of all, during the disasters, corporations changed hands, new executives were in and new systems – everything was altered. Fellows who were your prop men were now running the studio. Your position was gone. You had to re-establish yourself, begin all over again. It was difficult. And embarrassing.

Did you have any idea it would be like that?

No, I didn't give it a thought. But you can't stop making pictures for three years and come back without somebody saying, 'What was your last credit?' And if it was back far enough, they'd say, 'Oh, hell, that was back in Noah's time. That's too far back.' So you'd have to start all over again.

HOLLYWOOD PARTY (1934)

Every star on the MGM lot was in this picture and every director on the lot had done a piece of it. But when they finally tried to put it together, it just wouldn't jell. It was nothing. So I was invited over by Eddie Mannix to look at it and see if I could do anything with it. So I went into a projection room – nobody else was there – and they started to run this movie for me. Thousands of feet of film, all disconnected

Still: Henry Kendall in Counsel's Opinion *(1933), one of Dwan's British pictures.*

stuff. Even Mickey Mouse was in it. And after a while, I was conscious of people coming in and sitting down close to me, but I couldn't see who they were, and I paid no attention to them anyway. I figured it was just somebody curious who worked at the studio. Finally it ended, and they hadn't even turned the lights up when somebody beside me – who turned out to be Mannix – said, 'Well, what do you think of it?' And I said, 'It's a nightmare.' And from behind, a pair of arms were thrown around my shoulders and a voice said, 'A genius! At last we've got a genius! Now we've got something.' And the lights went up and it was Louis B. Mayer. I had to shut up because I didn't know what I had done that made me a genius, but he said, 'That's just what it is – it's a nightmare – we make it a nightmare.' He looked at me. 'How are you going to do it?' Jimmy Durante was in the footage and I couldn't think of anything else real quick, so I said, 'Durante has a dream. He dreams all this stuff, so it's mixed up and it doesn't have to tie together because it's a dream.' 'Wonderful! Wonderful! How will you get him to the dream – he's going to the party – he can't be sleeping at the party.' I said, 'No, but he's waiting for his wife to get dressed. Did you ever wait for your wife to get dressed?' He said, 'Ah, yes, I see. Wonderful! Wonderful! So who will play his wife?' Well, they sent for the head of casting, and three or four other big executives came down to have a big conference about who could play Jimmy Durante's wife. Finally, they said to me, 'Have you a suggestion?' And I said, 'Yes.' 'Who?' 'His wife.' 'Great idea!' So they got his wife. And I went out and made the additional scenes that would tie this thing together – worked two or three days on it – and they gave me a nice fat cheque.

Still: schnozzolas for two – Jimmy Durante in Hollywood Party.

BLACK SHEEP (1935)

How did you get back to directing regularly after being forgotten?

I had to come back in as a writer. If you go in with material, you're always welcome. It's called a package deal today and it began then. They want somebody *with* a good piece of material – unless they've sent for you, and they weren't sending for *me*. So I wrote a story called *Black Sheep*, which they liked for Claire Trevor and I said, 'But I want to direct it.' And that's how it happened.

HUMAN CARGO (1936)

Rita Cansino was a little dancer – she and her father had an act – we saw them down in

Stills: Dwan's Claire Trevor movies. Left – Black Sheep. *Above –* Song and Dance Man *(1936). Right –* Human Cargo, *with Brian Donlevy and Rita Cansino (later Rita Hayworth).*

Tijuana. That's where we engaged her. She became Rita Hayworth, though she was Cansino on my picture. And she'd get so nervous – she'd cry – very frightened about working around the others who seemed to be more pro. And it bothered her to be rushed or ignored too. But she soon got over it, and got along pretty well.

Did you work on the scripts of all these Fox films – Human Cargo, High Tension [1936], 15 Maiden Lane [1936], Woman-Wise [1937] – *or were they just assigned to you?*

Well, they *were* assigned to me, but I still worked on the scripts – always with two things in mind – budget and speed, tempo. I'd eliminate stuff that was extraneous and speed up stuff that was written slowly. A writer stretches a story out, and you've got to fix it up. Make it move. Take a scene of two people sitting in a room and try to figure how you can get them

Stills: Fox, 1936–37. Above – Glenda Farrell and Brian Donlevy in High Tension. *Left – Cesar Romero and Claire Trevor in* 15 *Maiden Lane. Right – Rochelle Hudson and Robert Kent in* That I May Live.

walking down the street and maybe bumping into a person now and then or getting separated as people go between them – anything to break it up. Give it a sense of motion. That's what you do with any script you get ahold of. Because we write with the camera, not with a pencil or pen and we've got to remember that and not get trapped by the fellow who writes with words.

Well, then do you agree that films are a director's medium?

I think no individual ever makes a motion picture – it's a team. Nobody ever writes one. You can put words on paper, but that isn't what people see when they go to the theatre. They listen to a few of the words, but they see movement and personalities and production and photography and backgrounds. And then some fellow wants to say, 'I wrote this – this is mine – I built the world.' They want to play God. Everybody wants to be God in this business.

But wouldn't you say that the closest thing to God on a picture is the director?

No, I'd go back further than that – I think the story is the number one thing. The whole business is based on that – they would rather have what they call a good property than anything else – even a star. Next in importance is the interpretation, which comes down through various branches: the actor is an interpreter and the director is his assistant, though he can control it. He's the fellow who's running the engine, but the engine has to be there to run. If the director wrote the story or the screenplay then he's much more important than if he is just interpreting somebody else's.

Of course, a bad director can wreck a good story. That's true. And a bad actor can. And a bad producer can if he interferes. A lot of people can hurt it and a lot of them can help it. If you've got a good team working, you're lucky. But if you haven't got any story, you've got nothing. What can you do? And if you do your best, people will still say, 'Well, it was well done, but it was a lousy story – I didn't like the picture.' And they won't tell their friends to go see it. And that's what makes pictures successful. We can't do anything without public acceptance – no matter who we are or what we are – it always goes right back to the public.

THAT I MAY LIVE (1937)

I saw that again recently – it was horrible.

Generally, how do you feel seeing your old pictures?

Well, if they're good I like them. But most of them are brand new to me – I sometimes don't even remember the people who were in them. I say, 'Well, that's a damn good scene', as if it were somebody else's picture and not mine at all. There are a few pictures I recall entirely, and they must have been ones I liked a great deal. But I don't like most pictures I did. I scarcely looked at them. In later years – almost the last thirty years of making pictures – I never even looked at dailies.

Why?

There were too many other people looking at them – all the executives would run down to see them, so why should I? They had their opinions and had their cutters put them together the way they wanted it. I'd look at the finished thing and seldom have much to say about it. 'Fine – if that's the way they like it, it's good.' In the beginning, we had to do it all – we had to look at it and cut it, decide everything and make every move. Later on, they had so many executives around doing it

that we just stepped back and did our end
– which was to direct it and turn it in. If they
liked it – fine. If they didn't they said so, and
we did it again whichever way they wanted it.
*I get the feeling you were happier making pictures
in the 'tens and 'twenties than any time afterwards.*
Well, it's possible, but I've always been happy
making pictures. I just love to make pictures.
I was happier before sound came in because I
thought they were truer motion pictures then.
But when did you feel most creative?
Well, I can't say I ever *felt* creative – I don't

Stills: One Mile from Heaven (*1937*), *the last of
Dwan's series of Fox movies with Claire Trevor.*

think any creator ever feels it – he may be
inspired to do something and he does it. Afterwards, looking back, he may say, 'That was my
best work', but I don't know what inspiration
is, as a matter of fact. You just have a hunch to
do something.
Well, when did you have most of your hunches?
They must have come early, when we *had* to
have them. There wasn't any comparison –
there was nothing we could do except 'make it

104

up' – and that's inspiration. Later, we began to be parasites, in a sense. We got books or plays that were well written and changed them into our form, and it doesn't require much to do that. You take a big Broadway hit and all you do is put it on film. In fact, the less creativity you have, the better – you won't spoil it. But at first we were building from the ground up. We had nothing to go by. A picture like *Robin Hood* was all fiction. Somebody jumped on Doug after we finished it and said, 'It's a very good picture, but you didn't stick to the book at all.' And Doug wanted to know what book they were talking about – there never was a book. But you might say that before the creative reins were taken away from us and given to the producers, we were happier working and did better work. Because then we were actually creating it ourselves. When the job was being handed to us on paper and the rules were laid down and our stuff was being inspected daily by executives, we became just members of the crew. And the fun went out. We did our job as we saw it, but we always had a mentor over us saying, 'I like it' or 'I don't like it'. So I still enjoyed making pictures, but it wasn't the same

Stills: Heidi – *Jean Hersholt as the grandfather with (right) Shirley Temple.*

thing. You didn't have to exert yourself. We used to mould a scene the way we wanted it, but we couldn't after we got scripts. 'It's there on paper – stick to the script' is all they'd say.

HEIDI (1937)

Shirley Temple was starting to slip. They hadn't made very good stuff with her, and *Heidi* was an effort to boost her back, and it worked.

Whose idea was it to do that story?

I proposed that we make it. And since it was a Shirley Temple picture, we were able to

splurge a little. But it was a fake bigness. We picked up sets around the Fox lot and dolled them up. Raymond Griffith was the associate producer. He was a very good comedian in silent pictures, but his vocal chords had been injured, so he could barely whisper. He was a good friend of Zanuck, and to help him along, Zanuck made him an associate producer. And he was fine. He understood pictures because he'd been in them and knew all the problems.

And he was excellent at gags – suggesting bits and stuff during the preparation. We seldom saw him on the set. But he had an effervescent attitude and we were able to get the story to bubble. It could have been a very heavy-footed thing, but it turned out all right.

It seemed to have an almost tongue-in-cheek quality.

Well, you have to in a way because it's to be seen by adults, and yet you don't destroy what the kids see – they don't catch that significance. But it was a very grim, heavy story, you know, father in prison, beating the kid, practically kidnapping her and selling her into slavery in a rich man's home. Mean old housekeeper and the aunt who sold her down the line. All those awful things, like 'Uncle Tom's Cabin', really gruesome. So we made it funny. We had pratfalls for the mean housekeeper – she slid across the hall because it was too slippery. None of

Photograph: Dwan (seated in foreground) directing Jean Hersholt in Heidi.

those things were in the novel of *Heidi* – we put them in – and the monkey, and other little odds and ends that speeded it up. The whole idea was to keep it light, because it can get awfully sticky if you really make those kind of stories seriously. And I've seen a couple. I saw two different *Heidis* later, and none of them had any fun in them.

How was Shirley Temple to work with?

Just absolutely marvellous – greatest in the world – you couldn't describe her. One in a hundred million. She was fun all the time. Very often she'd have other children around, and we had to have discipline on the set, so I created a police department and had some badges made. She was the Chief of Police. I was only Captain. And everybody around her had to wear a badge and salute, and the Chief had to keep discipline – so she behaved herself. And I'd say to her, 'Chief, the electricians are pretty slow today', and she'd go and bawl them out and they'd speed up. I got pinched for speeding one day. The cop said, 'I'm gonna give you a ticket.' I

108

said, 'It isn't going to do you any good to write a ticket because I'll report this to my Chief and you'll be in trouble,' and I flashed my badge at him. And he got burned and said, 'What is it?' It read 'Shirley Temple – Police Chief' and he said, 'My God, where did you get this?' I said, 'I'm the captain of it – would you like to have it?' He said, 'Sure, go ahead, drive out – my kid will go crazy about this.' I got out of a lot of trouble with that badge.

REBECCA OF SUNNYBROOK FARM (1938)

They owned the book, which was again sort of a *Pollyanna* – pretty sticky. I said, 'This *could* be made into something interesting.' And I had Raymond Griffith again so I was able to say, 'Let's go after this with an update attitude –

Still: Shirley Temple, Slim Summerville and Gloria Stuart in Rebecca of Sunnybrook Farm.

put some music in it – give Shirley something to sing – let's get radio in.' Radio was very popular then. And we injected all that. The book, *Rebecca of Sunnybrook Farm*, is nothing like that. In fact, when we were through, all we had left was the title and the names of the characters.

How did you work with Temple to get a performance?

Well, to a degree, you worked through her mother who had a great influence over her and used to work with her at home at night on the things she was to do the following day. And

with Shirley, you'd just tell her once and she'd remember the rest of her life – whatever it was she was supposed to do, she'd do it. She was always on the job and ready – knew all of her 'words', as she called dialogue – and her songs and dances. So it was very simple working with her – she was ready ahead of us. And if one of the actors got stuck, she'd tell him what his line was – she knew it better than he did.

You never had to resort to tricks?

No. If she'd been playing hard and it wasn't easy for her to get into the mood of crying, you'd simply say to her, 'Now, Shirley, I want you to think you'll never see your mother again. She's gone.' And, boy, the tears would boil out of her. She was very realistic about her thinking.

How did she avoid becoming swell-headed?

Well, I think her mother took care of that – taught her modesty, kept her down. And her father invested her money and did doggone well with it – he was a pretty shrewd fellow. So by the time Shirley was ready to quit, she was a pretty rich girl. And she always will be. One time, at the Beverly Hills Hotel, I got out of my car and as I turned to go in, a beautiful young girl ran up and threw her arms around my neck and gave me a nice smack and said oh, she's so happy to see me and how am I. I didn't know who it was – not for several seconds. It was Shirley. Grown up woman. But she didn't look like Shirley any more. And she's got Shirleys of her own – she's almost a grandmother now. I can't get over it. I'd expect to walk out now and see Shirley Temple as she always was. I can't believe the years have gone by. I see old women who were beautiful young leading women in my pictures and it shocks me. Men don't, but women do. The ageing of a woman is always a shock when you haven't seen her in a number of years. They're attractive, but they're somebody else – brand-new personalities. Men don't seem to change that way. They're idiots in the beginning and never get over it.

SUEZ (1938)

Zanuck cooked up the idea of making it, they developed it, and he assigned it to me. The cast was good and the special effects were unusually good – there was some remarkable stuff of the cyclone destroying the canal. In one instance, I had to have a windstorm come up, blow away some buildings and actually blow the people through the air. So I got about a hundred of those huge airplane prop fans we use to make

Stills: Opposite – Simone Simon in Josette *(1938). This page –* Suez. *Tyrone Power, Annabella.*

wind and lined them up. And those things were practically cyclones – if you walked through them, they'd knock you off your feet. At first they were blowing sand, but I had to discard that because it would cut the skin off people, so instead we used ground up cereal that we threw in front of the blades. The people had to move through that all day long, and I'm telling you, that was an ordeal. Everybody got beaten up good – particularly Ty Power and Annabella.

Still, left: Suez. *Building the canal. Photograph, above: shooting the aftermath of the storm.*

In one scene, he was supposed to be knocked unconscious, and she ties him to a post, and then the wind whips her away. We had to put her on a wire and fling her through the air. It was drastic.

Did you work on the script with Philip Dunne?

In the sense of suggesting this and that, and I'd

113

take out some incidents that were a little over-written or would have cost too much money. They squawked about that, but I suggested we try it without them and Zanuck said, 'You're right.' It would have cost another couple of hundred thousand dollars to do. Because you start one of those things, you don't know when to quit. There's a limit to effects. You can blow too many things down – you still have your story. And anything like a cyclone is a momentary

Stills, left: Suez. *Photograph, above: Dwan directing Tyrone Power and Joseph Schildkraut.*

interruption. It's a means to an end – destroys something so that afterwards you will say, 'Will we go on or are we finished ?' And your story's got to go from then on. They had overwritten it by two reels – got fascinated by destruction. And, of course, a lot of the special effects were miniatures.

What particularly appealed to you about the film?
Well, I liked the human story. Whether the canal was built or not was of no importance to me. It had a peculiar experience in France. The De Lesseps family – he was the builder of the canal, played by Power – started to sue me. We gave him a romance with Eugenie, and they objected to that, so they took it to court. And the court told them that this picture did so much honour to France that no matter what they thought as a family, the case must be discarded, and they threw it out of court.

Would you consider it one of your favourite films?
Well, as an example of what can be done to put history on the screen, yes. I thought it was great. But a little thing like *Big Brother* was of more interest to me as a story than that was. Or *Manhandled*. They're simple, honest stories that happen to people.

THE THREE MUSKETEERS (1939)

Was it your idea to parody the Fairbanks films with the Ritz Brothers version of The Three Musketeers?
Yes, in a sense. Many years had passed and so we kidded it. We were looking for something we could do with them – they were under contract and had to get a picture – so we came up with this idea, that three cooks by accident are made into musketeers. With them, you could do anything – clown your head off. For balance, we put in Don Ameche as D'Artagnan. Not exactly a Fairbanks, but he could sing and was attractive and popular in those days. It made a good combination and worked out well – there were a lot of good gags in it. My favourite scene, which I cooked up, had Binnie Barnes in

Photograph, during Suez. *Left – Dwan and Annabella with (bottom) Tyrone Power and the cinematographer J. Peverell Marley. Right – a scene in the House of Commons with Power standing in the gallery.*

it. She's English, a real fun girl, and she had to play the lady who had the secret documents – which she thrust into her bosom. So the three Ritz Brothers wanted to know, 'Where are they?' They were gentlemen so they wouldn't dare touch her there, but finally they turned her upside down and started to shake them out. And four or five papers fell out every time and each time he'd pick it up and it was a love note from some other guy. I loved that.

What were the Ritz Brothers like?
Harry was a hard worker. I remember the other two wanted to get off early one day to go to the race track, and it was always hard to get them on, so finally I got impatient and said, 'Go ahead – go to the track – I'd rather work here alone with Harry. And by the way, you don't need to come back tomorrow either because this sequence I'm starting will run on. So take tomorrow off at the track too and let Harry do

it alone – he can do a hundred per cent better – you two fellows get in his way. Glad to have you go.' They didn't go to the track. That was the only way I could handle them.

FRONTIER MARSHAL (1939)

I liked Randolph Scott and practically everybody in the cast. I think it was well done. When I had made *Suez* out there at Fox, I put about a million tons of sand on the back lot to make

Stills: the Ritz Brothers with Binnie Barnes in The Three Musketeers *(left) and with Bela Lugosi in* The Gorilla *(also 1939).*

a desert. Wagon-loads and wagon-loads came up from the beach and filled the place with sand for over half-a-mile wide. And at the time someone said to me, 'Well, what are we going to do with this sand when you get through?' I said, 'Well, some sucker will have to move it

119

out of here.' Now, when *Frontier Marshal* came along, I induced Zanuck to let me build a western street back there. And in order to do it, the sand had to be moved. So *I* was the sucker! By the way, normally, building a western street would have been prohibitive – two or three hundred thousand dollars. I told Zanuck I'd put one up for twenty thousand if he'd let me have *carte blanche* and do it my way. I knew where there were all kinds of western fronts around the lot that had been put there way back in the time of Tom Mix – I'd used them in the old days. So I didn't use studio personnel, I got a regular moving company to come over at night with their trucks, and we took them all – in the form they were in – dragged them over and put them up in two cross-streets. I just

Stills. Left – Randolph Scott in Frontier Marshal. *This page –* Young People (*1940*) *with Jack Oakie, Shirley Temple and Charlotte Greenwood.*

shoved the sand back out of the way. But this wonderful western street cost peanuts. It lasted there quite a while.

Was the picture really based on Wyatt Earp's life?

No, Zanuck just decided to call him Wyatt Earp, and I remember that in order to do that we had to clear it with any living relative he had. There was some woman in San Francisco who was related and they made a deal with her, gave her five thousand dollars or something to let us use the name Wyatt Earp because it wasn't in public domain. Some stunt of that kind. But when we got through, she started to sue the company because of what we had done with Wyatt Earp. Given him a love-affair with Nancy Kelly and all that – she said it was misrepresentation, that it never happened and she was right. We never meant it to *be* Wyatt Earp. We were just making *Frontier Marshal* and that could be any frontier marshal.

TRAIL OF THE VIGILANTES (1940)

That started out to be a real western melodrama; it was written very seriously. I went with a company clear up to a location in the mountains and started it, and I hadn't made three scenes before it struck me that this was not a good drama and that if it were made into a drama, it would be a miserable thing. I hadn't paid much attention to it in script form, but when I got these actors in front of me, I saw that the situation was humorous, not serious. So just on a hunch I closed up the company and took them back to the studio. It was very shocking to Universal when I appeared and told them, 'Frankly, it isn't going to work. We've got to change it.' And I was going to be taken off it because I said, 'If you're going to make it this way, I don't want to make it', and finally they began to ask me, 'What would you do with it? We're in it – the money is going out – people are committed.' 'Well,' I said, 'let

me pick a writer and go to work.' So I got hold of a writer and in a few hours we adjusted the script into the same story done with a tongue-in-cheek approach as a comedy. The characters who were supposed to be rough, tough, murderous kind of people were for the most part just clowns. The cowboys were making mistakes – everything was going wrong. They weren't trying to be funny people – they were just doing funny things. We went right back into it that way, and it turned out to be a pretty good, entertaining picture that made some money. But it would have been a terrific flop if we hadn't.

Were you left alone after that?

They had to leave me alone – I had the secret – it was in my vest pocket. I was the only one who knew what was happening – but the actors got onto the fact that it was going to be humorous and they went all out with it.

LOOK WHO'S LAUGHING (1941)

M.C.A. wanted to get their people into motion pictures – they were beginning to build into this giant outfit they eventually became. And they did it by making packages. Instead of just representing people, they put people together. They had Edgar Bergen and 'Fibber McGee and Molly' – big radio stars and they bought me away from my agent so I'd be one of their clients and part of a package, and so when they went to RKO, they supplied the whole works – stars, director and everything. That was their method. At that time, Lew Wasserman was my personal agent. Anyway, I made several pictures that way – cooked up the stories and shot them – *Look Who's Laughing* was the first. And I was always a leech, going around looking at standing sets and seeing how I could use them. Because a lot of your money goes into building the sets and if they're there, why

Photograph, above: Allan Dwan and Charlie McCarthy, Edgar Bergen's dummy. Stills: left – Franchot Tone, Charles Trowbridge and Broderick Crawford in Trail of the Vigilantes; *top right – Linda Darnell, George Murphy and Jack Oakie in* Rise and Shine *(1941); bottom right – Kay Kyser and Joan Davis in* Around the World *(1943).*

not use them? So, since we were on the RKO
lot, I saw Orson Welles's sets from *The Magnificent Ambersons* and used them for the sequel
to *Look Who's Laughing, Here We Go Again*
[1942].

FRIENDLY ENEMIES (1942)

I was hired by Eddie Small – it was the
begining of my relationship with him over a
series of pictures. We were going to do *Up in
Mabel's Room* but there was some difficulty in
clearing it properly, and he was committed to
me and to a couple of actors, so he was in

trouble. And there would be a considerable delay. What to do? He'd have to pay us all off – so I said to him, 'Do you have another piece of material around here that we could do instead?' And he mentioned several things, among them this play, *Friendly Enemies*. I sat down and read it within the next half hour or so, and said, 'I think this could be cooked up into a picture pretty quickly if you want to.' He said, 'Well, we've got to get a script written – take months.' I said, 'No, it won't.' I was talking to him, say, on a Monday. The following Monday we started to shoot *Friendly Enemies* with a good

Stills: Friendly Enemies *with Charles Winniger and* (above) *Charles Ruggles. Photograph – Dwan with Winniger and Nancy Kelly.*

script and a good cast on a set we inherited from Paramount. And we made it in about nine days.

How!?

Well, the play had been a successful New York show, so we got all our dialogue from it, and just put it into script form real fast. And invented some exteriors. In fact, I could have shot it from the play except the actors had to

125

have something in their hands.

But also that's what interested me about the whole project. The challenge. Not because I would ever have said, 'Let's go out of our way and make *Friendly Enemies* – or get writers and try to make it better.' It was just 'bang', and it was effective. In several cases, I've had to do that with pictures – and not waste time or money on them, because they aren't worth it. You don't know what you're going to get back out of it. In this case, he got a good profit because it turned out to be an acceptable picture.

ABROAD WITH TWO YANKS (1944)

That was a lot of fun – Bendix and O'Keefe dressed up like girls. We used a theatre in Hollywood for some of the interiors, right next to the Brown Derby. Now, it was such a hell of a job putting on that make-up and harnessing on those clothes, that they kept them on when we all went out to lunch. And I walked into the Brown Derby with two broads. Well, there was

Stills: Up in Mabel's Room (*1944*). *Dennis O'Keefe with Marjorie Reynolds (dream sequence, above), Mischa Auer and Gail Patrick (right).*

a panic. Can you imagine – two broads like
that ? The head waiter nearly dropped dead. We
finally got stuck in a booth, and people kept
looking and weren't sure. Thought maybe they
were a couple of pansies out camping. Of course,
they were cutting up, playing coy.
*Did you improvise a great deal on the four farces
you made for Small?*
Oh, yes, lots of off-the-cuff. You'd be surprised
how little script we had. On *Abroad with Two*

Stills: Abroad with Two Yanks – *William
Bendix and Dennis O'Keefe.*

Yanks, Small had writers sitting with him while
I was shooting. And around two or three in the
afternoon he'd send down the pages that were
supposed to have been shot that morning, but
I'd already shot what I wanted to shoot and
we'd just file the script away. So I was always
off-the-cuff and he was about a day behind me

129

with the script all the way through. He laughed about it later. 'Why the hell was I sitting up there battling with writers and firing them and getting this stuff on paper, and you're down there shooting this other thing.' And that's the way it was made, so that was fun. And it was difficult, but that's the way we like to make pictures. And Eddie Small was a good guy to work with – he was a pro. A great showman and not an interfering guy. He knows his way.

Stills: Brewster's Millions. *Mischa Auer, June Havoc, 'Rochester' and Dennis O'Keefe.*

BREWSTER'S MILLIONS (1945)

That's probably one of the best pieces of material I ever had. The idea that a man – without being able to tell a living soul anything about it – has to spend a million dollars in a year and have absolutely nothing to show for it when he's done. And if he does it, he gets another seven million from his uncle's will. Now that sounds like the most simple thing on earth – I know it can be done – I've done it – but, you see, he had to legitimately spend that money and then have *nothing* to show for it – which is what's tough.

How much did you work on the script?
Oh, quite a lot – you have to. Not so much on the story, but the movement – what comes next. There's so many things you had to eliminate because they would destroy the tempo. For instance, he finances a musical show that's supposed to be a flop and wasn't. So we had a scene on the stage, and they wanted to expand that into a big musical number. But that would interrupt the flow. I had to fight those things constantly.

GETTING GERTIE'S GARTER (1945)
Getting Gertie's Garter looked like it had the same set as Up in Mabel's Room *re-dressed.*
We had a strike of set dressers and designers and carpenters. So you had to go around and doll up what you could. They probably *were* the same sets, with a few little alterations that we could handle without the aid of any of those union men.

You also had a dream sequence in both of them that couldn't have been in the plays.
No, we put them in. We had to do things with the plays. We had those characters to play with, but they hadn't much to do – they'd make an entrance and an exit – we had to see what they were doing off-stage. Maybe the best things happen then, and they aren't *in* the play. They're indicated in the dialogue but they're not there – so we show them. You say, 'Where did he go and what is he doing?' He's going to come back in a little while with jam on his face. How did he get it there?

My main reason for doing all those farces was because I knew they'd be seen by a lot of kids at war, and in army camps – and they'd cheer them up. That whole series was made with them in mind. I didn't give a damn what the people who bought tickets saw or liked. I was thinking about those kids. And they went nuts about

Stills: Getting Gertie's Garter – Dennis O'Keefe and Marie 'The Body' MacDonald with Barry Sullivan and Jerome Cowan (top right) and Binnie Barnes (bottom right); top left – dream sequence. Photograph, below: O'Keefe, Dwan and MacDonald with a visitor, aviator Glenn Martin, pilot on A Girl of Yesterday *(1915) – see p34.*

them. And, of course, people at home would enjoy them because they were light. So they were very big hits. And even did well in Europe.

RENDEZVOUS WITH ANNIE (1946)
That was Mary Loos's idea – she and her husband, Dick Sale, and I discussed it and each of us would contribute a little thought, inject this or that. Then we got Eddie Albert in it and after I got acquainted with him – he wasn't anybody then – I found what his talents were so I'd add things for him. I let him sing, which wasn't

in the script; and many things turned out to be much more humorous because I found he was a comedian.

But I liked the idea of the story. A fellow has gone AWOL to sneak home and have a honeymoon with his wife, and nobody finds out about it. Then when his wife gets pregnant, he's got to *prove* he was there or the child must be a bastard. It was a fun picture too. We even had Mike Frankovich in there; he was breaking into the business at the time. He had been an aviator all through the war, and became our technical adviser. Then when we needed a

Photograph, left: Dwan with Mary Loos. Still, above: Eddie Albert and William Frawley in Rendezvous with Annie.

pilot for one scene, I said, 'All right, you're going to be the pilot.' And he played the role, and played it naturally.

That was your first of many pictures for Republic – did you have a lot of freedom there?

Well, yes, I had all the freedom in the world, except that the final decision as to whether a story would be made or not, and what the cast would be, was up to Herbert Yates, the head of

the company. A fine man, a good businessman and a *lousy* producer. That was the trouble with Republic – the top man's taste – and it wasn't the best. So, of course, we were handcuffed in that sense. We wanted to bring in better people and we had them wanting to come in. But he was pushing other people and we were forced for the sake of harmony and the dollar to do what he liked. The only other alternative would have been to walk away, and that wasn't always smart.

But after we got the go-ahead, it was all ours – nobody bothered us. Of course, they still

135

Photographs. Left: Calendar Girl. *Above: Herbert Yates (front, centre), Vera Hruba Ralston, Dwan, Nelson Eddy and others at Republic during shooting of* Northwest Outpost.

looked at rushes. And we played tricks on them. We'd do fake scenes with dialogue that makes today's sound like a blushing bride. Just to drive them nuts. They'd see them in the projection room and gasp and come rushing down. 'You can't use that!' And we'd say, 'Why? What's the matter with it?'

Yates had bought his studio from Mack Sennett, and it was fine – a nice place to work, good facilities, and he had nice people around the place. But he kept himself in the B-class for no reason. If you wanted to go out and hire a hundred thousand dollar star – wow. Even if it would help sell the picture and enable you to build up and make a good big picture, Yates would fight it down. He made me think of the old Universal days when Laemmle's two button-hole-making nephews came out to take charge of the studio. And they asked a director one day, 'Why did you go all the way out to Chattsworth Park to shoot?' And he said, 'Because I wanted

to get that fine scenery – the trees out there and those beautiful rocks.' They said, 'A tree is a tree, a rock is a rock – shoot it in Griffith Park.' In other words, do it here, do it in the backyard. That's the picture business.

I was at Republic to make more or less what I wanted, but I got to be accommodating. The old man was pleasant and he had a girl [Vera Hruba Ralston] he was trying to build into a star, and we were all trying to help him do it and stubbing our toes. Every now and then we'd get ahold of a good piece of material and make it.

Rendezvous with Annie *and* Driftwood *and* The Inside Story *are more your kind of pictures than* Calendar Girl *and* Northwest Outpost.

Yes, well, the first three you mentioned were original with us – we created the stories and got Yates to say O.K. to them. And I think they were as near our own as we ever got. Nice, simple stories. Later on, they would bring me a story and say, 'We'd like you to make it.' So, having nothing else to do, I'd make it. They wanted the musicals and that amused me – I like musicals – so we made a few little musicals.

NORTHWEST OUTPOST (1947)

That really was a peculiar one. We made a deal with Rudolf Friml to write the music, and we

Stills: Northwest Outpost. *Nelson Eddy with Jay Silverheels (above), Ilona Massey (right) and the Herman Wall chorus.*

got Robert Armbruster – a fine young musician to handle it. But I don't think Friml wrote three notes for the whole show. This fellow Armbruster had to go up to Friml's house and milk him for anything he could get, and then bring it back and do the best he could to put it together. Friml was living a soft life up there and wasn't inspired to compose. Armbruster had to play phrases on the piano or have him play little phrases out of some song he hadn't finished and Armbruster would pick it up and finish it. A real struggle, because it was tough to get the kind of grand music you'd expect from Friml. Whatever was good actually came from Armbruster. Friml took the bow.

I felt you were definitely making fun of the material in the film, and of the stars, particularly Nelson Eddy.

Yes, of course. Nelson Eddy was the ham of hams – a nice guy, but he wanted to play a cowboy above all things. So he got as near to a cowboy as he could in this. But the whole subject matter was peculiar – Russian atmosphere up in California – which did exist – but we had an English woman playing a Russian princess and a German playing a Russian – all kinds of dialects playing Russians. And a lot of White Russians. The best thing in the picture was the Easter episode in the church, which was authentic because I just turned the Russians loose and said, 'I want a real Russian Easter', and they put it on. Even provided all the food and conducted the church services the way they should be. We got ahold of a good Orthodox priest of theirs who was hiding somewhere behind his beard. We had fun with that. But Nelson Eddy riding down the street into town with a lot of Cossacks singing 'hallabaloo' – that's for the birds.

So you made fun of it?

Why not? Why suffer? In anything, you're always on that banana peel. I don't care what you're doing – the most vicious drama on earth is just on the ragged edge of being very funny.

DRIFTWOOD (1947)

Mary Loos discovered some information about a virus carried by squirrels that hits people in a certain section of the country and that intrigued her. So we got involved in that and brought in a young doctor who's developing a serum, and a little girl – an orphan with a dog. But what

intrigued me after we got going was the ability of the child we found – little Natalie Wood. She had a real talent for acting, an ability to characterise and interpret, and that was a pleasure. She had already been in a picture, and she was a natural. Her folks were Russian and her mother was ambitious for her daughter to be a ballet dancer. Any Russian would rather have their daughter become a ballet dancer than anything else. Anyway, it was a nice picture to make, but I don't remember much of it.

THE INSIDE STORY (1948)
At that time, there was a lot of financial trouble going on in the world, and I thought it would be a pretty good idea to hit the topic in some way, and to enlighten the people that the worst place for money to be was in a bank – that

Stills: Driftwood – *Natalie Wood, Francis Ford.*

141

money ought to work. I tried to show what a thousand dollars would do if it moved fast enough, from person to person. From you to the person you bought from, to the person he paid, and so on right down the line. Well, Mary Loos and Dick Sale and I created a story based on that thought. And the same thousand dollars did some amazing things – solved everybody's problem. It was a lot of fun – the crew used to come in and say, 'Who's got the

thousand today?' We got a lot of good reactions from the financial world. Not much from the public, because they never *saw* a thousand dollars. But I liked doing that – it was done real fast, for a very small amount of money – and there were a lot of good people in it.

What was your average shooting schedule at Republic?

Between 18 and 25 days. Anything over 25 days was dangerous.

SANDS OF IWO JIMA (1949)

The producer, Eddie Grainger, had the idea to make a picture about the Marines and taking Iwo Jima, and got Harry Brown to write the script. They had no foundation for it – they had to take it out of history, develop it, and they came up with a good script. Then Eddie started to work on Yates, who said he could make it for around one hundred and fifty thousand to two hundred thousand dollars, which was impossible. So he

Stills: The Inside Story – *Charles Winniger with Roscoe Karns, Allen Jenkins, William Haade and Hobart Cavanaugh.*

struggled with him – how to get a bigger budget. Finally, he got his father, Jim Grainger – who was head of sales at Republic and an old friend of mine – to go to bat for him. And Jim told Yates, 'Look, we'll put a good director on it and we'll get Wayne in it . . . ' 'No', Yates

said, 'I've got Wayne playing in the next picture with Vera Ralston.' 'Well', Jim said, 'we'll get *someone* big.' Finally, he let them go, said all right. Then Jim came to me and said, 'Would you go over with Eddie ?' I had a contract to do my own pictures, but I read the script and said, 'Sure, I'd like to do this. It looks good.' And I didn't ask about Wayne – because I thought there were three or four actors who could play it. There's no part in the world that only one actor can play. But Eddie wanted Wayne, so I said, 'Go and get him – fight for him.' Well, Eddie tried to induce Wayne – not

to play the part – that was easy – but it was hard to get him to go to Yates and say, 'I insist on doing it.' He didn't feel secure enough. But it worked. And after that picture, he was the kingpin – he'd go and tell him, 'Mr. Yates, I like your office better than I do my dressing-room – you go over to the dressing-room, I'll take the office.' He became a big shot, because the picture was a big success for him. And I don't think anyone could have been any better.
How was Wayne to work with?
Oh, he was fine. He came to me the second day and said, 'You're my kind of director', shook

144

hands and that was the end – I don't think there was a bit of friction. The only trouble was Wayne *used* to like to stay up at the bar quite late – and he could put away a lot – he had a terrific capacity. But some of these young actors in the cast – fellows like John Agar – used to try to stay along with him and they'd be a pathetic sight in the morning. At least, they *were* the first morning. I didn't lecture them. I just asked

Still, left: Thomas Gomez, Adele Mara, John Carroll and Alfonso Bedoya in Angel in Exile (*1948*). *Photograph: shooting* Sands of Iwo Jima.

General Erskine, the commandant down at Fort Pendleton, to give me the toughest drill sergeant there, and he sent me a big, husky guy – six foot, eight – who could have lifted any two of the men in my company. He said, 'What do you want, sir?' I said, 'I want you to make Marines out of these actors – full packs and rifles – and I want you to drill them. Give them the full routine including double-time. I want them to get into physical shape.' He eyed the hangovers doubtfully. I said, 'You think they look like Marines now?' And he said, 'No, sir. They don't.' Very firm

about it – he hated their guts. I said, 'Well, they're all yours', and I told the boys, 'Fellows, go on over there to the sergeant. He's going to teach you how to be Marines.' They grumbled and away they went – about twenty of them. Well, he worked them for two solid hours until they fell on their faces. Then he let them sleep a little while and got them up and worked them some more. Well, after the third day, they were pleading for mercy, but they were Marines. And not one of them ever stayed up late again – they crawled into that hay at 10 o'clock, and they avoided Wayne like a plague. Even Agar got straightened out – and he was a tough one because he liked the bottle. But they all hardened up, and it even got so the Marines around there didn't mind them any more.

Photographs: the making of Sands of Iwo Jima; *left – Dwan and John Wayne.*

Did Wayne ever take a hand in directing, as he does now?

No. He's particularly good at faking punches. And I let him and Forrest Tucker slug it out. They'd talk over their fight scenes and work them out. And I know one time these two kids weren't doing exactly what I wanted and they were a little sulky about it. And all of a sudden, over my shoulder, Wayne said, 'God damn it! Will you bastards do what he tells you!' And they did it then. I said, 'Thanks.'

But up to the day before I started the picture, we weren't sure we had Wayne. As a matter of fact, when I was down there getting things ready, we were so unsure of who was going to play the sergeant that I asked General Erskine if he'd play it. He was the perfect type for it, and his wife was trying to urge him to do it. He said, 'I'm not good enough to play a sergeant again.' And finally Wayne came down and brought James Edward Grant along to rewrite his scenes for him. The script was perfect for Wayne, except that he wants to say things in a certain way, and a writer sometimes writes a phrase a little differently. Wayne's very simple and very plain, and he seemed to think that Grant was the only man who could put the words the way he ought to say them. A lot of actors just can't handle it the way it's written and they say the same thing another way, that's all. And if it doesn't change the meaning, you let them do it. Some hardheads make them stick to the script, which is brutal because it's hard for them and it doesn't work out – it isn't a good show.

Sands of Iwo Jima had a larger budget than most of your films.

It couldn't have been made on a smaller budget. Cost a million – would be five or six million today, of course. And we wouldn't have

147

dared do it, but Grainger, as sales manager, gave us the assurance that he could get it back if it was good enough. And it did – made a big profit. You'd think that would stimulate Yates and he'd say, 'Let's go for some more of those', but never again. He had heart failure when he had that much money tied up in one picture.

SURRENDER (1950)

Oh, boy. That's another one of those with two great actors in it – John Carroll and Vera Hruba Ralston. I can't tell you what I think about it – it should be buried some place! Yates loaned

Carroll some money and that was one way of getting it back – give him a lot of work.

Was Yates simply blind to Vera Ralston's inadequacies?

What else? A man goes nuts about a woman – what can you say? It's a hopeless situation. She was a Czechoslovakian champion skater – and he saw her skating in a café. Very graceful. The first thing he did when he got her over here was to build a skating rink in one of the little stages and have her give him skating lessons. It's a wonder he didn't break his ass. Eventually he married her and wanted her to have a big

career, which she wanted too.
Didn't he pretty much wreck his studio with her?
Well, I wouldn't want to say he did, but I
would say that he wrecked a lot of my pictures.

BELLE LE GRAND (1951)

I liked the period. I've been crazy about
Virginia City anyway – its history – so it was a
pleasure to work in that background. I like the
romance of it – queer, strange, weird history.
They were looking for silver, and throwing all
that grey mud away until they found out it was
silver. They'd had it all the time. And a
character like Comstock – a little unwashed hobo
who came up there and actually never discovered anything – only got about twelve dollars
for all the work he did – and the *fortunes* that
were made because of him. The beginning of
all those famous western families came out of
Virginia City. Making allowances for the cast –
Carroll and Vera Ralston again – it was a
pleasant picture. Of course, she tried very hard

*Stills: Vera Hruba Ralston. Left – with William
Ching, Jane Darwell and Maria Palmer in*
Surrender. *Right – with John Carroll in* Belle le
Grand. *Photograph, below – with Dwan and
Wendell Corey on* The Wild Blue Yonder.

and was a very nice girl. She just hadn't been
trained to be an actress long enough to star in
pictures. You can't just come off the ice and
be a dramatic actress – unless you slide off with
the right finish. But those are penances –
making those pictures. We were getting pun-
ished for something we did.

THE WILD BLUE YONDER (1951)

The only thing I liked about that was the B-29
bomber. It did such a great job in the Second
World War – *ended* the war really. And that
intrigued me. I don't remember the story or the
people except what they did in the B-29. We
went down to a base in Tucson, Arizona, where
they kept the old planes in mothballs. And I
wanted to have an interior of the B-29 to work
with back at the studio. Well, the great red
tape started. They'd have to go to Washington
and Washington would have to dig up Lincoln
and find out if he would agree and so after an

149

I DREAM OF JEANIE (WITH THE LIGHT BROWN HAIR) (1952)

Somebody said, 'Can you give us a musical?' 'Fine.' But the music had to be something in public domain, because it takes a lot of money to do a musical, and we didn't have any. We had to make one on our kind of budget and Stephen Foster was a great composer in his day and the stuff was free. So we went to work, cooked up a story about him and tried to get all of his songs into one little picture.

You didn't seem overly concerned with the realities of Foster's life.

No, he was a very unfortunate fellow – you wouldn't want to make his life – it's too sad. He was badly kicked around, and kicked himself around too.

This was your first feature in colour – what did you think of it?

Well, I think colour photography has taken the art out of pictures because no skill in lighting is required. The colour takes care of itself – paint colour on things, turn the light on and there you are. Once in a while, you can get an effect, but you usually lose the colour when you do. The art's gone. In the black-and-white, you had to get the highlights and shadows. You had to work on it. In *Robin Hood*, for instance, we got some effects using ten mirrors. We were painting with the light. And I liked that kind of work. But you can't do that now – that's gone. And anyone can shoot in colour – you take colour photographs and they're always great – but you shoot the same thing in black-and-white and it's mushy – there's no quality. You say, 'Why didn't they get a little highlight on the side or something?' But I know that colour has value – it's accepted publicly above black-and-white. So if I were going to work, I'd say, 'Do it in colour by all means.' Everything's colour – even television is all colour now. (Though I still run it in black-and-white.) And you *can* do remarkable things with colour if you don't over-colour

awful lot of it, I said to the technical man assigned to me by the Air Force, 'Why don't you put it on some of those big Air Force trucks you've got and bring it up.' General Lemay had given us *carte blanche* – we could use anything we wanted – so why not? Well, they transported the thing – drove right through the gates of the base, past the guards and all through Arizona and California to our studio – without a single permit. We stole a B-29. Well, first thing we did was cut it right down the middle so we could get in and photograph it from the side, and I had a perfect B-29, put it up on rockers so I could move it. After we were done it was stacked up in the backlot and our picture was released and nobody ever asked for the B-29. Finally MGM needed one for a picture and put in a bid, so we wound up selling it to them. And I don't know what happened to it after that. So ends the case of the B-29 that was never returned.

Stills. Opposite – I Dream of Jeanie. *Above* – *Forrest Tucker, Jack Lambert, Jane Russell and Scott Brady in what the studio's caption describes as an 'old tintype pose' in* Montana Belle.

it. When it first came in, they wanted every colour of the rainbow on every set, instead of just saying, 'We'll get a little touch of red in here', or something. And it became a conglomeration of colour movement that made you dizzy watching. Because the great weakness of colour photography is the movement of colour over colour. If you reproduce a fine painting, it

stands still – if it comes to life, the minute the colours start moving over each other, the effect goes. It becomes unpleasant.

WOMAN THEY ALMOST LYNCHED (1953)

How did you decide to play the whole picture as a parody?

Well, what else could it be? Again, you either suffer or you don't – take your choice. If you treat that seriously, where would you be?

Did you tell the actors what you were doing?

No – then they'd try to be funny. You tell some

151

of those characters, 'This is a very funny scene', they'd horse it up, put things in. But imagine – we had a gun fight between two gals – going down the street like the cowpunchers. If they'd had anything but skirts on, I'd have shot between their legs. I couldn't do that with girls. Of course, today they would strip for it!

Was the writer in on what you did?

I don't think he'd know *now* that it wasn't serious. If the actors said the words, it was O.K. with him.

And Yates?

He doesn't know it yet either.

Stills. Below and bottom left – Sweethearts on Parade (*1953*). *Other stills:* The Woman They Almost Lynched – *Virginia Christine watches as Ann Savage helps Joan Leslie on with her gunbelt; Audrey Totter and Brian Donlevy as Charles and Kate McCoy Quantrill.*

SILVER LODE (1954)

Ben Bogeaus had lost his shirt on a bunch of pictures he produced, and for a long time he did nothing. But he had been friendly with a fellow who became the general manager for RKO Studios under Howard Hughes, and when they decided to encourage independent producers to come in and make pictures, they also let Bogeaus in because of that previous relationship with the studio manager. The president of the company was, again, my old friend, Jim Grainger. Now Bogeaus was notoriously extravagant in the early days, and they weren't

too confident that he could safely handle the kind of budget he'd have to use, so to give himself some security, Grainger reached out for someone with experience to go in and work with Bogeaus. And I was elected. I went over and the first thing Bogeaus came up with was *Silver Lode*. I read the script and found out the budget was going to be about 750-800 thousand dollars. But the script and the schedule he had would cost at least four million. So without saying too much to him, I carefully went to work on the script to tailor it down to its proper size. Well, he got furious at me – I was interfering with his 'magnificent' script. It was a lousy script, but he thought it was magnificent. At any rate, we started to have a battle. He was going to throw me off, but they wouldn't let him, so we went ahead and made the picture within our budget. But he was disgruntled and angry: 'You'll never work for me again', and the rest. Anyway, the picture went out and made good. He put another director on his next picture, but about a week later he sent for me and I came in and took that one over, and then we started a very friendly relationship. In fact, I named him Marcelene. Marcelene was a famous clown who used to be in the Hippodrome in New York. And his trick was that he was a very, very

Stills. Below – Joan Leslie and Jeff Donnell in Flight Nurse (*1954*). *Left – Alan Hale Jr., John Payne, Dan Duryea, Harry Carey Jr. and Stuart Whitman in* Silver Lode.

helpful character who messed everything up. He'd try to help with the scenery and it would fall over into the audience – that sort of thing. So every time Bogeaus would do anything I didn't like, or come around with suggestions, I'd say, 'Well, Marcelene, I'm afraid I can't agree.' And he began to accept it and we had a very good relationship. We stayed together for ten pictures. I went in as a policeman and ended up friendly with him. We liked each other very much.

You kept the same crew on all those pictures – Van Nest Polglase as art director, John Alton as cameraman.

Van Polglase was head of that department at RKO and he'd had a misfortune. Started to hit the bottle pretty hard and by the time he got off it, people had lost confidence in him. But I'd known him to be a very fine art director and a practical one, which is the kind I like. A

Stills. Left – Silver Lode, Lizabeth Scott and John Payne, seated; Dolores Moran (Bogeaus's wife) and Dan Duryea, standing. Right – Cornel Wilde and two Yvonne de Carlos in Passion.

lot of them are very arty and cost you too much money. This was a great guy to take one set and transform it into another one for you with very little money. So I approved of him highly when he was proposed. RKO wouldn't employ him but we would. Once you've broken your slate with those people they never forgive you. But he was fine. And John Alton was a fine cameraman and we hit it off well. He was good for us because he's wonderful with lights – very economical. You know the platforms with lights on them that are up above the sets? We discarded those completely. And you work much quicker without them. The union still insisted on keeping men up there, but we used to tie them on so they wouldn't fall off while they were asleep not doing anything. Alton had tried to reform the lighting at MGM and finally they didn't want him around because the unions were getting stubborn about his not using this and not using that. When he'd light

a set, he'd mark those lights, spot them and leave them there all during the use of the set. The custom is to strike everything at night – shove it away. The reason is so that the labour will have to put it back again. It's a union trick – a pork barrel. We had to have a special electrician come in an hour earlier every morning just to light the dressing-rooms and make-up tables. A specialist. Any electrician could plug it in or push a switch – or I could. But the union stuck you with him. And, of course, that pork barrelling has wrecked the business. We could use tiny equipment for lighting – with a fifth as many men – and get a better effect. In the old days, if I wanted to make a shot of you coming out of a house on location, getting into a car and driving away, I could do it with a hand camera. I'd just say, 'Come on', and you'd do it and I'd photograph you. But now I've got to have a hundred and forty men to go out with me in twenty-five trucks. I have to buy them lunch and put up reflectors and great big lamps in the street. They don't light them. We don't need that amount of light, but that's the rule. You've got to go with a full crew – make-up staff and all. People say, 'Why do pictures cost so much and why are they being driven out of the country to Europe?' It's because of that pork barrel. That unnecessary gang around running up the costs.

PASSION (1954)

I didn't think much of the story – it was a contrived affair, but the shooting was one of our shrewd business manipulations. We rented magnificent Spanish sets Warner Bros. had built for some big picture, and then we moved over to Universal and used a lot of their sets. So we got a magnificent production for very little money. The rent was high, but we couldn't have built the smallest set in the picture for the rent of all our sets. In fact, whenever I saw a particularly good set, I'd contrive a situation to put into it. And we were

thieves too. We'd rent a certain section of a set on the lot, and if there was no one else working nearby, we'd pretty soon expand to a dozen sets instead of one little one. So we really got a picture that looked expensive and it wasn't. *Were the Bogeaus budgets always small?*
Never over around 800–850 thousand. About three weeks shooting each – fifteen days. That was the design. They were token pictures to keep the studio alive – Hughes wasn't interested in a big splurge. And none of our pictures warranted a big budget – they all went out and got their money back plus a profit.

CATTLE QUEEN OF MONTANA (1954)

We shot it up in the Glacier National Park area of Montana, and we got some real Blackfoot Indians to work with us. They weren't easy to get. We were going to be very kind to these poor, downtrodden red men who had been abused by the government, so we went around to make them gorgeous offers of about five dollars a day – if they'd bring their horses too. But we found we were dealing with a bunch of millionaires. Standard Oil Company had gone in there and paid every one of them about $30,000 cash just to explore their land for oil. And if they hit oil, they got a lot more. So they

were independent of us, and when we finally got a bunch to come over, they all came out in Cadillac cars. One of them had a brand-new Cadillac – he'd smashed his other one the day before and bought a new one. They never bothered to get them fixed – if they hit a post, they bought a new car. But they made a real good Blackfoot Indian camp for us.

Of course, in those days, Ronald Reagan wouldn't fly. Neither would John Alton. So they came to location by train – took them three days to get up there from Los Angeles. We flew up in a couple of hours.

How were Reagan and Stanwyck to work with?
She's a very remarkable girl – terrific worker – and a great friend to the working men on the crew. She was a real mixer, helped everybody. Reagan was a nice man, but he's got a temper. He's a good rider, but one time we got him on an Indian horse that wasn't broken and knew nothing about pictures. He was supposed to

ride down toward the camera and warn somebody – he came tearing along on his horse, and as he approached the camera he was supposed to pull up and veer off. Well, as he started to, the horse began to dance sideways and he wound up way over there. And all the time Reagan is hollering, 'Whoa! Whoa! Whoa!' As he went by the camera, he yelled out to me, mad as hell, 'I'm not one of those Hollywood riders who says he can ride and can't ride! This goddamn horse won't do what I tell him!' He's explaining himself to me as he flies by the camera. Of course, we're howling with laughter.

PEARL OF THE SOUTH PACIFIC (1954)
Oh, that was a terrible picture. It should never have been done. We tried to talk Bogeaus out of that one – I don't know how he got involved. And everything went wrong on that. It was a mess. But a comedy to me. I was laughing all the way through it, and Bogeaus couldn't understand why I was amused since it was tragedy. And I was howling. We rented a yacht – and I think the bottom was made out of tissue paper. Well, we went out to sea with Bogeaus and the whole crew and cast, but I had three taxi-boats to go with us. Bogeaus said, 'What do you want those boats for?' I said, 'Just in case. I want them close because this thing they playfully call a yacht is a sieve.' The owner of the boat was crocked – he was down below having the time of his life. And the actors would come up bleary-eyed – I thought they were seasick, but they were getting lit. Finally one of them came up and said, 'The water's coming in!' I said, 'Oh no, here it comes', and sure enough the damn thing started to sink. I signalled for the taxis and we deserted the ship. On that picture, even the boat balked! And we had a very effective scene in which one of our characters – a missionary, I think – rode majestically out on this raft. We had a double for it, Barbara Stanwyck's brother, and I told

him to just sit there with great dignity no matter what happened. So he rode out majestically and the damn thing started to sink. The natives all dove off, of course, and swam away from it, but this guy just sat there as the thing went down – because I'd said, 'Don't do anything'. And the water came right up over his

Stills. Opposite: Ronald Reagan and Barbara Stanwyck in Cattle Queen of Montana. *Above: David Farrar, Barbara Stanwyck and Robert Ryan in* Escape to Burma *(1955). Right: Virginia Mayo in* Pearl of the South Pacific.

dead-pan face and not a peep out of him until nothing was left but a floating hat. And I'm dying. I can't holler 'Cut' or anything because I'm laughing so hard. And Bogeaus was dying of heart failure. And the fellow would have gone right down and drowned but, of course, after he got under the natives grabbed him and pulled him up. You never saw a man obey like that in your life.

Buster Keaton did a gag like that in a short called The Boat.

Yes, launching a ship – that happened many years before ours.

Did you play the picture for laughs?

No, *I* was laughing at it, but it was supposed to be a very serious thing.

TENNESSEE'S PARTNER (1955)

Did you initiate any of the ten pictures you did with Bogeaus?

Tennessee's Partner was one. I can't remember any others I brought in because generally a producer likes to produce – pick his material and make it. But this was a good, honest story, and I liked Bret Harte. I always looked for things of his, and this seemed to be a natural and it was public domain. I believe the original story was more tragic than ours, but it was very definitely downbeat. And it was a short story, so we had to stretch it out some way or other.

You had four writers on it, but did you guide them?

Well, of course, the word 'writer' always indicates somebody tapping a typewriter or running a pencil across paper. I would give ideas or thoughts – sometimes I'd dictate to a secretary who'd hand it to the writers and say, 'Try to inject that'. So the actual writing was done by the writers, but the thinking was mine. And very often when I'm out making a picture I find things aren't running right, so I'll make the changes and present them to the actors right off-the-cuff on the set. Or, knowing where we're headed, write it up so we have a new scene to play a day later. You just can't put it all on

Stills: Tennessee's Partner. *Left – Rhonda Fleming, John Payne, Ronald Reagan. Below – Chubby Johnson, Rhonda Fleming and the young ladies of her Marriage Market including, right, Angie Dickinson.*

television that *must* come some day. Then the finest productions in the world can be made to fit that screen. And they'll be better than anything ever made for pictures because more money can be spent on them. More money will be coming in. Right now there's too many people trying to stop it. The theatre people don't want it, the picture people don't want it, television people don't want it – nobody wants it. Consequently, the lobbies against it are so

Stills. Left: Hold Back the Night. *Others:* Slightly Scarlet – *Dahl, Fleming, Payne.*

paper, have it perfect and walk out and shoot it that way – it's very hard to do that. You can do a play that way because you can rehearse, but not an action picture.

Did you cut all these pictures yourself?

Oh, I did the first cut. Then Bogeaus would come in and he fancied himself quite an editor, though he was really just Marcelene in the cutting room too. But we had Jim Leicester, who was a very good cutter, and when Bogeaus would tell him to change things, Jim would run it for him next day and say, 'Hey, I think that suggestion of yours was a big improvement' – and it was exactly the same – he hadn't touched it. And Bogeaus would say, 'You see, I told you . . . ' So he was kept under control pretty well.

In 1955 and 1956, you did two short TV films; what did you think of the procedure?

Oh, I didn't get into it enough to be affected. I thought it was very simple – a small motion picture – just a cute little cheater. We were back at the old one-reel days. That's all I could see – right back starting – television is what we did in the beginning. And it still is. The westerns they put out are all the little B-westerns we made. And they're not as good. But I like television. I think it can be good. If we can just get rid of Madison Avenue. Because I think television is as good a theatre as any if you design for it, stay within its limits. It's *pay*

162

vast that the public just isn't being considered at all. But pretty soon the public will put it on the ballot and they'll vote it in. Then I think we'll get some great stuff on television.

SLIGHTLY SCARLET (1956)

I didn't think much of that. We were hand-cuffed. There were things I wanted to do that were very hard to get by. Today, without censorship, it'd be easy. I remember in one

scene, a gangster came into a house, looked across the room and there was a couch, from behind which a woman's leg came up with a foot wiggling. And as he walked over, the leg disappeared; he came over to her, looked down and you knew he was looking down at an 'exposed' woman. Then she sat up and they carried on a scene – she was flirting with him and he didn't know who she was. Well, the censors said that leg coming up in the air wasn't allowed. Too suggestive. But that was the kind of picture it had to be and if we couldn't do it that way, the picture couldn't be done right. Because you couldn't be subtle about it. Arlene Dahl had to be a real tart – practically do a strip tease when she was half-drunk in one scene – and it was very hard to get anything like that done in those days – it was a handcuff job.

THE RIVER'S EDGE (1957)

I marvelled at Bogeaus sometimes – I don't know how he ever got the cast for *The River's Edge*. Ray Milland owed Fox a picture and they'd never found one he'd accept. Along came Bogeaus with this one and he liked it. Then he got Tony Quinn. Remarkable thing to pull those two together. And Fox said, 'Will you use Debra Paget?' So he took her – they played ball that way and we made the picture. But these are not the kind of things I like to be involved in. I don't enjoy putting a picture together. I enjoy making a picture. I'll contribute any ideas I have gladly. But I don't like to go out and find the money, or things like that. I enjoyed making it, and the idea was good, but one of the reasons I can't rave about it was Debra Paget. She's a nice little girl – I liked her – but I don't think she was the best person they could have had for that part. The two men were great, and they weren't balanced off by the girl, which annoyed me all the way through. The triangle wasn't right. With those two fellows you needed a girl who could hold up her end, because they knew all the tricks and were well balanced. That's what I liked about them – they were so different in their person-alities. She had enough sex as far as that's concerned, but nothing came out in the scenes – she was just wooden. And you can't put that into a person. You can't say, 'Roll your eyes a little more' – that won't do it. And since the three of them were together all the time, it was

Stills. Above – Arlene Dahl, the couch and Ted De Corsia in Slightly Scarlet. *Right – Debra Paget and Ray Milland in* The River's Edge.

important she be just right. I can name half a dozen girls who could have done it well, but she came with the rent. Fox wanted to use her, and Bogeaus accepted.

THE RESTLESS BREED (1957)

Was the producer aware that you were creating a comedy?
I don't know what he was aware of because we

It was just that type of picture – you know, it's your turn to peek. And one very hammy young guy we had in there peeked all the time.

When you make a film this way, do you think most of your audience realises it's a comedy or not?

Well, it's hard to say. I sneak into a theatre where it's playing and listen. Somebody will start laughing and somebody else will say, 'Shhh!' Then I know it's all right. One's taking it seriously, the other one's having a good time. If people start to laugh and get shushed, I know we've got it. One of those things – take your choice.

ENCHANTED ISLAND (1958)

I read Melville's 'Typee' and thought, well, if we just do what he wrote, maybe it'd work. But when you start to mess around with a book like that . . . Actually, 'Typee' had been started once by Allied Artists and was stopped for running out of hand. But 'Typee' was public domain, so Bogeaus grabbed it, though, because of an agreement with the Producers' Association, he couldn't call it 'Typee' – and wanted to get *away* from the book. He wanted to do 'Typee' without doing it. So he did *Enchanted Island*. And even then he had trouble with Allied Artists over it. But when they looked at the picture, they said, 'I guess we won't sue you for that.'

The movements were all right in the picture, and the backgrounds were good – it looked like a South Seas Island, though we faked it up down in Mexico. But I suffered through it with a drunken actor and a nice girl who didn't belong in it – Jane Powell – she just looked false as hell. She looked like a little girl pretending. If we had a real native kid or even a young Mexican girl, it would have been fine. Because the picture had an accent. But this sophisticated little prima donna couldn't bend herself down to it. And it didn't jell. It wasn't her fault – bad casting – she just didn't belong.

Still: Enchanted Island.

ignored him. We just went out and made it. And that really was a corner-cutter – we were doing that for peanuts. But what else could you do with it? Just had to be that way. Then, after it was finished, a very funny thing happened. Rhys Williams played a kindly old man who'd taken in this waif – Anne Bancroft – and been a father to her. Now, long after I'd left the picture, Alperson, the producer, got a painting of her in this low-cut dancing costume, put it on the wall, and made a scene with Rhys Williams looking at this painting with a lecherous leer, as though he wanted this girl. Well, when I saw that, I flipped. Just horrible bad taste – took all the gentility out of this nice old guy and made him a real dirty old man. But Alperson wanted some dirt in it.

What was the idea behind having everyone eavesdropping in the film?

MOST DANGEROUS MAN ALIVE (1961)
That again was a synthetic thing. In the first place, there was a deception about it. Even I got hooked. Bogeaus said that it was to be a pilot for a television series – in two episodes – and employed everybody on that basis. But when he presented the two parts to the syndicates in Mexico, they said, 'This is a script that's cut in half. It's a continuous story, so it is not a television film but a feature. Therefore you can't make it on TV terms, with a skeleton crew and everything at much lower rates. You must take a full crew and do it at full feature rates.' Well, as a matter of fact, that's what it was. He had just cut the script in half and was making the two parts. Pretty soon the actors got on to that and then the woole roof fell in on him and he didn't get away with his cheater. Which threw the budget completely out of the window – tripled it; to counterbalance that, it had to be done wham – fast. What should have been shot in five weeks was done in one. And everything in interiors – nothing built. The actors didn't want to stay. All they wanted to do was get home. And I was in the awkward position of trying to keep it together with all this schism going on around us. So I gritted my teeth and battled it. And that's not fun. Nobody cared a damn. So it was just get it in the box and get home. A misfit from start to end.

Since you made it in 1958, why wasn't it released until 1961?
They just didn't let it escape until then. They were probably short of a picture so they let it get out. It might have just been an accident. Though Bogeaus sold it to Columbia at a flat price that was more than it cost. The studio thought they were buying a big bargain – they didn't know how cheaply it had been made.

Bogeaus never made any more films.
No, he went out of the business for awhile and when he tried to come back he found that all of his old friends had gone out of the business or were dead. And he just didn't rate with the big outfits as someone they needed to have on their staff. He didn't have the material to promote anything and wasn't equipped to put it across. He tried several things. And he was always looking for a subject he could take to the majors and put over. And he just didn't have the standing with them. Even up to his death, he was still groping around, looking for the thing to make.

Have you enjoyed your retirement?
I've enjoyed it. I came out of it around 1966–67 and was going to do *Marine!* about General 'Chesty' Puller, for Warners. But the producer stalled around until Jack Warner sold the control of the studio and the picture went into mothballs and was never made. Yes, I've enjoyed the retirement, but I'm thinking of opening a free clinic for sick scripts and stories that people can't fix up, and see if I can help some of these young people get off the ground with their stuff. I'm helping a couple of fellows right now. But I'm not going to work, and I have no desire under today's circumstances to get back into the grind – the idiocy that's being perpetrated now. Still, you never get it out of your blood. You're always interested. Every book I read, I see a picture in my imagination.

Looking over your career, what kind of subjects would you say you were most drawn to?
Any human story. Adventure, movement and romance. I deplored tragedy. I didn't like violence – I used it occasionally to gain a point. And, of course, always hope. I hated an unhappy ending. I don't mean you can't make unhappiness occasionally, but I just don't like to aim at a downbeat end. Sometimes we'd have them wished on us and that was it. I know I made one great classic at Republic to please Yates, in which both the leading man and leading lady die in each other's arms in the last scene and the camera pulls gently away from them lying there in the mud. And I think the

picture's still lying there.

But I've always preferred stories of intimacy. Spectacle is only useful commercially – it's simply a mob-grabber – the Barnum and Bailey part of us. And a spectacle is no good anyway unless it's protected by a good, intimate story within. *Robin Hood* is a very simple story: king leaves town so his brother double-crosses him, and a young fellow comes along and saves the kingdom for the king till he comes back. In the meantime, he had a romance. Easy as that. You put it in a great big background of knights and palaces and crusades, but they're complementary, they wouldn't work if the intimate story wasn't right.

Over the years, which directors have you most admired?

Well, I like Hitchcock – I think he's done some good things. I like some of the excellent things Ford has done. I liked Capra, King Vidor, Frank Borzage. I liked Raoul Walsh's on-the-edge things very much. I admired Leo McCarey very much – he was a rebel and did some fine things. I think Hawks is good. And I admire Preminger's ability to keep going and putting things on – I think he's a good organiser. Of course, I used to go and see all the good pictures, or have them run at the studio. But I haven't seen many lately. I don't go anymore.

Which of your pictures would you want to be remembered by?

Oh, boy! Well, there are four or five I might want to see again or have anybody see again – *Robin Hood*, *Suez*, *Sands of Iwo Jima*, *Manhandled*, *Big Brother*. I don't know – I don't even remember the pictures so it's hard for me to say which ones I'd like to see again. If you read all the titles, I'd probably say, 'Put them all on!' Of course, the whole thing in this business is your last picture. You're judged on that. They used to say, 'You're as good as your last picture.' I always said, 'You're as good as your last producer.' But they *do* rate you from your last credit. That's all they remember. Not what you did before or since. And they don't understand very often that you're working for people and you're influenced by what those people want. So you're judged by the job you take. That's why so many people are finicky about what they'll do – they're trying to protect themselves. People call them temperamental, but they *should* be touchy. My weakness was that I'd take anything. If it was a challenge to me, I'd take a bad story and try to make it good. I did what I could to make it a picture. But you're limited if you haven't the material – a good story and a good cast is wonderful insurance for a director.

You never thought about posterity?

No, never. Not at all. Never gave it a thought. Hardly ever thought about *tomorrow*.

Is there anything you really regret in your career?

Well, that's hard to say. Of course, we made mistakes and regretted many things. I would never again sign a long-term contract with anybody – it would have to be individual pictures one by one. I'd do more independent work if I did it again. I would not get involved in so many poor pictures some producer wanted done. If you can get associated with a top producer, you're lucky – otherwise, do it yourself. A question of survival. Commit suicide or conquer. One or the other. But don't let another fellow murder you.

You feel you were murdered a few times?

Oh, sure. I got involved in contracts which made me do things I wouldn't do under any condition – wouldn't want to do – but had to. You're drawing a salary, you're assigned a thing and you do it the best you can. But in the early days, you were strictly on your own. What would I do differently if I were a young man starting out? My advice would be: Don't get involved in the other fellow's thing unless you know he's good . . . But I have no regrets about any of it.

Dwan's Career

FILMOGRAPHY

This filmography was compiled by Mae Woods from a previously published one in Présence du Cinéma, *No. 22–23 (Autumn, 1966), augmented by a considerable amount of new information gathered from publications of the time, the files of Universal Studios, the collection of the Academy of Motion Picture Arts and Sciences, the records of the National Film Archive in Washington and of the Directors Guild of America. Most of the material on the pictures Dwan made for the American Film Company was researched by Timothy J. Lyons of the University of Iowa.*

Allan Dwan was born Joseph Aloysius Dwan on 3 April 1885, in Toronto, Canada. His father, Joseph Michael Dwan, was a clothing merchant; his mother was the former Mary Hunt; they had one other son, the late Leo G. Dwan, who became a doctor. After a short stay in Detroit, Dwan's family moved to Chicago at the time of the 1893 World's Fair. There he attended Alcott School and North Division High School before entering Notre Dame University, where he studied electrical engineering and became a football star. He also played in amateur theatricals. After his graduation in 1907, he stayed on to coach football and teach mathematics and physics; in the following year, he joined the Peter Cooper Hewitt Company as an illuminating engineer. His work on the mercury vapour arc brought him in 1909 to Essanay Studios, where he became interested in the movies, sold the company several stories he had written in college, finally accepted a job as scenario editor.

When the American Film Company (also known as 'Flying A') was formed by several Essanay staff members in late 1910, Dwan joined them as chief scenario editor. He stayed at the Chicago headquarters for a while, but American's main production unit was filming in Tucson, Arizona, under the direction of Frank Beal, and Dwan was sent there as a kind of production manager. Eventually, the company was moved to California and in early 1911 Dwan replaced Beal. Over the next three years he directed over 250 films for American, supervising the production of as many more.

The following pictures he directed are listed by release date (which is not necessarily the order of production) and his company's location in California. Unless otherwise indicated, each is one reel in length. The few titles on which Dwan's direction could not be positively certified are followed by question marks. The cast and crew for these pictures – most of which were westerns – varied, but were made up from these people: Director-producer-writer: Allan Dwan. Business manager: Wallace Kerrigan. Photographer: Roy Overbaugh; assistant cameramen: R. D. Armstrong, Victor Fleming. Scenery: Sid Boldridge. Props: C. P. Morrison; prop assistant: Smith 'Slim' Wilson. Cast: J. Warren Kerrigan (leading man), Pauline Bush (leading lady), Marshall 'Steve' Neilan (juvenile lead), Jessalyn 'Toddles' Van Trump (ingénue), Louise Lester (character actress; later 'Calamity Anne'), George Periolat (character actor), Mrs Hathaway (character actress), Jack Richardson (heavy), Charlotte Burton (heavy), Peter, Carl and Chick Morrison (cowboys), J. A. Harrison, Little Helen Armstrong, Eugene W. Pallette, William J. Tedmarsh, Vera Sisson, M. B. Robbins.

Film titles shown in *italic* following a title in capital letters are alternative titles.

Page numbers shown in *italic* are references to illustrations.

169

1911: San Juan Capistrano

May 22   BRANDISHING A BAD MAN (comedy) and A WESTERN DREAMER (drama). A split reel. Dwan finished these films at Beal's old location before moving to:

1911: Lakeside

May 25   A DAUGHTER OF LIBERTY and A TROUPER'S HEART. A split reel.

May 29   RATTLESNAKES AND GUNPOWDER (comedy) and THE RANCH TENOR – *The Foreman's Fixup* (comedy). A split reel. *See p.* 18.

June 1   THE SHEEPMAN'S DAUGHTER (drama).

June 5   THE SAGEBRUSH PHRENOLOGIST (comedy) and THE ELOPEMENTS ON DOUBLE L RANCH (comedy). A split reel.

June 8 $5000 REWARD – DEAD OR ALIVE (drama).

June 12   THE WITCH OF THE RANGE (drama).

June 15   THE COWBOY'S RUSE (comedy) and LAW AND ORDER ON BAR L RANCH (comedy). A split reel.

June 19   THE YIDDISHER COWBOY (comedy) and THE BRONCHO BUSTER'S BRIDE (comedy). A split reel.

June 22   THE HERMIT'S GOLD (drama). Re-released: 17 February 1917.

June 26   THE ACTRESS AND THE COWBOYS (comedy) and THE SKY PILOT'S INTEMPERANCE (comedy). A split reel.

June 29   A WESTERN WAIF (drama).

July 3   THE CALL OF THE OPEN RANGE (drama)

July 6   THE SCHOOL MA'AM OF SNAKE (comedy) and THE RANCH CHICKEN (comedy). A split reel.

July 10   CUPID IN CHAPS (comedy).

July 13   THE OUTLAW'S TRAIL (drama).

July 17   THE RANCHMAN'S NERVE (drama).

July 20   WHEN EAST COMES WEST (comedy-drama).

July 24   THE COWBOY'S DELIVERANCE.

July 27   THE CATTLE THIEF'S BRAND (drama).

July 31   THE PARTING TRAILS (drama).

Aug. 3   THE CATTLE RUSTLER'S END (drama).

Aug. 7   CATTLE, GOLD AND OIL (comedy-drama).

Aug. 10   THE RANCH GIRL – *The Ranch Girl's Rustler* (drama).

Aug. 14   THE POISONED FLUME (drama). *See p.* 20.

Aug. 17   THE BRAND OF FEAR (drama).

Aug. 21   THE BLOTTED BRAND (drama).

Aug. 24   AUNTIE AND THE COWBOYS (comedy) and *Anne Harris in Chicago Swimming Marathon* (documentary). A split reel, the second title of which was directed by one of American's Chicago staff.

Aug. 28   THE WESTERN DOCTOR'S PERIL (drama).

Aug. 31   THE SMUGGLER AND THE GIRL – *The Diamond Smugglers* (drama).

Sept. 4   THE COWBOY AND THE ARTIST (drama).

Sept. 7   THREE MILLION DOLLARS (comedy). *See pp.* 6, 24.

Sept. 11   THE STAGE ROBBERS OF SAN JUAN (comedy-drama).

Sept. 14   THE MOTHER OF THE RANCH (drama).

Sept. 18   THE GUNMAN (drama).

Sept. 21   THE CLAIM JUMPERS – *The Range Squatter* (drama).

Sept. 25   THE CIRCULAR FENCE (comedy).

Sept. 28   THE RUSTLER SHERIFF (comedy-drama).

Oct. 2   THE LOVE OF THE WEST – *Western Love* (drama).

No date   THE TRAINED NURSE AT BAR Z (comedy).

1911: La Mesa

Oct. 5   THE MINER'S WIFE (drama).

Oct. 9   THE LAND THIEVES (drama).

Oct. 12   THE COWBOY AND THE OUTLAW (drama).

Oct. 16   THREE DAUGHTERS OF THE WEST (comedy-drama) and CAVES OF LA JOLLA (documentary). A split reel.

Oct. 19   THE LONELY RANGE (drama).

Oct. 23   THE HORSE THIEF'S BIGAMY (drama).

Oct. 26   THE TRAIL OF THE EUCALYPTUS (drama).

Oct. 30   THE STRONGER MAN (drama).

Nov. 2   THE WATER WAR (drama).

Nov. 6   THE THREE SHELL GAME (drama).

Nov. 9	THE MEXICAN (drama).	Feb. 15	AN INNOCENT GRAFTER (drama).
Nov. 13	THE EASTERN COWBOY (comedy).	Feb. 19	SOCIETY AND CHAPS (comedy).
Nov. 16	THE WAY OF THE WEST (comedy-drama).	Feb. 22	THE LEAP YEAR COWBOY – *February 29* (comedy).
Nov. 20	THE TEST (drama).	Feb. 26	THE LAND BARON OF SAN TEE (drama).
Nov. 23	THE MASTER OF THE VINEYARD (drama).	Feb. 29	AN ASSISTED ELOPEMENT (comedy).
Nov. 27	SLOPPY BILL OF THE ROLLICKING R – *Jolly Bill of the Rollicking R* (comedy). Made at Lakeside.	March 4	FROM THE FOUR HUNDRED TO THE HERD (drama).
Nov. 30	THE SHERIFF'S SISTERS (drama).	March 7	THE BROKEN TIES.
Dec. 4	THE ANGEL OF PARADISE RANCH – *The Girl of the Ranch* (drama).	March 11	AFTER SCHOOL (drama).
		March 14	A BAD INVESTMENT (drama).
Dec. 7	THE SMOKE OF THE FORTY-FIVE (drama).	March 18	THE FULL VALUE (drama).
		March 21	THE TRAMP'S GRATITUDE.
Dec. 11	THE MAN HUNT (drama).	March 25	FIDELITY (drama).
Dec. 14	SANTA CATALINA, MAGIC ISLE OF THE PACIFIC (documentary).	March 28	WINTER SPORTS AND PASTIMES OF CORONADO BEACH – *Coronado New Year's Day* (documentary).
Dec. 18	THE LAST NOTCH (drama).	April 1	THE MAID AND THE MAN (comedy-drama).
Dec. 21	THE GOLD LUST (drama).		
Dec. 25	THE DUEL OF THE CANDLES (drama).	April 4	THE COWBOY SOCIALIST – *The Agitator* (drama).
Dec. 28	BONITA OF EL CAJON (drama).	April 8	CHECKMATE and THE RANCHMAN'S MARATHON (comedy). A split reel.
No date	THE LAWFUL HOLDUP (comedy-drama)?		
No date	BATTLESHIPS (documentary)?	April 11	THE COWARD (drama).
No date	DAMS AND WATERWAYS (documentary)?	April 15	THE DISTANT RELATIVE (comedy-drama).
		April 18	THE RANGE DETECTIVE (drama).
1912: La Mesa		April 22	DRIFTWOOD (drama). Title used again for Dwan's 1947 feature.
Jan. 1	A MIDWINTER TRIP TO LOS ANGELES (documentary).	April 25	THE EASTERN GIRL – *Her Mountain Home*.
Jan. 4	THE MISADVENTURES OF A CLAIM AGENT and BRONCHO BUSTING FOR FLYING A PICTURES – *Bucking Horses* (drama). A split reel.	April 29	THE PENSIONERS (drama).
		May 2	THE END OF THE FEUD (drama).
		May 6	THE WEDDING DRESS – *Her Wedding Dress* (comedy-drama).
Jan. 8	THE WINNING OF LA MESA (drama).	May 9	MYSTICAL MAID OF JAMASHA PASS (drama).
Jan. 11	THE LOCKET (drama).	May 13	THE OTHER WISE MAN (drama).
Jan. 15	THE RELENTLESS OUTLAW (drama).	May 16	THE HATERS (comedy).
Jan. 18	JUSTICE OF THE SAGE (drama).	May 20	THE THREAD OF LIFE (drama).
Jan. 22	OBJECTIONS OVERRULED (comedy-drama).	May 23	THE WANDERING GYPSY (drama).
		May 27	THE REWARD OF VALOR (comedy). Marshall Neilan's first film with Dwan.
Jan. 25	THE MORMON (drama).		
Jan. 29	LOVE AND LEMONS (drama).	May 30	THE BRAND (drama).
Feb. 1	THE BEST POLICY (comedy).	June 3	THE GREEN EYED MONSTER (comedy-drama).
Feb. 5	THE REAL ESTATE FRAUD (drama).		
Feb. 8	THE GRUBSTAKE MORTGAGE (drama).	June 6	CUPID THROUGH PADLOCKS (comedy).
		June 10	FOR THE GOOD OF HER MEN (drama).
Feb. 12	WHERE BROADWAY MEETS THE MOUNTAINS (drama).	June 13	THE SIMPLE LOVE (drama).

June 17	THE WEAKER BROTHER (drama) and FIFTY MILE AUTO CONTEST – *Auto Race-Lakeside* (comedy). A split reel.	Sept. 19	THE FORECLOSURE.
		Sept. 23	WHITE TREACHERY (drama).
		Sept. 26	THEIR HERO SON (drama).
June 20	THE WORDLESS MESSAGE.	Sept. 30	CALAMITY ANNE'S WARD (drama). The first of what began a popular series featuring Calamity Anne, a tough frontier woman played by Louise Lester; she was Dwan's invention. Re-released: 23 November 1916.
June 24	THE EVIL INHERITANCE (drama).
June 27	THE MARAUDERS (drama).
July 1	THE GIRL BACK HOME (drama).
July 4	UNDER FALSE PRETENSES.
July 8	WHERE THERE'S A HEART (drama).
July 11	THE VANISHING RACE – *The Vanishing Tribe* (drama).	Oct. 3	FATHER'S FAVORITE – *The Favored Son* (drama).
July 15	THE FATAL MIRROR (drama) and POINT LOMA, OLD TOWN (documentary). A split reel.	Oct. 7	JACK OF DIAMONDS – *Queen of Hearts* (drama).
		Oct. 10	THE REFORMATION OF SIERRA SMITH – *The Lost Watch* (drama).
July 18	THE TELL TALE SHELLS (drama).	Oct. 14	THE PROMISE (drama).
July 22	INDIAN JEALOUSY (drama) and SAN DIEGO (documentary). A split reel.	Oct. 17	THE NEW COWPUNCHER (drama).
		Oct. 21	THE BEST MAN WINS.
July 25	THE CANYON DWELLER (drama).	Oct. 24	THE WOOERS OF MOUNTAIN KATE – *Mountain Kate* (drama).
July 29	IT PAYS TO WAIT (comedy-drama).
Aug. 1	A LIFE FOR A KISS (drama).	Oct. 28	ONE, TWO, THREE (comedy).
Aug. 5	THE MEDDLERS (drama).	Oct. 31	THE WANDERER (drama).
Aug. 8	THE GIRL AND THE GUN (drama).	Nov. 4	MAIDEN AND MEN (drama).
Aug. 12	THE BATTLEGROUND (drama). 2 reels.	Nov. 7	GOD'S UNFORTUNATE (drama).
		Nov. 11	MAN'S CALLING (drama).
Aug. 14	THE BAD MAN AND THE RANGER (drama).	Nov. 14	THE INTRUSION AT LOMPOC (drama).
Aug. 15	THE OUTLAW COLONY (drama).	Nov. 18	THE THIEF'S WIFE (drama).
Aug. 19	THE LAND OF DEATH (drama).
Aug. 22	THE BANDIT OF POINT LOMA (drama).

At this time, Dwan formed a second production company in Santa Barbara, headed by Wallace Reid. Dwan served only as supervisor for these one-reel productions, which are not included below.

Aug. 26	THE JEALOUS RAGE (drama).	Nov. 21	THE WOULD-BE HEIR (drama).
Aug. 29	THE WILL OF JAMES WALDRON (drama).	Nov. 25	JACK'S WORD – *A Man's Word* (drama).
No date	THE HOUSE THAT JACK BUILT (drama) ?	Nov. 28	HER OWN COUNTRY (drama).
		Dec. 2	PALS.
No date	CURTISS'S SCHOOL OF AVIATION (documentary) ?	Dec. 5	THE ANIMAL WITHIN (drama).
		Dec. 9	THE LAW OF GOD (drama).
No date	THE STEPMOTHER (drama) ?	Dec. 12	NELL OF THE PAMPAS (comedy).
No date	THE ODD JOB MAN (drama) ?	Dec. 16	THE DAUGHTERS OF SENOR LOPEZ (drama).
No date	THE LIAR (drama) ?
		Dec. 19	THE POWER OF LOVE (drama).

The rest of the American releases were shot in Santa Barbara, where the company had moved in July, 1912.

		Dec. 23	THE RECOGNITION (drama).
1912: SANTA BARBARA		Dec. 26	BLACKENED HILLS (drama).
Sept. 2	THE GREASER AND THE WEAKLING (drama).	Dec. 30	LONELINESS OF NEGLECT (drama).
		No date	PAID IN FULL (drama).
Sept. 5	THE STRANGER AT COYOTE (drama).	No date	RANCH LIFE ON THE RANGE (drama).
Sept. 9	THE DAWN OF PASSION (drama).	No date	THE MAN FROM THE EAST (drama).
Sept. 12	THE VENGEANCE THAT FAILED (drama).
Sept. 16	THE FEAR (drama).	No date	THE HORSE THIEF (drama).

No date   THE GOOD LOVE AND THE BAD (drama).

1913: SANTA BARBARA
Jan. 4   THE FRAUD THAT FAILED (drama).
Jan. 6   ANOTHER MAN'S WIFE (drama).
Jan. 11   CALAMITY ANNE'S INHERITANCE (comedy). Re-released: 16 February 1917.
Jan. 13   THEIR MASTERPIECE (drama).
Jan. 18   HIS OLD-FASHIONED MOTHER and *The English Walnut Industry*. A split reel, the second title of which was directed by Samuel Hutchinson.
Jan. 20   WHERE DESTINY GUIDES.
Jan. 23   THE SILVER PLATED GUN (drama).
Jan. 25   A ROSE OF OLD MEXICO.
Jan. 30   BUILDING THE GREAT LOS ANGELES AQUEDUCT (documentary).
Feb. 1   WOMEN LEFT ALONE (drama).
Feb. 3   ANDREW JACKSON. 2 reels.
Feb. 8   CALAMITY ANNE'S VANITY (comedy). Re-released: 30 November 1916.
Feb. 10   THE FUGITIVE.
Feb. 15   THE ROMANCE (comedy-drama).
Feb. 17   THE FINER THINGS (drama).
Feb. 22   LOVE IS BLIND (drama).
Feb. 24   WHEN THE LIGHT FADES.
March 1   HIGH AND LOW (drama).
March 3   THE GREATER LOVE.
March 6   THE JOCULAR WINDS (comedy-drama).
March 8   THE TRANSGRESSION OF MANUEL.
March 10   CALAMITY ANNE, DETECTIVE (comedy). Re-released; 23 February 1917.
March 15   THE ORPHAN'S MINE.
March 17   WHEN A WOMAN WON'T.
March 22   AN EASTERN FLOWER (drama).
March 24   CUPID NEVER AGES (drama).
March 29   CALAMITY ANNE'S BEAUTY (comedy).
March 31   THE RENEGADE'S HEART.
April 3   MATCHES (comedy-drama).
April 5   THE MUTE WITNESS.
April 7   CUPID THROWS A BRICK (comedy-drama). Re-released: 3 March 1917.
April 12   WOMAN'S HONOR (drama).
April 14   SUSPENDED SENTENCE.
April 17   IN ANOTHER'S NEST (drama).
April 19   THE WAYS OF FATE.
April 21   BOOBS AND BRICKS (comedy).
April 26   CALAMITY ANNE'S TRUST (comedy). Re-released: 2 March 1917. *See pp.* 6, 24.
April 28   OIL ON TROUBLED WATERS (drama). 2 reels. *See pp.* 26–27.
May 3   THE ROAD TO RUIN (drama).
May 5   THE BROTHERS.
May 8   HUMAN KINDNESS (drama).
May 10   YOUTH AND JEALOUSY.
May 12   ANGEL OF THE CANYONS.
May 17   THE GREAT HARMONY (comedy-drama).
May 19   HER INNOCENT MARRIAGE.
May 22   CALAMITY ANNE PARCEL POST (comedy).
May 26   THE ASHES OF THREE (drama).
May 29   ON THE BORDER.
May 31   HER BIG STORY (drama).
June 2   WHEN LUCK CHANGES.
June 5   THE WISHING SEAT (comedy).
June 12   HEARTS AND HORSES.
June 14   THE REWARD OF COURAGE.
June 16   THE SOUL OF A THIEF. 2 reels.
June 21   THE MARINE LAW (drama).
No date   THE ROAD TO SUCCESS (drama).

In mid-1913, Dwan signed with Universal Pictures in Los Angeles (*see pp.* 28–29), taking both his Flying A production units with him. At the new company, he again supervised the work of Wallace Reid and Marshall Neilan, who alternated as directors (a few of these titles are included below as token evidence). In one filmography, Dwan is credited as scenarist on a series of ten pictures directed at Universal by Otis Turner during 1913 and 1914; this is erroneous.

1913: THE SPIRIT OF THE FLAG (Universal-Bison).
Director: Allan Dwan. Writer: Wallace Reid. 2 reels. Released: June 7.
With Reid (American doctor), Pauline Bush (American teacher), Jessalyn Van Trump (Bonita), Arthur Rosson (her father), David Kirkland (Spanish renegade).
   An American doctor in the Philippines teaches the natives to defend their settlement from the Spaniards.

1913: THE CALL TO ARMS – *In Love and War* (Universal-Bison).
Director-writer: Allan Dwan. 2 reels. Released: June 17.
With Pauline Bush (girl), Marshall Neilan (lawyer), Wallace Reid (journalist).
   A Northerner who cannot pass the physical goes to the front as a journalist and proves himself a hero.

1913: WOMEN AND WAR (Universal-Bison).
Director: Allan Dwan. Writer: Wallace Reid. 2 reels.
Released: June 21.
With Pauline Bush (girl), Jessalyn Van Trump (younger
sister), Wallace Reid (neighbour), Marshall Neilan (stay-
at-home).

Engaged to the girl next door, a Virginia soldier goes
into the Civil War and returns loving the sister.

1913: THE POWDER FLASH OF DEATH (Universal-
Bison).
Director-writer: Allan Dwan. 2 reels. Released: July 8.
With Wallace Reid (Union soldier), Marshall Neilan
(Confederate soldier), J. D. Kirkland (neutral), Pauline
Bush (Dixie girl), Jessalyn Van Trump (girl of the
crossroads).

A Dixie girl is loved by a Rebel, a Yankee and a
neutral.

1913: THE PICKET GUARD (Universal-Bison).
Director: Allan Dwan. Scenarist: Arthur Rosson, from
poem by Ethelin Elliot Beers. 1,830 feet. Released:
July 15.
With Wallace Reid (sentry), Pauline Bush (Mary, his
wife), Marshall Neilan (officer), Jessalyn Van Trump
(his wife), David Kirkland (Confederate picket).

A federal sentry dies defending his post in the Civil
War.

1913: MENTAL SUICIDE (Universal-Powers).
Director: Allan Dwan. Writer: Wallace Reid. 1 reel.
Released: July 25.
With Pauline Bush (invalid), Jessalyn Van Trump (her
sister), Marshall Neilan (architect), Wallace Reid, David
Kirkland (contractors).

An architect accepts a contractor's bribe to provide
for his fiancée's invalid sister.

1913: MAN'S DUTY (Universal).
Director: Allan Dwan. Writer: M. de la Parelle. 955 feet.
Released: August 10.
With Wallace Reid (Bill), Marshall Neilan (Joe), Jessalyn
Van Trump (Flora), Pauline Bush (blind girl).

In a western town, a blind girl convinces a selfish man
to fulfil his obligations to another woman.

1913: THE ANIMAL (Universal-Rex).
Director-writer: Allan Dwan. 995 feet. Released:
August 17.
With Wallace Reid (husband), Pauline Bush (wife),
Marshall Neilan (her former suitor), Jessalyn Van
Trump, D. Barlow (other couple).

A husband kidnaps his own child.

1913: *The Harvest of Flame* (Universal-Rex).
Director-writer: Wallace Reid. Producer: Allan Dwan.
1,500 feet. Released: August 21.
With William Walters (capitalist), Pauline Bush (his
daughter), Marshall Neilan (the smoker), Wallace Reid
(inspector).

1913: THE WALL OF MONEY (Universal-Rex).
Director: Allan Dwan. Writer: Marshall Neilan. 2 reels.
Released: September 21.
With Marshall Neilan (man of ideas), Pauline Bush (his
sister), Jessalyn Van Trump (his sweetheart), James
McQuarrie (monopolist), Wallace Reid (his son).

A rich industrialist's son turns against his father for
mistreating his factory workers.

1913: THE ECHO OF A SONG (Universal-Rex).
Director: Allan Dwan. Writer: M. de la Parelle. 1 reel.
Released: October 12.
With Pauline Bush (organist), Murdock MacQuarrie
(the modern Fagin), Jessalyn Van Trump, Gertrude
Short (his children).

An old man teaches slum children to steal.

1913: CRIMINALS (Universal-Rex).
Director: Allan Dwan. Writer: M. de la Parelle. 2 reels.
Released: October 19.
With Murdock MacQuarrie (Richard Wainwright/John
Dick), Pauline Bush (his daughter), Arthur Rosson,
Richard Rosson (his followers), Jessalyn Van Trump
(their sister), William Lloyd (James Stevens), William
Walters (policeman).

A notorious safe cracker masquerades as the town
benefactor.

1913: THE RESTLESS SPIRIT (Universal-Victor).
Director-scenarist: Allan Dwan, from Thomas Gray's
'Elegy Written in a Country Churchyard'. Photography:
Walter Prichard. 3 reels. Released: October 21.
With J. Warren Kerrigan (husband), Pauline Bush
(wife), Jessalyn Van Trump (woman), William Worthing-
ton (stranger).

Visualisation of Gray's poem. (Working title: *Paths
of Glory*.) See pp. 6, 30, 63.

1913: JEWELS OF SACRIFICE (Universal).
Director: Allan Dwan. Writer: M. de la Parelle. 1 reel.
Released: November 2.
With Pauline Bush.

A selfish woman must sacrifice her jewellery to save
her baby's life.

1913: BACK TO LIFE (Universal-Victor).
Director: Allan Dwan. Writer: M. de la Parelle. 2 reels.
Released: November 24.
With J. Warren Kerrigan (Jim), William Worthington

(gambler), Pauline Bush (his wife), Lon Chaney (rival), Jessalyn Van Trump (charmer).

A gambler prefers dance-hall girls to his sickly wife; Jim comes to the rescue. *Lon Chaney's first of over sixteen films for Dwan. See pp. 30–31.*

1913: RED MARGARET, MOONSHINER
(Universal-Gold Seal).
Director: Allan Dwan. Writer: Jeanie MacPherson. 2 reels. Released: December 9.
With Pauline Bush (Red Margaret), Lon Chaney (her mountain lover), Murdock MacQuarrie (government agent), James Neill (sheriff).

A daring, red-headed young girl is the leader of a band of Tennessee moonshiners. (Working title: *Warrington's Honor;* re-issued as a one-reeler, *Moonshine Blood*, on 21 December 1916.)

1913: BLOODHOUNDS OF THE NORTH
(Universal-Gold Seal).
Director: Allan Dwan. Writer: Arthur Rosson. 2 reels. Released: December 23.
With William Lloyd (embezzler), Pauline Bush (his daughter), James Neill (refugee), Murdock MacQuarrie, Lon Chaney (Mounties).

An embezzler and his daughter are pursued by the Mounties in the Northwestern wilderness.

1913: HE CALLED HER IN (Universal).
Director-scenarist: Allan Dwan, from poem by James Whitcomb Riley. 1 reel.
With Pauline Bush (wealthy girl), Jessalyn Van Trump (girl of nature), Murdock MacQuarrie (rich man).

Before she dies, a dispirited girl discovers happiness in nature.

1913: THE MENACE (Universal).
Director-writer: Allan Dwan. 1 reel.
With Wallace Reid (Captain Bruce Douglas), Pauline Bush (his sweetheart), Marshall Neilan (Jed), Jessalyn Van Trump (Sue), David Kirkland (tavern keeper).

A Dixie boy is torn between his love for a girl and his desire to be a soldier.

1913: THE CHASE (Universal).
Director: Allan Dwan. 2 reels.

1913: THE BATTLE OF WILLS (Western Feature Film Company).
Director: Allan Dwan. 2 reels.

1913: *The Ways of Fate* (Western Feature Film Company).
Director: Wallace Reid. Producer: Allan Dwan. 3 reels.

With Reid, Vivian Rich.

1914: THE LIE (Universal-Gold Seal).
Director: Allan Dwan. Writer: Jeanie MacPherson. 2 reels. Released: January 6.
With Murdock MacQuarrie (MacGregor), Pauline Bush (his daughter), Lon Chaney (his son), William Lloyd (MacGregor's brother), Richard Rossen, Arthur Rosson (youths), Fred McKay (their father), James Neill (gambler).

A stern religious Scotsman must lie to protect his innocent daughter.

1914: THE HONOR OF THE MOUNTED (Universal-Gold Seal).
Director: Allan Dwan. Writer: Arthur Rosson. 2 reels. Released: February 17.
With Pauline Bush (Marie Laquox), Lon Chaney (her brother Jacques), Murdock MacQuarrie (MacTavish), James Neill (commandant), Gertrude Short.

In a small town in the Rockies, a Mountie recruit has to arrest his best friend.

1914: REMEMBER MARY MAGDALENE
(Universal-Victor).
Director-writer: Allan Dwan. 1 reel. Released: February 23.
With Pauline Bush (woman), Murdock MacQuarrie (minister), Lon Chaney (orphan).

A minister defends a wronged woman.

1914: DISCORD AND HARMONY (Universal-Gold Seal).
Director: Allan Dwan. Writer: Arthur Rosson. 3 reels. Released: March 17.
With Murdock MacQuarrie (Felix, the composer), Lon Chaney (sculptor), Pauline Bush (girl), Allen Forrest (artist), James Neill (symphony conductor), John Burton.

An old musician befriends a young girl.

1914: THE MENACE TO CARLOTTA
(Universal-Rex).
Director: Allan Dwan. Writer: Lon Chaney. 1 reel. Released: March 22.
With W. C. Dowlan (Tony), Pauline Bush (his sister), Murdock MacQuarrie (his father), Lon Chaney (Giovanni Bartholi), John Burton (vulture).

An Italian comes to join his friends in America.

1914: THE EMBEZZLER (Universal-Gold Seal).
Director-writer: Allan Dwan. 2 reels. Released: March 31.
With Murdock MacQuarrie (John Spencer), Pauline

Bush (his daughter), Lon Chaney (J. Roger Dixon), William C. Dowlan (Arthur Bronson), William Lloyd (William Perkins), Richard Rosson (Dick, the penman), Gertrude Short.

An embezzler is blackmailed for his daughter's hand in marriage.

1914: THE LAMB, THE WOMAN, THE WOLF (Universal-101 Bison).
Director-writer: Allan Dwan. 3 reels. Released: April 4.
With Pauline Bush (woman), Lon Chaney (the wolf), Murdock MacQuarrie (the lamb).

A girl must choose between two suitors – one gentle, one brutish.

1914: THE END OF THE FEUD (Universal-Rex).
Director: Allan Dwan. Writer: Richard Rosson. 1 reel.
Released: April 12.
With Murdock MacQuarrie (Hen Dawson), Pauline Bush (Jane Dawson), Lon Chaney (Wood, her cousin), William Lloyd (Jed Putnam), William C. Dowlan (Joel Putnam).

Two children from feuding small-town families fall in love.

1914: TRAGEDY OF WHISPERING CREEK (Universal-101 Bison).
Director: Allan Dwan. Scenarist: Lon Chaney, from story by Elliott J. Clawson. Photography: L. O. Bartholomew. 2 reels. Released: May 2.
With Pauline Bush (orphan), Lon Chaney (the greaser), Murdock MacQuarrie (stranger), William C. Dowlan (Bashful Bill), George Cooper (kid), Mary Ruby (his sweetheart), John Burton, Doc Crane, William Lloyd (prospectors).

A madman menaces a village of prospectors.

1914: THE UNLAWFUL TRADE (Universal).
Director: Allan Dwan. Writer: George Cooper. 1 reel.
Released: May 14.
With Pauline Bush (Amy Tate), William Lloyd (Ol' Tate), George Cooper (Young Tate), William C. Dowlan (Newton Haugh), Lon Chaney ('Cross Blood'), Murdock MacQuarrie (revenue man).

A man protects his sister from an unscrupulous suitor.

1914: THE FORBIDDEN ROOM (Universal-101 Bison).
Director: Allan Dwan. Writer: Bess Meredyth. Photography: L. O. Bartholomew. 3 reels. Released: June 20.
With Murdock MacQuarrie (Dr Gibson), Pauline Bush (his sister/his niece), William C. Dowlan (prosecuting attorney), Lon Chaney (John Morris), John Burton (Dr Jarvis).

A man tries to keep his niece from learning of her mother's insanity. (Working title: *The Web of Circumstance*.)

1914: THE HOPES OF BLIND ALLEY (Universal-101 Bison).
Director: Allan Dwan. Writers: Dwan, Murdock MacQuarrie; continuity by Grace Johnson. Photography: L. O. Bartholomew. 3 reels. Released: July 4.
With Murdock MacQuarrie (Old Jean Basse), Pauline Bush (Pauline, his grand-daughter), George Cooper (janitor), William C. Dowlan (artist).

An old pedlar inherits a valuable painting.

1914: THE GREAT UNIVERSAL MYSTERY (Universal-Nestor).
Director: Allan Dwan. 1 reel. Released: July 10.
With King Baggott, Pauline Bush, Ford Sterling, William Clifford, Lois Weber, Lee Moran, Ella Hall, Hobart Henley, William Welsh, Betty Schade, Leah Baird, Howard Crampton, Al Christie, Carl Laemmle, Maurice Fleckes, Herman Fichtenberg, Allen Curtis, Florence Lawrence, Francis Ford, Bob Leonard, Cleo Madison, Victoria Forde, Murdock MacQuarrie, Ethel Grandin, Alexander Gadin, Rupert Julian, Edna Maison, Edmund Mortimer, Frank Crane, J. C. Graham, Wilfred Lucas, F. A. Van Husan, J. V. Bryson, Henry McRae, J. Warren Kerrigan, Grace Cunard, Herbert Rawlinson, Phillips Smalley, Eddie Lyons, William Shay, Irene Wallace, Matt Moore, Marie Walcamp, Frank Smith, William C. Dowlan, Herbert Brenon, Isadore Bernstein, Otis Turner, Bob Thornby, David Horsley, Fred Balshofer.

A promotional film with the entire Universal Studio participating, filmed in California, and at Coytesville Studio, New Jersey; Imp factory, Bayonne, New Jersey; Victor Studio, New Jersey; Imp Studio, New York and the executive offices of the company at 1600 Broadway, New York.

1914: RICHELIEU (Universal-101 Bison).
Director-scenarist: Allan Dwan, from story by E. Bulwer Lytton. 6 reels. Released: September 26.
With Pauline Bush (Julie de Mortemar), Murdock MacQuarrie (Cardinal Richelieu), William C. Dowlan (Adrien de Mauprat), Lon Chaney (Baradas), Robert Chandler (Sieur de Beringham), Edna Maison (Marion de Lorme), James Neill (King), Edythe Chapman (Queen), William Lloyd (Joseph), Richard Rosson (Francois), Frank Rice (Huget), John Burton.

Conspirators attempt to defame the Cardinal and gain control of the French throne. *Dwan's first feature-length movie.*

Though several of his Universal films were still to be released, Dwan signed in 1914 with the Famous Players Company in New York, where he went to work.

1914: WILDFLOWER (Famous Players).
Director: Allan Dwan. Scenarists: Dwan, Eva Unsell, from story by Mary Germaine. 4 reels. Released: October 15.
With Marguerite Clark (Letty Roberts), Harold Lockwood (Arnold Boyd), James Cooley (Gerold Boyd, his brother), Jack Pickford (Arnold's valet).
Romance about a New Yorker who rescues a naïve country girl from his own brother. *See p. 33.*

1914: THE COUNTY CHAIRMAN (Famous Players).
Director-scenarist: Allan Dwan, from play by George Ade. 5 reels. Released: October 26.
With Maclyn Arbuckle (Jim Hackler), Wellington Playter (Whittaker), Harold Lockwood (Wheeler), Daisy Robinson (Lucy Rigby), William Lloyd (Elias Rigby), Helen Aubrey (Mrs Rigby), Willis P. Sweatnam (Sassafras Livingston).
In 1880, a rural political campaign involves the whole town.

1914: THE SMALL TOWN GIRL (Universal-101 Bison).
Director: Allan Dwan. Writer: Beatrice Van. Photography: L. O. Bartholomew. 3 reels. Released: November 7.
With William Lloyd (hotel proprietor), Richard Rosson (clerk), Pauline Bush (proprietor's niece), Rupert Julian (snob), Murdock MacQuarrie (his father), Lon Chaney (procurer).
A small town girl is lured to the big city, then deserted.

1914: THE STRAIGHT ROAD (Famous Players).
Director: Allan Dwan. Writer: Clyde Fitch. 4 reels. Released: November 12.
With Gladys Hanson (Mary O'Hara), William Russell (Bill Hubbell), Arthur Hoops (Douglas Aines), Iva Shepard (Lazy Liz), Lorraine Huling (Ruth Thompson).
An alcoholic woman reforms.

1914: THE CONSPIRACY (Famous Players).
Director: Allan Dwan. From play by Robert B. Baker, John Emerson. 4 reels. Released: December 10.
With John Emerson (Winthrop Clavering), Lois Meredith (Margaret Holt), Francis Byrne (Victor Holt, her brother), Harold Lockwood (newspaper reporter), Iva Shepherd (Juanita), Hal Clarendon (Morton), Dodson Mitchell (Detective Bill Flynn), Edward Durand (Savellie).
A mystery writer unravels a real crime.

1914: THE UNWELCOME MRS. HATCH (Famous Players).
Director: Allan Dwan. From play by Mrs. Burton Harrison. 4 reels.
With Henrietta Crosman, Walter Craven, Harold Lockwood, Lorraine Huling, Gertrude Norman.
A girl from a divorced home is finally reunited with her mother.

1914: THE MAN ON THE CASE (Famous Players).
Director: Allan Dwan. 2 reels.
With Jack Devereaux.

In 1915, Dwan married his former leading lady, Pauline Bush; they were divorced five or six years later. His second wife (they were married in the early twenties) was Marie Shelton, a former Ziegfeld Follies girl; they remained married until her death in 1954. Dwan has no children.

1915: THE DANCING GIRL (Famous Players).
Director: Allan Dwan. Writer: Henry Arthur Jones. 5 reels. Released: January 11.
With Florence Reed (Drusilla Ives), William Russell (her Quaker sweetheart), Fuller Mellish (her father), Eugene Ormonde (Duke of Guiseberry).
A girl forsakes her Quaker background for life in London society.

1915: *The Country Boy* (Famous Players-Lasky).
Director: Fred A. Thomson. Producer: Allan Dwan. From play by Edgar Selwyn, Cecil B. DeMille. 5 reels. Released: February 18.
With Marshall Neilan, Loyola O'Connor, Florence Dagmar, Dorothy Green, H. B. Carpenter, Edward Lewis.

1915: DAVID HARUM (Famous Players).
Director: Allan Dwan. From novel by Edward Noyes Westcott. Photography: Hal Rosson. Editor: William Le Baron. Filmed at Nyack, New Jersey. 5 reels. Released: February 22.
With William H. Crane (David Harum), Kate Meeks (Aunt Polly), Harold Lockwood (John Lennox), May Allison (May Blake), Hal Clarendon (Chet Timson), Russell Bassett (General Woolsey).
Rural comedy-romance about a gruff eccentric who is actually the town philanthropist. *See pp. 7, 33–34.*

1915: THE LOVE ROUTE (Famous Players).
Director: Allan Dwan. Writer: Edward Peple. 4 reels. Released: February 25.
With Harold Lockwood, Winifred Kingston, Donald Crisp.
A new railroad line disrupts a girl's ranch.

1915: THE COMMANDING OFFICER (Famous Players).
Director: Allan Dwan. 4 reels. Released: March 11.
With Donald Crisp, Alice Dovey, Marshall Neilan, Jack Pickford.

A girl rejects two suitors and marries the post commandant.

1915: MAY BLOSSOM (Pathe-Famous Players).
Director: Allan Dwan. From play by David Belasco. 4 reels. Released: April 15.
With Gertrude Robinson (May Blossom), Donald Crisp, Marshall Neilan, Russell Bassett, Gertrude Norman.

Believing that her true love has been killed, a girl marries another.

1915: THE PRETTY SISTER OF JOSE (Famous Players).
Director: Allan Dwan. From novel by Frances Hodgson Burnett. 5 reels. Released: May 31.
With Marguerite Clark (Pepita), Jack Pickford (Jose), Rupert Julian (Sebastiano, the bull fighter), Teddy Sampson, Gertrude Norman, Dick Rosson, William Lloyd, Edythe Chapman.

A young girl who hates men falls for a young matador.

1915: A GIRL OF YESTERDAY (Famous Players).
Director: Allan Dwan. Producer-scenarist: Mary Pickford, from story by Wesley C. MacDermott. 4 reels. Released: October 7.
With Mary Pickford (Jane Stuart), Marshall Neilan (Stanley Hudson), Jack Pickford (John Stuart), Frances Marion (city girl), Glenn Martin (pilot), Donald Crisp, Douglas Gerard, Kenneth Douglas, Al Kaufman.

An old-fashioned girl becomes a young modern. See pp. 34-35, 132.

1915: THE FOUNDLING (Famous Players).
Director: Allan Dwan. Producer: Mary Pickford. Writer: Frances Marion. 5 reels.
With Mary Pickford, Robert Cain, Gertrude Norman.

Scheduled for release on December 27, this film was completed in August and had been reviewed by the trade papers when it was accidentally destroyed in a studio fire. A partially new cast was brought in to re-shoot, and this version, directed by John B. O'Brien, was released in 1916.

Dwan left Famous Players to join the Triangle Company, where his productions were under the supervision of D. W. Griffith. See pp. 35-39.

1915: JORDAN IS A HARD ROAD
(Fine Arts-Triangle).
Director-scenarist: Allan Dwan, from novel by Sir Gilbert Parker. Producer: D. W. Griffith. 5 reels. Released: December 19.
With Frank Campeau (Bill Minden), Dorothy Gish (Cora Findley), Owen Moore (Mark Sheldon), Sarah Traux (Mrs. Findley), Ralph Lewis (Jim Starbuck), Mabel Wiles (Lady Alicia Fairfax), Fred Burns, Lester Perry, Jim Kid (the McMahons), Walter Long (agent), Joseph Singleton (Pete Findley).

A reformed train robber conceals his true identity from his daughter. See p. 40.

1916: BETTY OF GREYSTONE (Fine Arts-Triangle).
Director: Allan Dwan. Producer: D. W. Griffith. Writer: F. M. Pierson. 5 reels. Released: February 20.
With Dorothy Gish (Betty Lockwood), George Fawcett (Jim Weed), Kate Bruce, Albert Tavernier, Kid McCoy, John Beck, Owen Moore, Warner P. Richmond, Grace Rankin, Macey Harlan, Eugene Ormonde, Leonore Harris.

The daughter of Greystone Gables' caretaker provokes gossip in the town. See p. 37.

1916: Her Father's Keeper (Fine Arts-Triangle).
Supervisor: Allan Dwan. 5 reels. Released: April 1.
With Irene Howley, Frank Currier, Jack Devereaux, Jack Raymond, John Hanneford, Walter Russell.

1916: THE HABIT OF HAPPINESS – Laugh and the World Laughs (Fine Arts-Triangle).
Director-writer: Allan Dwan. Producer: D. W. Griffith. Scenarists: Dwan, Shannon Fife. 5 reels. Released: April 2.
With Douglas Fairbanks (Sunny Wiggins), George Fawcett (Jonathan Pepper), Dorothy West (Elsie Pepper), George Backus (Mr Wiggins), Grace Rankin (Clarice Wiggins), Macey Harlan (Foster), William Jefferson (Jones).

A high-spirited optimist teaches others that laughter can cure their troubles. Dwan's first of eleven films with Douglas Fairbanks. See pp. 7, 40-42.

1916: THE GOOD BAD MAN – Passing Through (Fine Arts-Triangle).
Director: Allan Dwan. Producer: D. W. Griffith. Writer: Douglas Fairbanks. Photography: Victor Fleming. 5 reels. Released: May 7.
With Douglas Fairbanks ('Passin' Through'), Joseph Singleton ('Weazel'), Bessie Love (Amy), Sam De Grasse (Bud Frazer), Mary Alden (Jane Stuart), George Beranger (Thomas Stuart), Pomeroy Cannon (marshal), Fred Burns (sheriff).

An eccentric outlaw aids unfortunate children. *See p. 7.*

1916: AN INNOCENT MAGDALENE (Fine Arts-Triangle).
Director: Allan Dwan. Producer: D. W. Griffith. Scenarist: Roy Sumerville, from story by Granville Warwick (pseudonym for Griffith). 5 reels. Released: June 18.
With Lillian Gish (Dorothy Raleigh), Spottiswoode Aitken (Col. Raleigh), Sam De Grasse (Forbes Stewart), Mary Alden (woman), Seymour Hastings (preacher), Jennie Lee (Mammy), William de Vaull (Old Joe).

A Southern belle leaves her family to marry a gambler, then discovers he may be a bigamist. *See pp. 7, 37, 38.*

1916: THE HALF-BREED (Fine Arts-Triangle).
Director: Allan Dwan. Producer: D. W. Griffith. Scenarist: Anita Loos, from story by Bret Harte. 5 reels. Released: July 30.
With Douglas Fairbanks (Lo Dorman), Alma Rubens (Teresa), Sam De Grasse (Sheriff Dunn), Tom Wilkinson (Curson), Jack Brownlee (Winslow Wynn), George Beranger (Jack Brace), Jewel Carmen (Nellie).

A half-breed outcast befriends a girl who gets lost in the forest. (Working title: *The Carquinez Woods.*) *See pp. 8, 42, 43.*

1916: MANHATTAN MADNESS (S. A. Lynch Enterprises-Fine Arts-Triangle).
Director: Allan Dwan. Producer: D. W. Griffith. Writer: Charles T. Dazey, from story by E. V. Durling. 5 reels. Released: October 1.
With Douglas Fairbanks (Steve O'Dare), Jewel Carmen (girl), George Beranger (butler), Ruth Darling (maid), Eugene Ormonde (Count Marinoff), Macey Harlan (villain), Warner P. Richmond (Jack Osborne), John Richmond (Cupid Russell), Albert MacQuarrie.

A rancher finds New York dull so his friends stage a mock-kidnapping. *See pp. 7, 42.*

1916: FIFTY-FIFTY (Fine Arts-Triangle).
Director-writer: Allan Dwan. Producer: D. W. Griffith. Scenarist: Robert Shirley. 5 reels. Released: October 22.
With Norma Talmadge (Naomi), J. W. Johnston (Frederic Harmon), Marie Chambers (Helen Carew), Ruth Darling (Louise O'Malley), H. S. Northrup (man from Sing Sing), Frank Currier (judge), Dodson Mitchell (detective), Warren P. Richmond (man about town).

A man forsakes his wife and child for another woman.

Dwan continued to supervise some productions at Triangle as he branched out to various independent

companies, among them Fairbanks's newly formed unit at Mary Pickford's Artcraft Company.

1917: PANTHEA (Talmadge-Selznick Pictures).
Director-scenarist: Allan Dwan, from play by Monckton Hoffe. Photography: Roy Overbaugh, Harold Rosson. Assistant directors: Erich Von Stroheim, Arthur Rosson. 78 minutes. Released: January.
With Norma Talmadge (Panthea), Roger Lytton (impressario), Earle Fox (husband), Murdock Mac-Quarrie (police agent), George Fawcett (police official), Erich Von Stroheim (lieutenant), Frank Currier (doctor), Norbert Wicki, Herbert Barry, Jack Meredith, Henry Thorpe, William Abbington, Winifred Harris, Elaine Persey, Stafford Windsor, William Lloyd, Dick Rosson, J. S. Furey.

Drama set in Russia, England and Paris, in which a woman sacrifices herself for her husband's career. *See pp. 8, 42–44.*

1917: *The Man Who Made Good* (Fine Arts-Triangle).
Director: Arthur Rosson. Supervisor: Allan Dwan. Writer: Robert Shirley. Photography: Roy Overbaugh. 58 minutes. Released: May 13.
With Jack Devereaux, Winifred Allen, Henry P. Dixon, Barney Gilmore.

1917: *American – That's All* (Fine Arts-Triangle).
Director: Arthur Rosson. Supervisor: Allan Dwan. Writer: Robert Shirley. Photography: Roy Overbaugh. Assistant director: Dick Rosson. 58 minutes. Released: June 3.
With Winifred Allen, Blanche Davenport, Charles Mussett, George Rennavent, Jack Raymond, Walter Walker, Miss Cummins.

1917: *Her Excellency, The Governor* (Triangle).
Supervisor: Allan Dwan. 5 reels. Released: June 17.
With Wilfred Lucas, Hedda Hopper, Joseph Kilgour, Regan Hughston, Walter Walker, Edith Speare, Albert Perry.

1917: *A Successful Failure* (Triangle).
Director: Arthur Rosson. Supervisor: Allan Dwan. Scenarist: Robert Shirley, from novel by Michael Kane. Photography: Roy Overbaugh. 68 minutes. Released: August 2.
With Jack Devereaux, Winifred Allen, George Senaut.

1917: *The Food Gamblers* (Triangle).
Director: Albert Parker. Supervisor: Allan Dwan. Released: August 9.
With Wilfred Lucas.

1917: *Grafters* (Triangle).
Director: Arthur Rosson. Supervisor: Allan Dwan.
Writer: James W. Adams. Photography: Roy Over-
baugh. Assistant director: Dick Rosson. 52 minutes.
Released: August 30.
With Anna Lehr, Jack Devereaux, Frank Currier,
George A. Siegmann, Irene Leonard, Robert Crimmins.

1917: *The Haunted House* (Triangle).
Director: Albert Parker. Supervisor: Allan Dwan.
Released: September 20.
With Winifred Allen, Richard Rosson.

1917: THE FIGHTING ODDS (Goldwyn Picture
Company).
Director: Allan Dwan. Writers: Roy Cooper Megure,
Irvin S. Cobb. Photography: Rene Guissart. 5 reels.
Released: October 7.
With Maxine Elliott (Mrs Copley), Henry Clive (Mr
Copley), Charles Dalton (John W. Blake), George Odell
(Egan), Regan Hughston (Jewett), William T. Carleton
(district attorney), Eric Hudson (Detective Butler).
When a businessman is jailed on false charges, his
wife goes after the real villain. *See p. 44.*

1917: *Cassidy* (Triangle).
Director: Arthur Rosson. Supervisor: Allan Dwan. 5
reels. Released: October 21.
With Dick Rosson, Frank Currier, Pauline Curley, Mac
Alexander, Eddie Sturgis, John O'Connor.

1917: *The Man Hater* (Triangle).
Director: Albert Parker. Producer: E. A. Martin.
Supervisor: Allan Dwan. Scenarist: Mary Brecht
Pulver, from story by James Oliver Curwood. 5 reels.
Released: October 28.
With Winifred Allen, Jack Meredith, Harry Neville,
Jessie Shirley, Anna Lehr.

1917: *The Jinx Jumper* (Triangle).
Supervisor: Allan Dwan.
With Jack Devereaux.

1917: *'Melia No Good* (Triangle).
Supervisor: Allan Dwan.
With Winifred Allen.

1917: A MODERN MUSKETEER (Artcraft-Famous
Players-Lasky).
Director-scenarist: Allan Dwan, from 'D'Artagnan of
Kansas' by F. R. Lyle, Jr. Producer: Douglas Fairbanks.
Photography: Victor Fleming. Exterior locations at
Grand Canyon, Canyon de Chelly, Arizona. 5 reels.
Released: December 31.

With Douglas Fairbanks (Ned Thacker), Marjorie Daw
(Dorothy Moraine), Frank Campeau (Navajo), Kathleen
Kirkham (Mrs Moraine), Tully Marshall (Philip
Marden), Eugene Ormonde (Raymond Peters), ZaSu
Pitts.
A gallant young man from a small Kansas town
pursues adventure in the wide world. *See pp. 8, 45–48,
45–48.*

1918: *Headin' South* (Artcraft-Famous Players-Lasky).
Director: Arthur Rosson. Supervisor-writer: Allan
Dwan. Producer: Douglas Fairbanks. Photography:
Hugh McClung, Harry Thorp. 5 reels. Released:
February 25.
With Douglas Fairbanks ('Headin' South'), Frank
Campeau (Spanish Joe), James Mason (his aide),
Catherine MacDonald (girl), Jack Holt, Marjorie Daw.

1918: MR. FIX-IT (Artcraft-Famous Players-Lasky).
Director-scenarist: Allan Dwan, from story by Ernest
Butterworth. Producer: Douglas Fairbanks. Pho-
tography: Hugh McClung. 5 reels. Released: April 15.
With Douglas Fairbanks (Dick Remington), Wanda
Hanley (Mary McCullough), Marjorie Daw (Marjorie
Threadwell), Frank Campeau (Uncle Henry Burroughs),
Catherine MacDonald (Georgiana Burroughs), Leslie
Stuart (Reginald Burroughs), Ida Waterman (Aunt
Agatha Burroughs), Alice Smith (Aunt Priscilla Bur-
roughs), Mrs H. R. Hancock (Aunt Laura Burroughs),
Mr Russell (Butler Jarvis), Fred Goodwin (Gideon Van
Tassell), Margaret Landis (Olive Van Tassell).
Comedy about a young man who impersonates his
best friend. *See p. 8.*

1918: BOUND IN MOROCCO
(Artcraft-Famous Players-Lasky).
Director-writer: Allan Dwan. Producer: Douglas Fair-
banks. 5 reels. Released: August 5.
With Douglas Fairbanks (George Travelwell), Pauline
Curley (Ysail), Tully Marshall (Ali Pah Shush), Edythe
Chapman (Ysail's mother), Frank Campeau (Basha El
Harib, governor of Province of Harib), Jay Dwiggins
(Kaid Mahedi el Menebhi, Lord High Ambassador to
Court of El Harib), Marjorie Daw.
Comedy about an American traveller who rescues a
beautiful harem girl. *See pp. 8, 48–49, 48.*

1918: HE COMES UP SMILING (Artcraft-Famous
Players-Lasky).
Director: Allan Dwan. Producer: Douglas Fairbanks.
Scenarist: Frances Marion, from novel by Charles
Sherman. Photography: Joseph August. 5 reels.
Released: September 15.
With Douglas Fairbanks (Jerry Martin), Herbert

Standing (Mike), Bull Montana (Baron Bean), Albert MacQuarrie (Batchelor), Marjorie Daw (Billie), Frank Campeau (John Bartlett), Jay Dwiggins (general), Kathleen Kirkham (Louise).

A bank clerk leaves his dull job and becomes a hobo. *See p. 8.*

1919: CHEATING CHEATERS (Select Pictures Corp.).
Director: Allan Dwan. Producer: Lewis J. Selznick. Scenarist: Kathryn Stuart, from play by Max Marcin. Photography: Arthur Edeson. 5 reels. Released: February 1.
With Jack Holt (Tom Palmer), Clara Kimball Young (Ruth Brockton), Tully Marshall (Ira Lazarre), Frank Campeau (Steven Wilson), Edwin Stevens (Mr Palmer), Anna Q. Nilsson (Grace Palmer), Frederick Burton (George Brockton), Nicholas Dunsew (Antonio Verdi), Mayme Kelso (Mrs Brockton), Jess Singleton (Phil), Eleanor Hancock (Mrs Palmer), W. A. Carroll (Ruth's chauffeur).

Living side by side, two groups of crooks impersonate rich people, each planning to rob the other. *See pp. 49, 49.*

1919: GETTING MARY MARRIED (Cosmopolitan-Select).
Director: Allan Dwan. Producer: Marion Davies. Writers: John Emerson, Anita Loos. 5 reels. Released: April 19.
With Marion Davies (Mary), Norman Kerry (James Winthrop), Frederick Burton (Amos Bussard), Matt Moore (Ted Barnacle), Amelia Summerville (Mrs Bussard), Constance Beaumar (Matilda Bussard), Elmer Grandin (John Bussard).

When she marries, a girl loses her inheritance.

1919: *Sahara* (W. W. Hodkinson).
Director: Arthur Rosson. Producer: Allan Dwan. Released: July 12.
With Louise Glaum.

1919: THE DARK STAR (Cosmopolitan-Artcraft-Famous Players-Lasky).
Director: Allan Dwan. From novel by Robert W. Chambers. 7 reels. Released: August 16.
With Marion Davies (Rue Carew), Norman Kerry (Jim Neeland), Dorothy Green (Princess Naia), Matt Moore (Prince Alik), Ward Crane (French secret agent), George Cooper (Mr Brandes), Arthur Earle (Mr Stull), G. Butler Conblough, Emil Hoch (German spies), James Laffey (ship captain), William Brotherhood (steward), Fred Hearn (Reverend William Carew).

Drama involving a fabulous jewel known as 'the dark star'. *See p. 49.*

1919: SOLDIERS OF FORTUNE (Mayflower-Realart).
Director: Allan Dwan. Producer: W. W. Hodkinson. From novel by Richard Harding Davis. Exterior locations at San Diego Fairgrounds, Balboa Park, California. 7 reels. Released: November 22.
With Norman Kerry (Robert Clay), Anna Q. Nilsson (Alice Langham), Ward Crane (Reginald King), Pauline Stark, (Hope Langham), Melbourne McDowell (Mr Langham), Wallace Beery (Mendoza), Wilfred Lucas (President Alvarez), Philo McCullough (Captain Stuart), Herold Lindsay (Mrs Alvarez), Frank Wally (Teddy Langham), Fred Kohler (McWilliams), Ogden Crane (Burke).

Revolutionary forces win their independence in a South American republic. *See pp. 8, 49–50.*

1920: THE LUCK OF THE IRISH (Mayflower-Realart).
Director: Allan Dwan. Scenarist: Harold MacGrath 6,500 feet. Released: January 15.
With James Kirkwood (William Grogan), Anna Q. Nilsson (Ruth Warren), Ward Crane (Norton Colburton), Harry Northrup (Camden), Ernest Butterworth ('Kid').

A plumber inherits $28,000 and starts on an adventurous world cruise. *See pp. 51, 51.*

1920: *A Splendid Hazard* (Mayflower).
Director: Arthur Rosson. Producer: Allan Dwan. Scenarist: Harold MacGrath. Photography: Glen McWilliams. 6 reels. Released: September 26.
With Henry B. Walthall, Rosemary Theby, Ann Forrest, Hardee Kirkland.

1920: THE FORBIDDEN THING (Associated Producers).
Director-producer: Allan Dwan. Scenarists: Dwan, Lillian Ducey, from story by Mary Mears. Photography: Tony Gaudio. 6 reels. Released: November 7.
With James Kirkwood (Abel Blake), Helen Jerome Eddy (Joan), Marcia Manon (Glory Prada), King Baggott (Dave), Gertrude Claire (Mrs Blake), Jack Roseleigh (Jose), Arthur Thalasso (Joe Portega), Newton Hall (gamin), Harry Griffith (Ryan), Katherine Norton (Mrs Ryan). *See p. 52.*

1921: A PERFECT CRIME (Dwan Productions-Associated Producers).
Director-producer-scenarist: Allan Dwan, from story by Carl Clausen. Photography: Lyman Broening. Assistant director: Wilfred Buckland. 5 reels. Released: March 27.
With Monte Blue (Wally Griggs), Jacqueline Logan (Mary Oliver), Stanton Heck ('Big Bill' Thaine), Hardee Kirkland (Halliday).

A timid bank messenger who fantasises adventurous stories solves a real crime. *See pp.* 51–52.

1921: A BROKEN DOLL (Dwan Productions-Associated Producers).
Director-producer-scenarist: Allan Dwan, from story, 'Johnny Cucabod' by Wilbur Hall, adapted by Lillian Ducey. Photography: Lyman Broening, L. William O'Connell. 4,594 feet. Released: June 12.
With Monte Blue (Tommy Dawes), Mary Thurman (Harriet Bundy), Mary Jane Irving (Rosemary), Les Bates (Bill Nyall), Lizette Thorne (Mrs Nyall), Arthur Millette (Sheriff Hugh Bundy), Jack Riley (Knapp Wyant).
When he sets out to buy a new doll for his sweetheart, a ranch hand is mistaken for an escaped convict.

1921: THE SCOFFER (Mayflower-First National).
Director-producer: Allan Dwan. Scenarist: Lillian Ducey, from story by Val Cleveland. Photography: Lyman Broening. 7 reels. Released: September 6.
With Mary Thurman (Margaret Haddon), James Kirkwood (Dr Stannard Wayne), Philo McCullough (Dr Arthur Richards), Rhea Mitchell (Alice Porn), John Burton (Old Dabney), Noah Beery (Boorman), Eugenie Besserer (his wife), Georgie Stone (their son), Bernard Durning (Reverend Carson), Ward Crane ('The Albany Kid').
A cynical physician regains his faith when a sick child is saved. *See p.* 52.

1921: THE SIN OF MARTHA QUEED (Mayflower-Associated Exhibitors).
Director-producer-writer: Allan Dwan. Photography: Tony Gaudio. 6 reels. Released: October 6.
With Mary Thurman (Martha Queed), Joseph J. Dowling (Marvin Queed), Eugenie Besserer (Alicia Queed), Frank Lee (Georgie Queed), Niles Welch (Arnold Barry), George Hackathorne (Atlas), Frank Campeau (David Boyd), Gertrude Claire (grandmother).
Compromised by gossip, a woman is forced to marry a man she hates.

1921: IN THE HEART OF A FOOL (Mayflower-First National).
Director-producer: Allan Dwan. Scenarist: Lillian Ducey, from novel by William Allen White. Photography: Lyman Broening. 7 reels. Released: November.
With James Kirkwood (Grant Adams), Anna Q. Nilsson (Margaret Muller), Mary Thurman (Laura Nesbit), Philo McCullough (Tom Vandorn), Ward Crane (Henry Fenn), John Burton (Dr Nesbit), Margaret Campbell (Mrs Nesbit), Percy Challenger (Daniel Sands),

Arthur Hoyt (Martie Sands), Kate Tancray (Mary Adams), Emmet King (Amos Adams), Maryland Moore (Violet Manling).
An aetheist is redeemed; inspired by the Biblical quotation, 'A fool hath said in his heart there is no God'.

1922: THE HIDDEN WOMAN (Nanuet Amusement Corporation-American Releasing Corp.).
Director-producer: Allan Dwan. 4,626 feet. Released: April 2.
With Evelyn Nesbit (Ann Wesley), Crauford Kent (Bart Andrews), Murdock MacQuarrie (Iron MacLoid), Ruth Darling (Vera MacLoid), Albert Hart (Bill Donovan), Russell Thaw (Johnny Randolph), Mary Alden (Mrs Randolph), Jack Evans (derelict).
A frivolous New York society girl loses her fortune and goes to live in a settlement in the Adirondacks.

1922: SUPERSTITION (Artlee).
Director-producer: Allan Dwan. 60 minutes. Released: September.
With Jack Devereaux, Veta Searle, Stafford Windsor.
An old sea captain recounts a mutiny. *Made for Triangle in 1917, this picture was not released by the time the company folded, and was therefore sold to Lee Bradford, who distributed it on a States Rights basis.*

1922: ROBIN HOOD (Fairbanks Picture Corporation-United Artists).
Director: Allan Dwan. Producer: Douglas Fairbanks. Scenarist: Lotta Woods, from story by Elton Thomas (pseudonym for Fairbanks), based on the tales of Robin Hood. Photography: Arthur Edeson; second cameraman: Charles Richardson. Art director: Wilfred Buckland; assistant art directors: Irvin J. Martin, Edward M. Langley. Costumes: Mitchell Leisen. Editor: William Nolan. Special effects: Edeson, Martin. Assistant director: Richard Rosson. Literary consultant: Edward Knoblock. Research director: Dr Arthur Woods. 10,680 feet. Première (in Chicago): October 18; general release: 28 January 1923.
With Douglas Fairbanks (Robin Hood, Earl of Huntingdon), Wallace Beery (Richard the Lionhearted), Enid Bennett (Lady Marian Fitzwalter), Sam De Grasse (Prince John), Paul Dickey (Sir Guy of Gisbourne), William Lowery (High Sheriff of Nottingham), Roy Coulson (jester), Billie Bennett (Lady Marian's serving woman), Merrill McCormick, Wilson Benge (Prince John's henchmen), Williard Louis (Friar Tuck), Alan Hale (Little John), Maine Geary (Will Scarlett), Lloyd Talman (Alan-a-Dale), Kid McCoy, Bull Montana, Mary Pickford (townspeople).
During the Crusades, in the days of Richard the Lionhearted, a nobleman masquerades as a flamboyant

outlaw who robs the rich and gives to the poor. *The most expensive film made to that time, and still one of Dwan's handful of favourites. See pp.* 8, 53–56, 54–63, 150, 168.

1923: THE GLIMPSES OF THE MOON (Famous Players-Lasky-Paramount).

Director-producer: Allan Dwan. Scenarists: E. Lloyd Sheldon, Edfrid Bingham, from novel by Edith Wharton. Photography: Hal Rosson. 6,502 feet. Released: March 25.

With Bebe Daniels (Susan Branch), Nita Naldi (Ursula Gillow), David Powell (Nick Lansing), Maurice Costello (Fred Gillow), Rubye De Remer (Mrs Ellie Vanderlyn), Charles Gerard (Lord 'Streffy' Altringham), William Quirk (Bob Fulmer), Pearl Sindelar (Grace Fulmer), Beth Allen, Mrs George Peggram, Dolores Costello, Millie Muller, Beatrice Coburn, Fred Hadley, Robert Lee Keeling, Barton Adams, Freddie Veri.

An attractive couple go to Europe prepared to give each other up if a wealthy opportunity presents itself. *See p.* 65.

1923: LAWFUL LARCENY (Famous Players-Lasky-Paramount).

Director-producer: Allan Dwan. Scenarist: John Lynch, from a play by Samuel Shipman. Photography: Hal Rosson. 5,503 feet. Released: September 2.

With Hope Hampton (Marion Dorsey), Conrad Nagel (Andrew Dorsey), Nita Naldi (Vivian Hepburn), Lew Cody (Guy Tarlow), Russell Griffin (Sonny Dorsey), Yvonne Hughes (Billie Van de Vere), Dolores Costello (Nora, a maid), Gilda Gray, Florence O'Denishawn, Alice Maison (dancers at the Rendez-Vous).

A wife strives to recover a bad cheque her husband wrote to pay a gambling debt. *See pp.* 64, 65.

1923: ZAZA (Famous Players-Lasky-Paramount).

Director-producer: Allan Dwan. Scenarist: Albert Shelby Le Vino, from play by Pierre Berton, Charles Simon. Photography: Hal Rosson. 7,076 feet. Released: September 16.

With Gloria Swanson (Zaza), H. B. Warner (Bernard Dufresne), Ferdinand Gottschalk (Duke de Brissac), Lucille La Verne (Aunt Rosa), Mary Thurman (Florianne), Yvonne Hughes (Nathalie, the maid), Riley Hatch (Rigault), Roger Lytton (stage manager), Ivan Linow (Apache), Helen Mack.

A Paris music-hall entertainer falls in love with a married diplomat. *Dwan's first of eight films with Gloria Swanson. See pp.* 65–66, 66.

1923: BIG BROTHER (Famous Players-Lasky-Paramount).

Director-producer: Allan Dwan. Scenarist: Paul Sloane,

from story by Rex Beach. Filmed on New York City's East Side. 7,080 feet. Released: December 23.

With Tom Moore (Jimmy Donovan), Edith Roberts (Kitty Costello), Raymond Hatton (Cokey Joe Miller), Joe King (Big Ben Murray), Mickey Bennett (Midge Murray), Charles Henderson ('Father Dan' Marron), Paul Panzer (Mike Navarro), Neill Kelley (Monk Manelli), William Black (probation officer), Martin Faust (Spike Doyle), Milton Herman (Izzy), Florence Ashbrook (Mrs Sheean), Yvonne Hughes (Navarro's girl, 'Fly-by-Night'), Charles Hammond (judge).

A gangster reforms in order to win the custody of a homeless boy. *Among Dwan's favourite films. See pp.* 8, 67–68, 67, 116, 168.

1924: A SOCIETY SCANDAL (Famous Players-Lasky-Paramount).

Director-producer: Allan Dwan. Scenarist: Forrest Halsey, from play, 'The Laughing Lady' by Alfred Sutro. Photography: Hal Rosson. 6,857 feet. Released: March 24.

With Gloria Swanson (Marjorie Colbert), Rod LaRocque (Daniel Farr), Ricardo Cortez (Harrison Peters), Allan Simpson (Hector Colbert), Ida Waterman (Mrs Maturin Colbert), Thelma Converse (Mrs Hamilton Pennfield), Fraser Coalter (Schuyler Burr), Catherine Proctor (Mrs Burr), Wilfred Donovan (Hamilton Pennfield), Yvonne Hughes (Patricia De Voe), Catherine Coleburn, Marie Shelton, Dorothy Stokes, Cornelius Keefe (Marjorie's friends).

When a divorce lawyer ruins a woman's reputation, she plots her revenge, but falls in love with him instead. *See pp.* 68–70, 68.

1924: MANHANDLED (Famous Players-Lasky-Paramount).

Director-producer: Allan Dwan. Scenarist: Frank W. Tuttle, from story by Arthur Stringer. Photography: Hal Rosson. Editor: William LeBaron. 6,998 feet. Released: August 4.

With Gloria Swanson (Tessie McGuire), Tom Moore (Jimmy Hogan), Lilyan Tashman (Pinkie Doran), Ian Keith (Robert Brandt), Arthur Housman (Chip Thorndyke), Paul McAllisher (Paul Garretson), Frank Morgan (Arno Riccardi), M. Collosse (Bippo), Marie Shelton (model), Carrie Scott (landlady), Frank Allworth, Ann Pennington, Brooke Johns.

Comedy about a shop-girl who impersonates a Russian princess in New York society and nearly loses her sweetheart. *One of Dwan's favourite works. See pp.* 8, 70–75, 69–72, 116, 168.

1924: HER LOVE STORY (Famous Players-Lasky-Paramount).

Director-producer: Allan Dwan. Scenarist: Frank W. Tuttle, from story, 'Her Majesty, the Queen', by Mary Roberts Rinehart. Photography: George Webber. 6,750 feet. Released: October 6.

With Gloria Swanson (Princess Marie), Ian Keith (Captain Rudi), George Fawcett (Archduke), Echling Gayer (King), Mario Majeroni (Prime Minister), Sidney Herbert (Archduke's adviser), Donald Hall (court physician), Baroness de Hademann (lady-in-waiting), Jane Auburn (Clothilde), Bert Wales (boy), General Lodijensky (Minister of War).

A Balkan queen secretly marries a soldier. *See pp. 73, 74.*

1924: WAGES OF VIRTUE (Famous Players-Lasky-Paramount).

Director: Allan Dwan. Scenarist: Forrest Halsey, from novel by Percival Christopher Wren. Photography: George Webber. 7,093 feet. Released: November 10.

With Gloria Swanson (Carmelita), Ben Lyon (Marvin), Norman Trevor (John Boule), Ivan Linow (Luigi), Armand Cortez (Guiseppe), Adrienne D'Ambricourt (Madame La Cantiniere), Paul Panzer (Sergeant Le Gros), Joe Moore (Le Bro-way).

In Algiers, a woman is torn between gratitude to her Italian benefactor and love for an American legionnaire. *See p. 75.*

1924: ARGENTINE LOVE (Famous Players-Lasky-Paramount).

Director-producer: Allan Dwan. Scenarist: Gerald Duffy, from story by Vicente Blasco-Ibanez, adapted by John Russell. Photography: Roy Hunt. 5,970 feet. Released: December 29.

With Bebe Daniels (Consuelo Garcia), Ricardo Cortez (Juan Martin), James Rennie (Philip Sears), Mario Majeroni (Senator Cornejo), Russ Whital (Emanuel Garcia), Alice Chapin (Mrs Garcia), Julia Hurley (La Mosca), Mark Gonzales (Rafael Cornejo), Aurelio Coccia (Pedro).

A wealthy Argentine landowner wants to marry the mayor's daughter, but she loves an American engineer. *See p. 74.*

1925: NIGHT LIFE OF NEW YORK (Famous Players-Lasky-Paramount).

Director-producer: Allan Dwan. Scenarist: Paul Schonfield, from story by Edgar Selwyn. Photography: George Webber. Filmed in New York City. 6,998 feet. Released: July 25.

With Rod LaRocque (Ronald Bentley), Ernest Torrence (John Bentley), Dorothy Gish (Meg), Helen Lee Worthing (Carrie Reed), George Hackathorne (Jimmy), Arthur Housman (Jerry), Riley Hatch (William Workman).

A bored young man goes to New York and finds romance. *See pp. 9, 76.*

1925: *Fifty-Fifty* (Associated Exhibitors).

Director-producer: Henri Diamant Berger. Writer: Allan Dwan. 5,531 feet. Released: August 1.

With Hope Hampton, Lionel Barrymore, Louise Glaum, J. Roy Bennett, Arthur Donaldson, Jean Val Jean.

A remake of Dwan's 1916 film for Triangle.

1925: COAST OF FOLLY (Famous Players-Lasky-Paramount).

Director-producer: Allan Dwan. Scenarist: Forrest Halsey, from novel by Coningsby Dawson, adapted by James Creelman. Exterior locations at Coronado and San Diego, California. 7,001 feet. Released: September 12.

With Gloria Swanson (Nadine/Joyce Gathway), Alec B. Francis (Count de Tauro), Anthony Jowitt (Larry Fay), Dorothy Cumming (Constance Fay), Jed Prouty (Cholly Knickerbocker), Eugenie Besserer (Nanny), Arthur Housman (reporter), Lawrence Gray (bather), Charles Clary, Richard Arlen.

Neglecting her daughter to live at a swanky Riviera resort, a woman later seeks to prevent her from making the same mistake with her own family. *See pp. 75–78, 76, 77.*

1925: STAGE STRUCK (Famous Players-Lasky-Paramount).

Director-producer: Allan Dwan. Scenarist: Forrest Halsey, from story by Frank R. Adams, adapted by Sylvia La Varre. Photography (with two sequences in Technicolor): George Webber. Exterior locations at New Martinville, West Virginia. 6,691 feet. Released: November 16.

With Gloria Swanson (Jennie Hagen), Lawrence Gray (Orme Wilson), Gertrude Astor (Lillian Lyons), Marguerite Evans (Hilda Wagner), Ford Sterling (Waldo Buck), Carrie Scott (Mrs Wagner), Emil Hoch (Mr Wagner), Margery Whittington (soubrette).

Comedy about a stage-struck waitress who joins a showboat. (Working title: *Screen Struck.*) *Dwan's first experience with colour film. See pp. 9, 78–79, 79.*

1926: SEA HORSES (Famous Players-Lasky-Paramount).

Director-producer: Allan Dwan. Scenarist: James Shelley Hamilton, from novel by Francis Brett Young, adapted by Becky Gardiner. Photography: James Howe. 6,565 feet. Première (in New York): February 22; general release: March 6.

With Jack Holt (George Glenville), Florence Vidor (Helen Salvia), William Powell (Lorenzo Salvia), George

Bancroft (Cochran), Mack Swain (Bimbo-Bomba), Frank Campeau (Senor Cordoza), Allan Simpson (Harvey), George Nichols (Marx), Mary E. Dow (Cina Salvia), Dick La Reno (Henry), Frank Austin (Cheadle).

Melodrama about a woman who goes to the tropics in search of her husband. *See pp. 79–81, 78.*

1926: PADLOCKED (Famous Players-Lasky-Paramount).
Director-producer: Allan Dwan. Scenarist: James Shelley Hamilton, from novel by Rex Beach, adapted by Becky Gardiner. Photography: James Howe. 6,700 feet. Released: August 4.
With Lois Moran (Edith Gilbert), Noah Beery (Henry Gilbert), Louise Dresser (Mrs Alcott), Helen Jerome Eddy (Belle Galloway), Allan Simpson (Norman Van Pelt), Florence Turner (Mrs Alice Gilbert), Richard Arlen ('Tubby' Clark), Charles Lane (Monte Hermann), Douglas Fairbanks, Jr ('Sonny' Galloway), Charlot Bird (Blanche Galloway), Josephine Crowell (Mrs Galloway), Andre Lanoy (Lorelli), Irma Kornelia (Pearl Gates).

The daughter of a Puritanical reformer becomes a Broadway cabaret dancer. *See p. 80.*

1926: TIN GODS (Famous Players-Lasky-Paramount).
Director-producer: Allan Dwan. Scenarist: James Shelley Hamilton, from play by William Anthony McGuire, adapted by Paul Dickey, Howard Emmett Rogers. Photography: Alvin Wyckoff. Associate producer: William LeBaron. 8,568 feet. Released: September 6.
With Thomas Meighan (Roger Drake), Renée Adorée (Carita), Aileen Pringle (Janet Stone), William Powell (Tony Santelli), Hale Hamilton (Dr McCoy), John Harrington (Dougherty), Joe King (first foreman), Robert E. O'Connor (second foreman), Delbert Emory Whitten, Jr (Billy).

In South America, a girl saves an American engineer from drink. *See pp. 80, 81.*

In the same year Dwan signed with William Fox's studio, where he was to work off and on until 1941.

1926: SUMMER BACHELORS (Fox).
Director-producer: Allan Dwan. Scenarist: James Shelley Hamilton, from 'Summer Widowers' by Warner Fabian. Photography: Joseph Ruttenberg. 6,727 feet. Released: December 18.
With Madge Bellamy (Derry Thomas), Allan Forrest (Tony Landor), Matt Moore (Walter Blakely), Hale Hamilton (Beverly Greenway), Leila Hyams (Willowdean French), Charles Winninger (Preston Smith), Clifford Holland (Martin Cole), Olive Tell (Mrs Preston Smith), Walter Catlett (first bachelor).

Romantic comedy about a secretary who will only date married men because she's averse to getting married.

1927: THE MUSIC MASTER (Fox).
Director-producer: Allan Dwan. Scenarist: Philip Klein, from play by David Belasco, based on novel by Charles Klein. Photography: George Webber, William Miller. Assistant director: Clarence Elmer. 7,754 feet. Released: January 23.
With Alec B. Francis (Anton von Barwig), Lois Moran (Helene Stanton), Neil Hamilton (Beverly Cruger), Norman Trevor (Andrew Cruger), Charles Lane (Richard Stanton), William T. Tilden (Joles), Helen Chandler (Jenny), Marcia Harris (Miss Husted), Kathleen Kerrigan (Mrs Andrew Cruger), Howard Cull (August Poons), Armand Cortez (Pinac), Leo Feodoroff (Fico), Carrie Scott (Mrs Mangenborn), Dore Davidson (pawnbroker), Walter Catlett (medicine show barker).

A Viennese musician searches for his long-lost daughter.

1927: WEST POINT (Fox Movietone News).
Director: Allan Dwan. 1 reel.
Dwan's first released sound film. *See pp. 83–84.*

1927: THE JOY GIRL (Fox).
Director-producer: Allan Dwan. Scenarist: Frances Agnew, from story by May Edington. Filmed in Palm Beach, Florida. 5,877 feet. Released: September 24.
With Olive Borden (Jewel Courage), Neil Hamilton (John Jeffrey Fleet), Marie Dressler (Mrs Heath), Mary Alden (Mrs Courage), William Norris (Herbert Courage), Helen Chandler (Flora), Jerry Wiley (clergyman), Frank Walsh (Hugh Sandman), Clarence Elmer (valet), Peggy Kelly (Isolde), Jimmy Grainger, Jr. (chauffeur).

Society comedy set in Palm Beach. *See pp. 9, 81–82.*

1927: EAST SIDE, WEST SIDE (Fox).
Director-scenarist: Allan Dwan, from novel by Felix Risenberg. Photography: George Webber. 8,154 feet. Released: October 22.
With George O'Brien (John Breen), Virginia Valli (Becka), J. Farrell McDonald (Pug Malone), June Collyer (Josephine), Holmes Herbert (Gilbert Van Horn), Dora Davidson (Channon Lipvitch), Sonia Nodalsky (Mrs Lipvitch), John Miltern (Gerrit Rantoul), Frank Dodge (Judge Kelly), Dan Wolheim (Grogan), John Dooley (one of Grogan's gang), John Hearney (policeman), Edward Garvey (second), Frank Allsworth ('Flash'), William Fredericks (Breen), Jean Armour (Mrs Breen), Gordon MacRae, Harold Levett (mechanics).

A slum kid from the East River becomes a builder of cities. *See p. 9.*

1927: FRENCH DRESSING (First National).
Director-producer: Allan Dwan. Scenarist: J. L. Campbell, from a story by Adelaide Heilbron, adapted by Pauline Forney. Photography: Ernest Haller. Editor: Terrell Morse. 6,344 feet. Première (in New York): December 10; general release: January 15, 1928.
With H. B. Warner (Phillip Grey), Clive Brook (Henri de Briac), Lois Wilson (Cynthia Grey), Lilyan Tashman (Peggy Nash), Hedda Hopper.

Comedy-drama about a woman who goes to Paris when she suspects her husband of loving someone else.

1928: *The Whip Woman* (First National).
Director: Joseph C. Boyle. Producer: Allan Dwan. Scenarist: Earle Roebuck, from story by Forrest Halsey, Leland Hayward. Photography: Ernest Haller. 6,058 feet. Released: February 11.
With Estelle Taylor, Antonio Moreno, Lowell Sherman, Hedda Hopper, Julianne Johnston, Jack Ackroyd, Loretta Young.

1928: *The Mad Hour* (First National).
Director: Joseph C. Boyle. Producer: Allan Dwan. Scenarist: Tom J. Geraghty, from 'The Man and the Moment' by Elinor Glyn. Photography: Ernest Haller. 6,625 feet. Released: March 17.
With Sally O'Neal, Alice White, Donald Reed, Larry Kent, Lowell Sherman, Norman Trevor, Eddie Clayton, James Farley, Rose Dione, Tully Marshall, Margaret Livingston, Jack Eagan, Kate Price, Mary Foy, Iona Holmes.

1928: THE BIG NOISE (First National).
Director-producer: Allan Dwan. Scenarist: Tom J. Geraghty, from story by Ben Hecht. Titles: George Marion, Jr. Photography: Ted Pahle. Editors: Doris Farrington, Terry Morse. 7,412 feet. Released: March 25.
With Chester Conklin (John Sloval), Alice White (Sophie Sloval), Bodil Rosing (Ma Sloval), Sam Hardy (Philip Hurd), Jack Egan (Bill Hedges), Ned Sparks (William Howard), David Torrence (managing editor).

An old man becomes famous when his subway injury is exploited by the newspapers.

1928: *Harold Teen* (First National).
Director: Mervyn LeRoy. Producer: Allan Dwan. Scenarist: Tom J. Geraghty, from comic strip by Carl Ed. Photography: Ernest Haller. 7,541 feet. Released: April 21.
With Alice White, Arthur Lake, Mary Brian, Lucien Littlefield, Jack Duffy, Jack Eagen, Ben Hall, William Bakewell, Lincoln Stedman, Jane Keckley, Hedda Hopper, Virginia Sale.

1929: THE IRON MASK (Elton Corporation-United Artists).
Director: Allan Dwan. Producer: Douglas Fairbanks. Scenarist: Lotta Woods, based on 'The Three Musketeers', 'Twenty Years After', and 'The Man in the Iron Mask' by Alexandre Dumas, père, and the memoirs of D'Artagnan, Richelieu and Rochefort. Titles and dialogue: Elton Thomas (pseudonym for Fairbanks). Photography: Henry Sharp. Production designer: Maurice Leloir. Art director: William Cameron Menzies. Set decorators: Lawrence Irving, Burgess Beall, Ben Carre, Miles Borg. Costumes: Leloir, Mary Hallett, Gilbert Clark. Editor: William Nolan. Assistant director: Bruce Humberstone. 8,659 feet (silent); 8,855 feet (with spoken prologue and epilogue). Released: March 9.
With Douglas Fairbanks (D'Artagnan), Marguerite de la Motte (Constance Bonacieux), Leon Barry (Athos), Belle Bennett (Anne of Austria), Dorothy Revier (Lady de Winter), Rolfe Sedan (Louis XIII), William Bakewell (Louis XIV/his twin), Gordon Thorpe (Louis XIV as a child/his twin), Vera Lewis (Madame Peronne), Nigel De Brulier (Cardinal Richelieu), Ulrich Haupt (Rochefort), Lon Poff (Father Joseph), Charles Stevens (Planchet), Henry Otto (King's valet), Stanley J. Standford (Porthos), Gino Corrado (Aramis), Robert Parrish (page), Florence Turner (abbess), Fred Cavens, Madame Chalif, Princess Galitzine, Baronne d'Estournelle de Constant.

D'Artagnan rescues the King of France from the treachery of his power-hungry twin. *See pp. 9, 57, 82–83, 83, 84.*

1929: TIDE OF EMPIRE (Metro-Goldwyn-Mayer).
Director: Allan Dwan. Scenarist: Waldemar Young, from novel by Peter B. Kyne; titles: John Colton, Joe Farnham. Photography: Merritt B. Gerstad. Editor: Blanche Sewell. Exterior locations at Baldwin Hills, California. 6,552 feet (part-talking). Released: March 23.
With Renée Adorée (Josephita), George Duryea (Derry D'Arcy), William Collier, Jr. (Rimaldo), George Fawcett (Don José), Fred Kohler (Cannon), James Bradbury, Sr. (Bejabers), Harry Gribbon (O'Shea), Paul Hurst (Poppy).

Searching for gold in California, a young man wins the heart of a fiery Spanish girl. *See pp. 85–86, 86, 87.*

1929: THE FAR CALL (Fox).
Director: Allan Dwan. Scenarists: Seton I. Miller, Walter Woods, from novel by Edison Marshall. Photography: Hal Rosson. Titles: H. M. Caldwell. 5,282 feet (silent) 5,313 feet (part-talking). Released: April 28.
With Charles Morton (Pal Loring), Leila Hyams (Hilda Larsen), Ulrich Haupt (London Nick), Dan Wolheim (Black O'Neil), Charles B. Middleton (Kris Larsen),

Arthur Stone (Schmidt), Stanley J. Sandford (Captain Storkerson), Pat Hartigan (Lars Johansson), Bernard Siegel (Aleutian chief), Charles Gorman (Haycox), Willie Fung (Wing), Warren Hymer ('Soup' Brophy), Frank Chew (Ling-Fu), Randolph Scott (Helms), Ivan Linow (Red Dunkirk), Harry Grip (Pete), Sam Baker (Tubal).

Pirate adventure in the Pacific. *See p. 85.*

1929: FROZEN JUSTICE (Fox).
Director: Allan Dwan. Scenarist: Sonya Levien, from story by Ejnar Mikkelsen. Photography: Harold Rosson. Editor: Harold Schuster. 7,170 feet. Released: October 13.
With Leonore Ulric (Talu), Robert Frazer (Lanak,) Louis Wolheim (Duke), Ulrich Haupt (Captain Jones), Laska Winter (Douglamana), Tom Patricola (dancer), Alice Lake (Little Casino), Gertrude Astor (Moosehide Kate), Adele Windsor (Boston teacher), Warren Hymer (barman), Neyneen Farrell (Yukon Lucy), El Brendel (Swede), Lou Morrison (proprietor), Charles Yudels (French sailor), Joe Rochay (the Jew), The Meyers Sisters (Harmony Duo), George MacFarlane (singer), Landers Stevens (Matelot Moore), Jim Spencer (sorcerer), Arthur Stone (French Pete), Jack Ackroyd (English Eddie), Gertrude Chorre (Talu's mother).

A sailor falls in love with an Eskimo girl. *Dwan's first all-talking film. See pp. 86–88, 88.*

1929: SOUTH SEA ROSE (Fox).
Director: Allan Dwan. Scenarist: Sonya Levien, from play by Tom Cushing; dialogue: Elliot Lester. Photography: Harold Rosson. Editor: Harold Schuster. 6,500 feet. Released: December 8.
With Leonore Ulric (Rosalie Dumay), Charles Bickford (Captain Briggs), Kenneth McKenna (Dr Tom Winston), J. Farrell McDonald (Hackett), Elizabeth Patterson (Sarah), Tom Patricola (Willie Gump), Ilka Chase (servant), George MacFarlane (inn-keeper), Ben Hall (cabin boy), Daphne Pollard (Mrs Nott), Roscoe Ates, Charlotte Walker, Emile Chautard.

A sea captain returns to England with a South Sea island bride.

1930: WHAT A WIDOW! (Gloria Productions-United Artists).
Director-producer: Allan Dwan. Executive producer: Joseph P. Kennedy. Scenarist: Josephine Lovett; dialogue: James Gleason, James Seymour. Photography: George Barnes. Music: Josiah Zuro; songs by Vincent Youmans. Editor: Viola Lawrence. 8,126 feet. Released: September 13.
With Gloria Swanson (Tamarind Brook), Owen Moore (Gerry Morgan), Lew Cody (Victor), Margaret Living-

ston (Valli), William Holden (Mr Lodge), Herbert Braggiotti (Jose Alvarado), Gregory Gaye (Baslikoff), Adrienne d'Ambricourt (Paulette), Nella Walker (Marquise), Daphne Pollard (masseuse).

Farce about a wealthy widow who snags an attractive husband in Paris. *See pp. 9, 89–90, 90, 91.*

1930: MAN TO MAN (First National).
Director: Allan Dwan. Scenarist: Joseph Jackson, from story, 'Barber John's Boy', by Ben Ames Williams. Photography: Ira Morgan. Music: Louis Silvers, Erno Rapee. Costumes: Earl Luick. Editor: George Marks. 68 minutes. Released: December 6.
With Phillips Holmes (Michael Bolton), Grant Mitchell ('Barber John' Bolton), Lucille Powers (Emily Saunders), Barbara Weeks (Michael's college girlfriend), Dwight Frye (Vint Glade), Russell Simpson (Uncle Cal Bolton), Paul Nicholson (Ryan), Robert Emmett O'Connor (sheriff), George Marion (Jim McCord), Otis Harlan (Rip Hendry), Bill Banker (Tom), Charles Sellon, James Hall, Johnny Larkins.

A young man is reunited with his father, who has been wrongly imprisoned for 18 years. (Working title: *Barber John's Boy). See p. 9.*

1931: CHANCES (First National).
Director: Allan Dwan. Scenarist: Waldemar Young, from story by A. Hamilton Gibbs. Photography: Ernest Haller. Art director: Esdras Hartley. Music: David Mendoza. Costumes: Earl Luick. Editor: Ray Curtiss. 71 minutes. Released: July 18.
With Douglas Fairbanks, Jr. (Jack Ingleside), Rose Hobart (Molly Prescott), Anthony Bushell (Tom Ingleside), Mary Forbes (Mrs Mary Ingleside), Florence Britton (Sylvia), Holmes Herbert (Major Bradford), Tyrell Davis (Archie), Edmund Breon (General), Harry Allen (Private Jones), Edward Morgan (Lt. Wickham), Billy Bevan (waiter at pub), Jeanne Fenwick, Robert Bennett, Jameson Thomas.

During World War I, two British soldiers are in love with the same girl. *See pp. 9, 92–93, 92.*

1931: WICKED (Fox).
Director: Allan Dwan. Scenarists: Kenyon Nicholson, Kathryn Scola, from story by Adela Rogers St. John. Associate producer: John W. Considine, Jr. Photography: J. Peverell Marley. Editor: Jack Dennis. Locations filmed at San Quentin Prison. 55 minutes. Released: October 4.
With Elissa Landi (Margo Rand), Victor McLaglen (Scott Burrows), Theodore von Eltz (Tony Rand), Una Merkel (Miss June), Allan Dinehart (Blake), Oscar Apfel (Judge Luther), Irene Rich (Mrs Luther), Blanche Payson, Kathleen Kerrigan, Eileen Percy, Mae Busch,

Blanche Frederici, Lucille Williams, Alice Lake, Ruth Donnelly, Edmund Breese.

When her husband is killed in a robbery attempt, an innocent woman goes to prison and must give up her newborn baby. *See pp. 9, 93–94, 93, 94.*

1932: WHILE PARIS SLEEPS (Fox).
Director: Allan Dwan. Writer: Basil Woon. Photography: Glen McWilliams. Editor: Paul Weatherwax. 66 minutes. Released: May 8.
With Victor McLaglen (Jacques Costaud), Helen Mack (Manon Costaud), William Bakewell (Paul Renoir), Jack La Rue (Julot), Rita Le Roy (Fifi), Maurice Black (Roca), Dot Farley (concierge), Eddie Dillon (her husband), Lucille La Verne (Madame Golden Bennett), Paul Porcasi (Kapas), George Irwin.

In France, an escaped convict sacrifices himself for his daughter. *See pp. 9, 94, 95.*

Dwan went to England, where he shot his next three films. *See pp. 94–95.*

1933: HER FIRST AFFAIRE (A St. George Sterling Production-Associated British).
Director: Allan Dwan. Producer: John Ducer. Scenarists: Brock Williams, Dion Titheradge. Photography: Geoffrey Faithfull. Art director: James Edler Wills. Costumes: Gilbert Clark. Editor: Dr Seabourne. Filmed in London. 71 minutes. Première, London, February 17; U.K. release: May 15.
With Ida Lupino (Anne), Arnold Riches (Brian), George Curzon (Carey Merton), Diana Napier (Mrs Merton), Harry Tate (Major), Muriel Aked (Anne's aunt), Kenneth Kove (dance instructor), Helen Haye (Lady Brogden), Melville Gideon (himself), The Blackburn Twins.

Comedy-romance about a young girl's infatuation with a middle-aged author. *See pp. 94–96, 95–97.*

1933: COUNSEL'S OPINION (London Films-Paramount).
Director: Allan Dwan. Writer: Gilbert Wakefield. 71 minutes. Released: April.
With Henry Kendall (Logan), Binnie Barnes (Leslie), Cyril Maude (Willock), Lawrence Grossmith (Lord Rocklawn), Francis Lister (James), Harry Tate (taxi driver), Mary Charles (Stella), Margaret Bairds (Saunders), Stanley Lathbury (George).

Adventures of a young British divorce attorney. *See p. 98.*

1934: THE MORNING AFTER (I SPY) (Wardour Films-Majestic Films).
Director: Allan Dwan. Writer: Arthur Woods (pseudo-nym for Fred Thompson). Music: Sidney Barnes. 62 minutes. Released: January 1.
With Sally Eilers (Countess Olga), Ben Lyon (Wally), H. F. Maltby (Herr Doktor), Harry Tate (George), Andrews Englemann (Commander), Harold Warrender (N.B.6), Dennis Hoey (M.N.T.), Henry Victor (K.P.O.), Marcelle Rogez (vamp).

An American is mistaken for an international spy.

Dwan returned to America and soon was back at Fox.

1934: *Hollywood Party* (Metro-Goldwyn-Mayer).
Directors (uncredited): Richard Boleslawski, Allan Dwan, Roy Rowland. Writers: Howard Dietz, Arthur Kober. Photography: James Wong Howe. Music and lyrics: Richard Rodgers, Lorenz Hart, Walter Donaldson, Gus Kahn, Nacio Herb Brown, Arthur Freed. Choreography: Seymour Felix, George Hale, David Gould. Cartoon sequence (Mickey Mouse): Walt Disney Studios. Editor: George Boemler. 70 minutes. Released: May.
With Jimmy Durante, Charles Butterworth, Polly Moran, Lupe Velez, Jack Pearl, Stan Laurel, Oliver Hardy, Frances Williams, Eddie Quillan, June Clyde, George Givot, Arthur Treacher, Ben Bard, Ted Healy, Richard Carle, Tom Kennedy, Three Stooges, Robert Young.

See pp. 9, 98–99, 99.

1935: BLACK SHEEP (Fox).
Director-writer: Allan Dwan. Producer: Sol M. Wurtzel. Scenarist: Allen Rivkin. Photography: Arthur Miller. Art director: Duncan Cramer. Music: Oscar Levant; lyrics by Sidney Clare. Costumes: Royer. Editor: Alexander Troffey. 75 minutes. Released: June 14.
With Edmund Lowe (John Francis Dugan), Claire Trevor (Janette Foster), Adrienne Ames (Mrs Millicent Caldwell Bath), Tom Brown (Fred Curtis), Herbert Mundin (Oscar), Eugene Pallette (Col. Upton Calhoun Belcher), Jed Prouty (Orville Schmelling), Ford Sterling (Mather), Joseph W. Reilly (customs inspector), Billy Bevan (Alfred Schmelling), David Torrence (Captain Savage), Robert Elliott, Reginald Sheffield, Maude Turner Gordon, Del Henderson.

Shipboard romantic comedy involving gamblers, millionaires and a jewel robbery. (Working title: *Star for a Night.*) *Dwan's first of a series of six films with Claire Trevor. See pp. 9–10, 100, 100.*

1935: NAVY WIFE (20th Century-Fox).
Director: Allan Dwan. Producer: Sol M. Wurtzel. Scenarist: Sonya Levien, from novel, *Beauty's Daughter*, by Kathleen Norris; additional dialogue: Edward T. Lowe. Photography: John Seitz, Rudolph Mate. Art

director: Duncan Cramer. Costumes: Rega. Editor: Alfred De Gaetano. 69 minutes. Released: November 29. With Claire Trevor (Vicky Blake), Ralph Bellamy (Dr Quentin Harden), Jane Darwell (Mrs Keats), Warren Hymer (Butch), Ben Lyon (Dr Pete Milford), Kathleen Burke (Serena Morrison), George Irving (Dr Keats), Anne Howard (Susan Harden), Jonathan Hale (Norton), Ruth Gillette (Mamie), John Kelly (Spike), Susan Fleming (Jenny), Jed Prouty (Dr Barratt), Murray Alper (Sam).

Romantic drama about a Navy nurse who marries a naval surgeon and finds he's always on duty. (Working title: *Beauty's Daughter*.) See p. 10.

1936: SONG AND DANCE MAN (20th Century-Fox). Director: Allan Dwan. Producer: Sol M. Wurtzel. Scenarist: Maude Fulton, from play by George M. Cohan. Photography: Barney McGill. Songs, 'You're My Favorite One', 'On A Holiday In My Playroom', 'Join The Party', 'Let's Get Going', 'Ain't He Good-looking?', and 'Dancing In The Open' by Sidney Clare, Lew Pollack. Editor: Alfred De Gaetano. 72 minutes. Released: March 13.
With Claire Trevor (Julie Carroll), Paul Kelly (Hap Farrell), Michael Whalen (Alan Davis), Ruth Donnelly (Patsy O'Madigan), James Burke (Lt Mike Boyle), Helen Troy (Sally), Lester Matthews (C. B. Nelson), Ralf Harolde (Crosby), Gloria Roy (Dolores), Margaret Dumont (Mrs Whitney), Billy Bevan (Curtis), Irene Franklin (Goldie McGuffey).

Story of a show-business marriage. See pp. 10, 100.

1936: HUMAN CARGO (20th Century-Fox). Director: Allan Dwan. Producer: Sol M. Wurtzel. Scenarists: Jefferson Parker, Doris Malloy, from novel, *I Will Be Faithful*, by Kathleen Shepard. Photography: Daniel B. Clark. Art director: Duncan Cramer. Costumes: William Lambert. Editor: Louis R. Loeffler. 66 minutes. Released: June 19.
With Claire Trevor (Bonnie Brewster), Brian Donlevy (Packy Campbell), Alan Dinehart (Lionel Crocker), Ralph Morgan (District Attorney Carey), Helen Troy (Susie), Rita Cansino (Carmen Zoro, a Mexican dancer), Morgan Wallace (Gilbert Fender), Herman Bing (Fritz Schultz), John McGuire ('Spike' Davis), Ralf Harolde (Tony Sculla), Wade Botelier (Bob McSweeney), Harry Woods (Ira Conklin), Wilfred Lucas (police chief).

Crime melodrama: two reporters uncover a vicious smuggling ring. See pp. 10, 100–102, 101.

1936: HIGH TENSION (20th Century-Fox). Director: Allan Dwan. Producer: Sol M. Wurtzel. Scenarists: Louis Breslow, Edward Eliscu, John Patrick, from story by J. Robert Bren, Norman Houston.

Photography: Barney McGill. Art director: Duncan Cramer. Costumes: William Lambert. Song, 'And That Woman Made A Monkey Out of Me', by Sidney Clare. Editor: Louis R. Loeffler. 63 minutes. Released: July 17.
With Brian Donlevy (Steve Reardon), Glenda Farrell (Edith McNeil), Norman Foster (Eddie Mitchell), Helen Wood (Brenda Burke), Robert McWade (President Stone), Theodore Von Eltz (Noble Harrison), Romaine Callender (Jasper Tuttle), Jasper Sawyer (Harry Madden), Hattie McDaniel (Hattie), Murray Alper (Chuck).

A troubleshooter for an undersea cable company lives it up when his girl leaves him. (Working title: *Trouble Makers*.) See pp. 10, 102, *102*.

1936: 15 MAIDEN LANE (20th Century-Fox). Director: Allan Dwan. Producer: Sol M. Wurtzel. Scenarists: Lou Breslow, David Silverstein, John Patrick, from story by Paul Burger. Photography: John Seitz. Art director: Duncan Cramer. Costumes: Herschel. Editor: Alex Troffey. Technical consultant: Eugene Mahy. 64 minutes. Released: October 30.
With Claire Trevor (Jane Martin), Cesar Romero (Frank Peyton), Douglas Fowley (Nick Shelby), Lloyd Nolan (Detective Walsh), Lester Matthews (Gilbert Lockhart), Robert McWade (John Graves), Ralf Harolde (Tony), Russell Hicks (Judge Graham), Holmes Herbert (Harold Anderson), Natalie Moorehead (shoplifter), Patricia Patrick.

A girl reporter feigns love for a diamond thief in order to break his robbery ring. See pp. 10, 102, *102*.

1937: WOMAN-WISE (20th Century-Fox). Director: Allan Dwan. Producer: Sol M. Wurtzel. Writer: Ben Markson. Photography: Robert Planck. Art director: Lewis Creber. Editor: Alfred De Gaetano. 70 minutes. Released: January 22.
With Rochelle Hudson (Alice Fuller), Michael Whalen (Tracey Browne), Thomas Beck (Clint DeWitt), Alan Dinehart (Richards), Douglas Fowley (Stevens), George Hassell (John DeWitt), Astrid Allwyn ('Bubbles' Carson), Chick Chandler (Bob Benton), Pat Flaherty (Duke Fuller).

A sports writer exposes a fixed fight racket. See pp. 10, 102.

1937: THAT I MAY LIVE (20th Century-Fox). Director: Allan Dwan. Producer: Sol M. Wurtzel. Scenarists: Ben Markson, William Conselman. Photography: Robert Planck. Art director: Lewis Creber. Costumes: Herschel. Editor: Louis R. Loeffler. 70 minutes. Released: April 30.
With Rochelle Hudson (Irene Howard), Robert Kent (Dick Mannion), J. Edward Bromberg (Tex Shapirok Jack La Rue (Charlie), Frank Conroy (Pop), Frank Kelsey (Abner Jenkins), George Cooper (Mack), DeWitt

Jennings (police chief), Russell Simpson (Bish Plivens), William Benedict (Kurt Plivens).

Against his will, an ex-convict is involved in a hold-up during which a policeman is killed. *See pp. 10, 103, 103.*

1937: ONE MILE FROM HEAVEN (20th Century-Fox).
Director: Allan Dwan. Producer: Sol M. Wurtzel. Scenarists: Lou Breslow, John Patrick, from stories by Judge Ben Lindsay, Robin Harris and Alfred Golden. Photography: Sidney Wagner. Art director: Bernard Herzbrun. Costumes: Herschel. Editor: Fred Allen. 68 minutes. Released: August 13.
With Claire Trevor (Lucy 'Tex' Warren), Sally Blane (Barbara Harrison), Douglas Fowley (Jim Tabor), Fredi Washington (Flora Jackson), Joan Carol (Sunny), Ralf Harolde (Moxie McGrath), John Eldredge (Jerry Harrison), Paul McVey (Johnny), Ray Walker (Mortimer Atlas), Russell Hopton (Peter Brindell), Chick Chandler (Charlie Milford), Eddie 'Rochester' Anderson (Henry Bangs), Howard Hickman (Judge Clarke), Bill Robinson (Officer Joe).

A newspaperwoman uncovers the facts about two women, both claiming to be mother of the same child. *See pp. 10, 104, 105.*

1937: HEIDI (20th Century-Fox).
Director: Allan Dwan. Producer: Darryl F. Zanuck. Associate producer: Raymond Griffith. Scenarists: Walter Ferris, Julien Josephson, from novel by Johanna Spyri. Photography: Arthur Miller. Art director: Hans Peters. Set decorator: Thomas Little. Costumes: Gwen Wakeling. Song, 'In Our Little Wooden Shoes', by Lew Pollack, Sidney Mitchell. Editor: Allen McNeil. 88 minutes. Released: October 15.
With Shirley Temple (Heidi), Jean Hersholt (Adolph Kramer), Marcia Mae Jones (Klara Sesemann), Sidney Blackmer (Herr Sesemann), Arthur Treacher (Andrews), Thomas Beck (Pastor Schultz), Pauline Moore (Frau Elsa Schultz), Helen Westley (Anna, the blind woman), Mary Nash (Fraulein Rottenmeier), Mady Christians (Aunt Dete), Sig Rumann (police captain), Delmar Watson (Peter), Egon Brecher (inn-keeper), Christian Rub, George Humbert, Greta Meyer, Bodil Rosing, Elsa Janssen, Victor Kolberg.

A little girl is taken from her grandfather's home in the Swiss Alps to live in a rich but cruel household. *Dwan's first of three films with Shirley Temple. See pp. 10, 106–109, 106–108.*

1938: REBECCA OF SUNNYBROOK FARM (20th Century-Fox).
Director: Allan Dwan. Producer: Raymond Griffith. Scenarists: Karl Tunberg, Don Ettlinger, from novel by Kate Douglas Wiggin. Photography: Arthur Miller. Art directors: Bernard Herzbrun, Hans Peters. Set decorator: Thomas Little. Costumes: Gwen Wakeling. Songs, 'An Old Straw Hat', by Mack Gordon, Harry Revel; 'Alone with You', 'Happy Ending', 'Crackly Grain Flakes', by Lew Pollack, Sidney D. Mitchell; 'Come and Get Your Happiness', by Sam Pokrass, Jack Yetten; 'Toy Trumpet', by Pollack, Mitchell and Raymond Scott. Choreography: Geneva Sawyer, Nick Castle. Editor: Allen McNeill. 81 minutes. Released: March 18.
With Shirley Temple (Rebecca Winstead), Gloria Stuart (Gwen Warren), Randolph Scott (Anthony Kent), Jack Haley (Orville Smithes), Phyllis Brooks (Lola Lee), Helen Westley (Aunt Miranda Wilkins), Bill Robinson (Aloysius), Alan Dinehart (Purvis), Slim Summerville (Homer Busby), J. Edward Bromberg (Dr Hill), William Demarest (Henry Kipper), William Wagner (Reverend Turner), Dixie Dunbar (receptionist), Carroll Nye, Gary Breckner, Sam Hayes (radio announcers), Paul Hurst (Mug), Ruth Gillette (Melba), Paul Harvey (Cyrus Bertlett), Franklin Pangborn (Hamilton Montmarcy), Clarence Hummel Wilson (Jake Singer), Eily Malyon (Mrs Tunner), Mary McCarty (Florabelle), Kate Douglas, Peter Sisters, Raymond Scott and His Quintette.

When a girl is sought by two rival cereal companies to do singing radio commercials, her stepfather attempts to cash in on her talent. *See pp. 10, 109–110, 109.*

1938: JOSETTE (20th Century-Fox).
Director: Allan Dwan. Producer: Gene Markey. Scenarist: James Edward Grant, from play by Paul Frank, George Fraser, based on the story of Ladislaus Vadnal. Photography: Harry Mescal. Art directors: Bernard Herzbrun, David Hall. Set decorator: Thomas Little. Costumes: Royer. Songs, 'May I Drop a Petal in Your Glass of Wine', 'In Any Language', 'Where in the World', by Mack Gordon, Harry Revel. 73 minutes. Released: June 3.
With Simone Simon (Josette-Renée Le Blanc), Don Ameche (David Brossard, Jr.), Robert Young (Pierre Brossard), Bert Lahr (Barney Barnaby), Joan Davis (May Morris), Paul Hurst (A. Adolphus Heyman), William Collier, Sr. (David Brossard, Sr.), Tala Birell (Mlle. Josette), William Demarest (Bill), Ruth Gillette (Belle), Armand Kaliz (Thomas), Ferdinand Gottschalk (Le Blanc), Lillian Porter (Toinette), Maurice Cass (furrier), Lynn Bari (Mrs Dupree), Jane Regan (Celeste), Zeffie Tilbury, Harry Holman, Raymond Turner.

Two sons go to New Orleans to rescue their father from a singer, and they fall in love with her themselves. *See pp. 10, 110.*

1938: SUEZ (20th Century-Fox).
Director: Allan Dwan. Producer: Darryl F. Zanuck. Associate producer: Gene Markey. Scenarists: Philip Dunne, Julien Josephson, from story by Sam Duncan. Photography: J. Peverell Marley. Art directors: Bernard Herzbrun, Rudolf Sternad. Set decorator: Thomas Little. Costumes: Royer. Special effects: Fred Sersen. Editor: Barbara MacLean. Second-unit director: Otto Brower. 104 minutes. Released: October 28.
With Tyrone Power (Ferdinand de Lesseps), Loretta Young (Countess Eugenie de Montijo), Annabella (Toni Pellerin), J. Edward Bromberg (Prince Said), Joseph Schildkraut (Vicomte Rene De Latour), Henry Stephenson (Count Mathieu de Lesseps), Sidney Blackmer (Marquis De Brey), Maurice Moscovich (Mohammed Ali), Sig Rumann (Sgt. Pellerin), Nigel Bruce (Sir Malcolm Cameron), Miles Mander (Benjamin Disraeli), George Zucco (Prime Minister), Leon Ames (Louis Napoleon), Raffaela Ottiano (Maria De Teba), Victor Varconi (Victor Hugo), George Renavent (bank president), Frank Reicher (General Nicolas Anne Theodule Changarnier), Carlos De Valdez (Count Halgfeldt), Jacques Lory (Millet), Albert Conti (M. Fevrier), Brandon Hurst (Franz Liszt), Marcelle Corday (Madame Paquine), Odette Myrtle (Duchess), Egon Brecher (doctor), Alphonse Martell (General Arnaud Jacques Leroy de Saint-Arnaud), Montague Shaw (Everill Lowe), Leonard Mudie (farmer).
The epic story of the man who built the Suez Canal, and of the two women who loved him. *Dwan's most expensive talking film to date. See pp. 10, 11, 111–116, 111-117, 119, 168.*

1938: *The Book of Esther* (unrealised project).
An adaptation of the Biblical story – to be done in a simple style. Dwan first got interested in the subject when he saw Griffith's *Judith of Bethulia* (1913), but never was able to make a deal. In 1960, his friend Raoul Walsh made *Esther and the King*.

1939: THE THREE MUSKETEERS (20th Century-Fox).
Director: Allan Dwan. Producer: Darryl F. Zanuck. Associate producer: Raymond Griffith. Scenarists: M. M. Musselman, William A. Drake and Sam Hellman, from novel by Alexandre Dumas, père; additional dialogue: Sid Kuller, Ray Golden. Photography: J. Peverell Marley. Art directors: Bernard Herzbrun, David Hall. Set decorator: Thomas Little. Costumes: Royer. Songs, 'Chicken Soup', 'Song of the Musketeers' and 'My Lady' by Samuel Pokrass and Walter Bullock. Editor: Jack Dennis. 73 minutes. Released: February 17.
With Don Ameche (D'Artagnan), Al Ritz, Jimmy Ritz,

Harry Ritz (three lackeys), Binnie Barnes (Milady de Winter), Lionel Atwill (De Rochefort), Gloria Stuart (Anne d'Autriche), Pauline Moore (Constance Bonacieux), Joseph Schildkraut (Louis XIII), John Carradine (Naveau), Miles Mander (Cardinal de Richelieu), Douglas Dumbrille (Athos), John King (Aramis), Russell Hicks (Porthos), Gregory Gaye (Vitray), Lester Matthews (Duke Buckingham), Egon Brecher (Logeur), Moroni Olsen (Bailli), George Renavent (Captain Fageon), Montague C. Shaw (ship captain), Jean Parry, Frederik Vogeding (guards).
Three cowardly lackeys find themselves mistaken for the famous trio of musketeers. *A parody remake of the 1921 Douglas Fairbanks film. See pp. 10, 111–119, 118.*

1939: THE GORILLA (20th Century-Fox).
Director: Allan Dwan. Producer: Darryl F. Zanuck. Associate producer: Harry Joe Brown. Scenarists: Rian James, Sid Silvers, from play by Ralph Spence. Photography: Edward Cronjager. Art directors: Richard Day, Lewis Creber. Set decorator: Thomas Little. Costumes: Gwen Wakeling. Music: David Buttolph. Editor: Allen McNeill. 66 minutes. Released: May 26.
With Jimmy Ritz (Garrity), Harry Ritz (Harrigan), Al Ritz (Mulligan), Anita Louise (Norma Denby), Patsy Kelly (Kitty), Lionel Atwill (Walter Stevens), Bela Lugosi (Peters), Joseph Calleia (stranger), Edward Norris (Jack Marsden), Wally Vernon (sailor), Paul Harvey (Conway), Art Miles (gorilla).
Farce about three detectives who go to a lonely country house to solve a murder. *See pp. 10, 119.*

1939: FRONTIER MARSHAL (20th Century-Fox).
Director: Allan Dwan. Producer: Sol M. Wurtzel. Scenarist: Sam Hellman, from 'Wyatt Earp, Frontier Marshal' by Stuart N. Lake. Photography: Charles G. Clarke. Art directors: Richard Day, Lewis Creber. Set decorator: Thomas Little. Costumes: Herschel. Editor: Fred Allen. 71 minutes. Released: July 28.
With Randolph Scott (Wyatt Earp), Nancy Kelly (Sarah Allen), Cesar Romero (Doc Holliday), Binnie Barnes (Jerry), John Carradine (Ben Carter), Ward Bond (sheriff), Edward Norris (Dan Blackmore), Eddie Foy, Jr (Eddie Foy), Lon Chaney, Jr (Pringle), Chris Pin Martin (Pete), Joe Sawyer (Curly Bill), Del Henderson (Dave Hall), Harry Hayden (Major Henderson), Ventura Ybarra (Pablo), Charles Stevens (Indian Charlie), Tom Tyler.
To help clean up the town, Wyatt Earp becomes marshal of Tombstone. (Working title: *Frontier Marshal, The Saga of Tombstone, Arizona*.) *Some of the same material formed the basis of John Ford's 1946 My Darling Clementine. See pp. 10, 119–122, 120.*

1940: SAILOR'S LADY (20th Century-Fox).
Director: Allan Dwan. Producer: Sol M. Wurtzel.
Scenarist: Frederick Hazlitt Brennan, from story by
Lt. Commander Frank 'Spig' Wead; additional dialogue:
Lou Breslow, Owen Francis. Photography: Ernest
Palmer. Editor: Fred Allen. 66 minutes. Released:
July 5.
With Nancy Kelly (Sally Gilroy), Jon Hall (Danny
Malone), Joan Davis (Myrtle), Dana Andrews ('Scrappy'
Wilson), Mary Nash (Miss Purvis), Larry 'Buster'
Crabbe (Rodney), Katherine Aldridge (Georgine), Harry
Shannon (Father McGann), Wally Vernon (Goofer),
Bruce Hampton ('Skipper'), Charles D. Brown (Captain
Roscoe), Selmer Jackson (Executive Officer), Edgar
Dearing (Chief Master-at-Arms), Edmund McDonald
(Barnacle), William B. Davidson (Judge Hinsdale), Kane
Richmond (Division Officer), Ward Bond (Marine).

To test the love of a sailor she's about to marry, a girl
borrows a baby and smuggles it aboard ship. *See p. 10.*

1940: YOUNG PEOPLE (20th Century-Fox).
Director: Allan Dwan. Producer: Harry Joe Brown.
Scenarists: Edwin Blum, Don Ettlinger. Photography:
Edward Cronjager. Art directors: Richard Day, Rudolph
Sternad. Set decorator: Thomas Little. Costumes:
Gwen Wakeling. Songs, '5th Avenue', 'Tra-La-La', 'I
Wouldn't Take a Million', 'The Mason-Dixon Line' and
'Young People', by Mack Gordon, Harry Warren.
Choreography: Nick Castle, Geneva Sawyer. Editor:
James B. Clark. 78 minutes. Released: August 30.
With Shirley Temple (Wendy), Jack Oakie (Joe
Ballantine), Charlotte Greenwood (Kit Ballantine),
Arleen Whelan (Judith), George Montgomery (Mike
Shea), Kathleen Howard (Esther Appleby), Minor
Watson (Dakin), Frank Swann (Fred Willard), Frank
Sully (Jed), Mae Marsh (Maria Liggett), Sarah Edwards
(Mrs Stinchfield), Irving Bacon (Otis), Charles Halton
(president), Arthur Aylesworth (porter), Olin Howlin
(station-master), Billy Wayne (state manager), Harry
Tyler (Dave), Darryl Hickman (Tommy), Shirley Mills
(Mary Ann), Diane Fisher (Susie), Bobby Anderson
(Jerry Dakin).

Vaudeville family leaves Broadway for life on a New
England farm, where they find themselves ostracised.
See pp. 10, 121.

1940: TRAIL OF THE VIGILANTES (Universal).
Director: Allan Dwan. Writer: Harold Schumate.
Photography: Joseph Valentine, Milton Krasner. Art
director: Jack Otterson. Costumes: Vera West. Editor:
Edward Curtiss. 75 minutes. Released: December 13.
With Franchot Tone (Tim Mason, 'Kansas'), Broderick
Crawford (Swanee), Peggy Moran (Barbara Thornton),
Andy Devine (Meadows), Warren William (Mark

Dawson), Mischa Auer (Dimitri Bolo), Porter Hall
(Sheriff Korley), Samuel S. Hinds (George Preston),
Charles Trowbridge (John Thornton), Paul Fix (Lefty),
Harry Cording (Phil), Max Wagner (Joe).

Comedy-western in which an Eastern lawman is sent
West to break up a gang of outlaws. *See pp. 10, 122, 122.*

1941: LOOK WHO'S LAUGHING (RKO Radio).
Director-producer: Allan Dwan. Writer: James V. Kern.
Photography: Frank Redman. Art director: Van Nest
Polglase. Music: Roy Webb. Special effects: Vernon L.
Walker. Editor: Sherman Todd. 78 minutes. Released:
November 21.
With Edgar Bergen (himself), Jim Jordan (Fibber
McGee), Marian Jordan (Molly McGee), Lucille Ball
(Julie Patterson), Lee Bonnell (Jerry), Dorothy Lovett
(Marge), Harold Peary (The Great Gildersleeve), Isabel
Randolph (Mrs Uppington), Walter Baldwin (Bill),
Neil Hamilton (Hilary Horton), Charles Halton
(Cudahy), Harlow Wilcox (Mr Collins), Spencer
Charters (director), Jed Prouty (Major), George
Cleveland (Kelsey), Bill Thompson (veteran).

Edgar Bergen and Charlie McCarthy wind up in
Fibber McGee and Molly's radio home town, Wistful
Vista. *See pp. 123–124.*

1941: RISE AND SHINE (20th Century-Fox).
Director: Allan Dwan. Producer: Mark Hellinger.
Scenarist: Herman J. Mankiewicz, from 'My Life and
Hard Times' by James Thurber. Photography: Edward
Cronjager. Art directors: Richard Day, George Dudley.
Set decorator: Thomas Little. Costumes: Gwen
Wakeling. Songs, 'I'm Making A Play For You',
'Central 2-2-0-0', 'I Want to be the Guy', 'Hail to
Bolenciewicz', 'Get Thee Behind Me, Clayton', by Leo
Robin, Ralph Rainger. Choreographer: Hermes Pan.
Editor: Allen McNeill. 92 minutes. Released: Novem-
ber 21.
With Jack Oakie ('Boley' Bolenciewicz), Linda Darnell
(Louise Murray), George Murphy (Jimmy McGonigle),
Walter Brennan ('Grandpa' Murray), Sheldon Leonard
(Menace), Donald Meek (Prof. Murray), Ruth Donnelly
('Mame'), Raymond Walburn (Colonel Bacon), Donald
McBride (Coach Graham), Emma Dunn (Mrs Murray),
Charles Waldron (president), William Haade (Butch),
Dick Rich (Gogo), John Heistrand (announcer at game),
Francis Pierlot (Prof. Schnauzer), Mildred Gerer (Mrs
Robertson), Claire Du Brey (Mrs Pinkham), Paul
Harvey (Orville Turner), Edward Deering (cheerleader),
James Flavin (policeman), Milton Berle ('Seabiscuit'),
Nester Paiva (gangster).

Comedy about a college football hero who is kidnapped
by mobsters to keep him out of the big game. *See pp. 10,
123.*

1942: FRIENDLY ENEMIES (Small Productions-United Artists).
Director: Allan Dwan. Producer: Edward Small. Scenarist: Adelaide Heilbrun, from play by Samuel Shipman, Aaron Hoffman. Photography: Edward Cronjager. Art director: John DuCasse Schulze. Set decorator: Edward G. Boyle. Costumes: Royer. Music: Lucien Moraweck. Editor: William Claxton. 95 minutes. Released: June 26.
With Charles Winninger (Karl Pfeiffer), Charles Ruggles (Heinrich Block), James Craig (Bill Pfeiffer), Nancy Kelly (June Block), Otto Kruger (Anton Miller), Ilka Gruning (Mrs Pfeiffer), Greta Meyer (Gretchen), Addison Richards (Inspector McCarthy), Charles Lane (Braun), John Piffle (Schnitzler), Ruth Holly (Nora), Murray Alper (delivery-man).
During World War I, the friendship of two German-born millionaires in America is split on the issue of loyalty to the fatherland. *The first of five films Dwan directed for Edward Small. See pp. 10, 124–126, 124, 125.*

1942: HERE WE GO AGAIN (RKO Radio).
Director-producer: Allan Dwan. Scenarists: Paul Gerard Smith, Joe Bigelow, from story by Smith. Photography: Frank Redman. Music: Roy Webb; songs, 'Delicious Delirium', 'Until I Live Again', by Mort Greene, Harry Revel. Special effects: Vernon L. Walker. Editor: Desmond Marquette. 77 minutes. Released: October 9.
With Edgar Bergen (himself), Jim Jordan (Fibber McGee), Marian Jordan (Molly McGee), Harold Peary (The Great Gildersleeve), Ginny Simms (Jean), Bill Thompson (Wimple), Gale Gordon (Caldwalader), Isabel Randolph (Mrs Uppington), Ray Noble and his orchestra.
Charlie McCarthy masquerades as an Indian and Bergen as a squaw when they go West, in this follow-up to the radio-inspired *Look Who's Laughing* (1941). *See p. 124.*

During 1943 Dwan worked in the U.S. Armed Services photographic division, organising and training camera units throughout the country to cover battle action for the national archives.

1943: AROUND THE WORLD (RKO Radio).
Director-producer: Allan Dwan. Writer: Ralph Spence. Photography: Russell Metty. Art directors: Albert S. D'Agostino, Hal Herman. Music: George Dunning; songs, 'Candlelight and Wine', 'They Chopped Down The Old Apple Tree', 'Don't Believe Everything You Dream', 'He's Got A Secret Weapon', 'Great News In The Making', 'A Moke From Shamokin', and 'Roodle-De-Doo', by Jimmy McHugh, Harold Adamson. Editor: Theron Warth. 81 minutes. Released: November.
With (as themselves) Kay Kyser, Mischa Auer, Joan Davis, Marcy McGuire, Georgia Carroll, Harry Babbitt, Ish Kabibble, Sully Mason, Julie Conway, Diane Pendleton, Kay Kyser Orchestra, Jack and Mae, Little Fred's Football dogs, Robert Armstrong, Wally Brown (clipper pilot), Alan Carney (Joe Gimpus).
A musical tour of the world. *See p. 123.*

1944: UP IN MABEL'S ROOM (Small Productions-United Artists).
Director: Allan Dwan. Producer: Edward Small. Scenarist: Tom Reed, from play by Otto Harbach, Wilson Collison; dialogue: Isobel Dawn. Photography: Charles Lawton, Jr. Art director: Joseph Sternad. Set decorator: Edward G. Boyle. Music: Michel Michelet. Special effects: George Emick. Editor: Richard Heermance. 76 minutes. Released: April 7.
With Marjorie Reynolds (Geraldine Ainsworth), Dennis O'Keefe (Gary Ainsworth), Gail Patrick (Mabel Essington), Mischa Auer (Boris), Charlotte Greenwood (Martha Weldon), Lee Bowman (Arthur Weldon), John Hubbard (Jimmy Larchmont), Binnie Barnes (Alicia Larchmont), Janet Lambert (Priscilla), Fred Kohler, Jr. (Johnny), Harry Hayden (Justice).
Before his wife can find out, a flustered professor tries to recover a romantically incriminating slip from a former girlfriend. *Previously filmed in 1926. See pp. 10–11, 124, 126, 127, 132.*

1944: ABROAD WITH TWO YANKS (Small Productions-United Artists).
Director: Allan Dwan. Producer: Edward Small. Scenarists: Charles Rogers, Wilkie Mahoney, Ted Sills, from story by Fred Guiol, adapted by Edward Seabrook. Photography: Charles Lawton, Jr. Art director: Joseph Sternad. Costumes: Odette. Editor: Richard Heermance. 80 minutes. Released: August 4.
With William Bendix (Biff Koraski), Helen Walker (Joyce Stuart), Dennis O'Keefe (Jeff Reardon), John Loder (Cyril), George Cleveland, Janet Lambert, James Flavin, Arthur Hunnicutt, Willard Jillson, Herbert Evans, William Forrest, John Abbott.
In England, two leathernecks try to outdo each other for the same girl's hand, but lose her to a Limey. *See pp. 11, 126–131, 128, 129.*

1945: BREWSTER'S MILLIONS (Small Productions-United Artists).
Director: Allan Dwan. Producer: Edward Small. Scenarists: Siegfried Herzig, Charles Rogers, Wilkie Mahoney, from novel by George Barr McCutcheon and

play by Winchell Smith and Byron Ongley. Photography: Charles Lawton, Jr. Art director: Joseph Sternad. Editor: Richard Heermance. 79 minutes. Released: April 7.

With Dennis O'Keefe (Monty Brewster), Helen Walker (Peggy Gray), Eddie 'Rochester' Anderson (Jackson), June Havoc (Trixie Summer), Gail Patrick (Barbara Drew), Mischa Auer (Michael Michaelovitch), Joe Sawyer (Macky Smith), Nana Bryant (Mrs Gray), John Litel (Swearengen Jones), Herbert Rudley (Nopper Harrison), Thurston Hall (Cluel Drew), Bryon K. Foulger (Judge), Barbara Pepper (taxi driver), Joseph Crehan (notary), Neil Hamilton (Mr Grant).

An eccentric relative leaves an ex-GI 7 million dollars *if* he can spend another million in two months and have nothing to show for it. *Filmed previously in 1914, 1921, and 1935 and as* Miss Brewster's Millions *in 1926. See pp. 11, 131–132, 130, 131.*

1945: GETTING GERTIE'S GARTER (Small Productions-United Artists).
Director: Allan Dwan. Producer: Edward Small. Scenarists: Dwan, Karen De Wolfe, from play by Wilson Collison, Avery Hopwood. Photography: Charles Lawton, Jr. Art director: Joseph Sternad. Set decorator: Henry Zane. Editors: Walter Hanneman, Truman K. Wood. 73 minutes. Released: November 30.
With Dennis O'Keefe (Ken), Marie 'The Body' McDonald (Gertie), Barry Sullivan (Ted), Binnie Barnes (Barbara), Sheila Ryan (Patty), J. Carroll Naish (Charles Boucher), Jerome Cowan (Billy), Vera Marshe (Anna, the maid), Don Beddoe (Clancy), Frank Fenton (Winters), Richard LeGrand (Dr Clark).

A newly married young scientist tries frantically to retrieve a garter from an old girlfriend. *Previously filmed in 1927. See pp. 10–11, 132–134, 132, 133.*

Toward the end of 1945, Dwan signed an exclusive deal with Republic Pictures, where he worked until 1954.

1946: RENDEZVOUS WITH ANNIE (Republic).
Director-associate producer: Allan Dwan. Writers: Mary Loos, Richard Sale. Photography: Reggie Lanning. Art director: Hilyard Brown. Set decorators: John McCarthy, Jr., George Milo. Costumes: Adele Palmer. Music: Joseph Dubin. Special effects: Howard and Theodore Lydecker. Editor: Arthur Roberts. 89 minutes. Released: July 22.
With Eddie Albert (Corporal Jeffrey Dolan), Faye Marlowe (Annie Dolan), Gail Patrick (Dolores Starr), Philip Reed (Lt. Avery), Sir Charles Aubrey Smith (Sir Archibald Clyde), Raymond Walburn (Everett Thorndyke), William Frawley (General Trent), James Millican (Captain Spence), Wallace Ford (Al Morgan), Will

Wright (Elmer Snodgrass), Lucien Littlefield (Ed Kramer), Edwin Rand (Phil Denim), Mary Field (Deborah), Richard Sale (Clarence), Bob Foy (radio operator), Mike Frankovich (pilot).

A soldier goes AWOL to spend a weekend secretly with his wife. Later, when she has a baby, he must prove he's the father. (Released in Great Britain as *Corporal Dolan AWOL.) See pp. 11, 134–138, 135.*

1947: CALENDAR GIRL (Republic).
Director-associate producer: Allan Dwan. Scenarists: Mary Loos, Richard Sale, Lee Loeb, from story by Loeb. Photography: Reggie Lanning. Art director: Hilyard Brown. Music: Leo Arnaud. Songs, 'A Lovely Night to Go Dreaming', 'I'm Telling You Now', 'Calendar Girl', 'At the Fireman's Ball', 'New York's a Nice Place to Visit', 'Let's Have Some Pretzels and Beer', and 'A Bluebird Is Singing to Me', by James McHugh, Harold Adamson. Special effects: Howard and Theodore Lydecker. Editor: Fred Allen. 88 minutes. Released: January 31.
With Jane Frazee (Patricia O'Neil), William Marshall (Johnny Bennett), Gail Patrick (Olivia Radford), Kenny Baker (Byron Jones), Victor McLaglen (Matthew O'Neil), Irene Rich (Lulu Varden), James Ellison (Steve Adams), Janet Martin (Tessie), Franklin Pangborn (Dillingsworth), Gus Schilling (Ed Gaskin), Charles Arnt (Captain Olsen), Lou Nova (Clancy), Emory Parnell (mayor).

Musical set in turn-of-the-century New York, about a struggling composer and a playboy who are both after the same girl. *See pp. 11, 136, 137.*

1947: NORTHWEST OUTPOST (Republic).
Director-associate producer: Allan Dwan. Scenarists: Elizabeth Meehan, Richard Sale, from story by Angela Stuart, adapted by Laird Doyle. Photography: Reggie Lanning. Art directors: Hilyard Brown, Fred Ritter. Set decorators: John McCarthy, Jr., James Redd. Music: Rudolf Friml (and uncredited: Robert Armbruster), lyrics by Edward Heyman; songs: 'One More Mile to Go', 'Raindrops on A Drum', 'Love is the Time', 'Nearer and Nearer', 'Tell Me With Your Eyes', 'Weary Convict Song', and 'Russian Easter Hymn'. Second-unit director: Yakima Canutt. Special effects: Howard and Theodore Lydecker. Editor: Harry Keller. Technical consultant: Alexis Davidoff. 91 minutes. Released: June 25.
With Nelson Eddy (Captain James Laurence), Ilona Massey (Natalie Alanova), Joseph Schildkraut (Igor Savin), Elsa Lanchester (Princess Tanya), Hugo Haas (Prince Nikolai Balinin), Erno Verebes (Kyril), Leonore Ulric (Baroness Kruposny), Peter Whitney (Volkoff),

Tamara Shayne (Olga), George Sorel (Baron Kruposny), Rick Vallin (Dovkin), Countess Rosanska, Dina Smirnova, Lola De Tolly, Antonia Barnett, Myra Sokolskaya, George Blagoi, Sam Savitsky, Igor Dolgoruki, Nestor Eristoff (nobles), The American G.I. Chorus.

In mid-19th century California, a young Russian girl, held captive by her husband, escapes with a dashing U.S. cavalryman. (Working title: *One Exciting Kiss*.) *See pp.* 12, 137–139, *137–139*.

1947: DRIFTWOOD (Republic).

Director: Allan Dwan. Writers: Mary Loos, Richard Sale. Photography: John Alton. Art director: Frank Arrigo. Set decorators: John McCarthy, Jr., George Milo. Costumes: Adele Palmer. Music: Nathan Scott; song, 'I Wish I Wuz a Mole in the Ground'. Special effects: Howard and Theodore Lydecker. Editor: Arthur Roberts. 90 minutes. Released: September 15.
With Ruth Warrick (Susan), Walter Brennan (Murph), Dean Jagger (Dr Steve Webster), Charlotte Greenwood (Mathilda), Natalie Wood (Jenny), Jerome Cowan (Mayor Snyder), H. B. Warner (Reverend Hollingsworth), Margaret Hamilton (Essie Keenan), Hobart Cavanaugh (Judge Beckett), Francis Ford (Abner Green), Alan Napier (Dr. Adams), James Bell (Sheriff Bolton), Howard Chamberlin (Hiram Trumbull), Teddy Infuhr (Lester Snyder), James Kirkwood (Reverend McDougal), Ray Teal (Perkins), Zeke Holland (Blaine).

A young orphan who's had little contact with 'civilised' people is adopted by a young physician. (Working title: *Heaven for Jenny*.) *See pp.* 11, *12*, 137, 139–141, *140*, *141*.

1948: THE INSIDE STORY (Republic).

Director-producer: Allan Dwan. Scenarists: Mary Loos, Richard Sale, from story by Ernest Lehman, Geza Herczeg. Photography: Reggie Lanning. Art director: Frank Arrigo. Set decorators: John McCarthy, Jr., George Milo. Costumes: Adele Palmer. Music: Nathan Scott. Editor: Arthur Roberts. 87 minutes. Released: March 14.
With Marsha Hunt (Francine Taylor), William Lundigan (Waldo Williams), Charles Winninger (Uncle Ed), Gail Patrick (Audrey O'Conner), Gene Lockhart (Horace Taylor), Florence Bates (Geraldine Atherton), Hobart Cavanaugh (Mason), Allen Jenkins (Eddie Hale), Roscoe Karns (Eustace Peabody), Robert Shayne (Tom O'Conner), William Haade (Rocky), Frank Ferguson (Eph), Tom Fadden (Ab Follansbee), Will Wright (Jay Jay Johnson).

An old Vermont man urges everyone to keep their cash in circulation. (Working titles: *End of the Rainbow*, *The Storm*.) *See pp.* 11, 137, 141–142, *142*, *143*.

1948: ANGEL IN EXILE (Republic).

Directors: Allan Dwan, Philip Ford. Producer: Herbert J. Yates. Writer: Charles Larson. Photography: Reggie Lanning. Art director: Frank Arrigo. Set decorators: John McCarthy, Jr., George Milo. Costumes: Adele Palmer. Music: Nathan Scott; song, 'Yo Me Alegro'. Special effects: Howard and Theodore Lydecker. Editor: Arthur Roberts. 90 minutes. Released: November 1.
With John Carroll (Charlie Dakin), Adele Mara (Raquel Chavez), Thomas Gomez (Dr Esteban Chavez), Barton MacLane (Max Giorgo), Alfonso Bedoya (Ysidoro Alvarez), Grant Withers (sheriff), Paul Fix (Carl Spitz), Art Smith (Ernie Coons), Howland Chamberlin (S. H. Higgins), Tom Powers (prison director), Ian Wolfe (health officer), Elsa Lorraine Zepeda (Carmencita), Mary Currier (nurse).

In a small Arizona town, the Mexican peasants hail an ex-convict as God when he 'discovers' a cache of gold. (Working title: *The Blue Lady*.) *Billed as co-director, Philip Ford shot for one week while Dwan was ill. See pp.* 11, *144*.

1949: SANDS OF IWO JIMA (Republic).

Director: Allan Dwan. Associate producer: Edmund Grainger. Scenarists: Harry Brown, James Edward Grant, from story by Brown. Photography: Reggie Lanning. Art director: James Sullivan. Set decorators: John McCarthy, Jr., Otto Siegel. Costumes: Adele Palmer. Music: Victor Young. Special effects: Howard and Theodore Lydecker. Editor: Richard L. Van Enger. Exterior locations at Camp Pendleton, California. 108 minutes. Première (in Los Angeles): December 31; general release: March 1, 1950.
With John Wayne (Sgt. John M. Stryker), John Agar (Pfc. Peter Conway), Adele Mara (Allison Bromley), Forrest Tucker (Corporal Thomas), Wally Cassell (Pfc. Ragazzi), James Brown (Pfc. Bass), Arthur Franz (Corporal Dunne), Julie Bishop (Mary), Richard Webb (Pfc. 'Handsome Dan' Shipley), James Holden (Pfc. Soames), Peter Coe (Pfc. Hellenopolis), Richard Jaeckel (Pfc. F. Flynn), Bill Murphy (Pfc. E. Flynn), George Tyne (Pfc. Harris), Hal Fieberling (Pvt. 'Ski' Choynski), John McGuire (Captain Joyce), Martin Milner (Pvt. Mike McHugh), Leonard Gumley (Pvt. Sid Stein), William Self (Pvt. L. D. Fowler, Jr.), Colonel D. M. Shoup, USMC, Lt-Colonel H. P. Crowe, USMC, Captain Harold G. Shrier, USMC, Rene A. Gagnon, Ira H. Hayes, John H. Bradley (themselves) and over 1,000 U.S. Marines.

During World War II, the tough training that a U.S. Marine sergeant gives a squad of rebellious recruits in New Zealand results in the heroic capture of Iwo Jima.

Dwan's most successful talking picture, and one of his favourites; John Wayne's first nomination for an Academy Award. See pp. 11, 12, 143–148, 145–147, 168.

1950: SURRENDER (Republic).
Director-associate producer: Allan Dwan. Producer: Herbert J. Yates. Scenarists: James Edward Grant, Sloan Nibley, from story by Grant. Photography: Reggie Lanning. Art director: James Sullivan. Set decorators: John McCarthy, Jr., Charles Thompson. Costumes: Adele Palmer. Music: Nathan Scott. Special effects: Howard and Theodore Lydecker. Editor: Richard L. Van Enger. 90 minutes. Released: July 31. With Vera Hruba Ralston (Violet Barton), John Carroll (Gregg Delaney), Walter Brennan (Sheriff William Howard), Francis Lederer (Henry Vaan), William Ching (Johnny Beauregard Hale), Maria Palmer (Janet Barton), Jane Darwell (Mrs Hale), Roy Barcroft (deputy sheriff), Paul Fix (Williams), Esther Dale (Aunt May), Edward Norris (Wilburn), Howland Chamberlin (gambling hall manager), Norman Budd (Carson), Nacho Galindo (Trigo), Jeff York (Canning), Michey Simpson (Pete), Cliff Lyons (Girard).

Period melodrama about a woman who exploits the friendship between her gambler-lover and her wealthy husband. *See pp. 11, 148, 148.*

1951: BELLE LE GRAND (Republic).
Director: Allan Dwan. Producer: Herbert J. Yates. Scenarist: D. D. Beauchamp, from story by Peter B. Kyne. Photography: Reggie Lanning. Art director: James Sullivan. Set decorators: John McCarthy, Jr., George Milo. Costumes: Adele Palmer. Music: Victor Young. Special effects: Howard and Theodore Lydecker. Editor: Harry Keller. 90 minutes. Released: January 27. With John Carroll (Lucky John Kilton), Vera Hruba Ralston (Daisy Henshaw, 'Belle le Grand'), William Ching (Bill Shanks), Muriel Lawrence (Nan Henshaw), Hope Emerson (Emma McGee), Henry Morgan (Abel Stone), John Qualen (Corky McGee), Stephen Chase (Montgomery Crane), Charles Cane (Cal), Marietta Canty (Daisy), Glen Vernon (Groom), Grant Withers (Shannon), Thurston Hall (Parkington).

In Virginia City, a beautiful lady gambler risks a fortune by backing a high-spirited mining engineer. *See pp. 12, 149, 149.*

1951: THE WILD BLUE YONDER (Republic).
Director: Allan Dwan. Producer: Herbert J. Yates. Scenarist: Richard Tregaskis, from story by Andrew Geer, Charles Grayson. Photography: Reggie Lanning. Art director: James Sullivan. Set decorators: John McCarthy, Jr., Charles Thompson. Costumes: Adele Palmer. Music: Victor Young. Songs, 'The U.S. Air Force', by Robert Crawford; 'The Heavy Bomber Song', by Young, Ned Washington; 'The Man Behind the Armor Plated Desk', lyrics by Dwan; 'The Thing', by Charles R. Grean. Special effects: Ellis F. Thackery, Howard and Theodore Lydecker. Editor: Richard L. Van Enger. 98 minutes. Released: December 5. With Wendell Corey (Captain Harold 'Cal' Calvert), Vera Hruba Ralston (Lt. Helen Landers), Forrest Tucker (Major Tom West), Phil Harris (Sgt. Hank Stack), Walter Brennan (Major General Wolfe), Ruth Donnelly (Major Ida Winton), Harry Carey, Jr. (Sgt. Shaker Shucker), Penny Edwards (Sgt. Connie Hudson), Wally Cassell (Sgt. Pulaski), James Brown (Sgt. Pop Davis), William Ching (Lt. Ted Cranshaw), Richard Erdman (Corporal Frenchy), Philip Pine (Sgt. Tony), Martin Kilburn ('Peanuts'), Hal Baylor (Sgt. Eric Nelson), Joe Brown, Jr. (Sgt. O'Hara), Jack Kelly (Lt. Jessup), Bob Beban (Sgt. Barney Killion), Peter Coe (Sgt. Pollio), Hal Bartlett (Lt. Jorman), William Whitney (General Curtis LeMay), David Sharpe (Sgt. 'Red' Erwin).

A story about the famous B-29 of World War II and the men who flew one of them. (Released in Great Britain as *Thunder Across the Pacific*.) *See pp. 11, 149–150, 149.*

1952: I DREAM OF JEANIE (WITH THE LIGHT BROWN HAIR) (Republic).
Director: Allan Dwan. Producer: Herbert J. Yates. Writer: Alan LeMay, inspired by the life of Stephen Foster. Photography (in Trucolor): Reggie Lanning. Art director: Frank Hotaling. Set decorators: John McCarthy, Jr., James Redd. Costumes: Adele Palmer. Songs by Stephen Foster: 'My Old Kentucky Home', 'Old Folks at Home', 'Oh Suzanna', 'Old Dog Tray', 'Ring de Banjo', 'Campton Races', 'Jeanie', 'Come Where My Love Lies Dreaming'; with lyrics by Dwan: 'A Ribbon in Your Hair', 'I See Her Still in My Dreams', 'Head Over Heels'; 'On Wings of Song' by Mendelssohn; arranger: Robert Armbruster. Choreography: Nick Castle. Special effects: Howard and Theodore Lydecker. Editor: Fred Allen. 90 minutes. Released: June 15. With Ray Middleton (Edwin P. Christy), Bill Shirley (Stephen Foster), Muriel Lawrence (Inez McDowell), Eileen Christy (Jeanie McDowell), Lynn Bari (Mrs McDowell), Richard Simmons (Dunning Foster), Robert Neil (Milford Wilson), Andrew Tombes (R. E. Howard), James Dobson (Spike), Percy Helton (Mr Horker), Glenn Turnbull (dancer), Louise Beavers (Mammy), James Kirkwood (doctor), Carl Dean 'Alfalfa' Switzer (Freddie), Freddie Moultrie (Chitlins), Rex Allen (Commentator Mister Tambo).

A fictionalised biography of nineteenth-century

composer Stephen Foster. *Dwan's first all-colour film. See pp.* 11, 150, *150.*

Republic loaned Dwan to Howard Hughes for one picture:

1952: MONTANA BELLE (RKO Radio).
Director: Allan Dwan. Producer: Howard Welsch. Associate producer: Robert Peters. Scenarists: Horace McCoy, Norman S. Hall, from story by M. Coates Webster, Welsch. Photography (in Trucolor): Jack Marta. Art director: Frank Arrigo. Set decorators: John McCarthy, Jr., George Milo. Costumes: Adele Palmer. Music: Nathan Scott. Song, 'The Gilded Lily', by Portia Nelson, Margaret Martinez. Special effects: Howard and Theodore Lydecker. 82 minutes. Released: November 11.
With Jane Russell (Belle Starr), George Brent (Tom Bradfield), Scott Brady (Bob Dalton), Forrest Tucker (Mac), Andy Devine (Pete Bivins), Jack Lambert (Ringo), Ray Teal (Emmett Dalton), Rory Mallinson (Gary), Roy Barcroft (Jim Clark), John Litel (boarder), Ned Davenport (bank teller), Dick Elliot (Rideout), Eugene Roth (Ripple), Stanley Andrews (Combo), Holly Bane (Ben).
Western fiction about the notorious Belle Starr who sang in saloons and robbed banks. *See pp.* 12, *151.*

1953: WOMAN THEY ALMOST LYNCHED (Republic).
Director: Allan Dwan. Scenarist: Steve Fisher, from story by Michael Fessier. Photography: Reggie Lanning. Art director: James Sullivan. Set decorators: John McCarthy, Jr., George Milo. Costumes: Adele Palmer. Music: Stanley Wilson. Songs, 'How Strange', by Victor Young, Peggy Lee, 'All My Life', by Sidney Mitchell, Sam Stept. Special effects: Howard and Theodore Lydecker. Editor: Fred Allen. 90 minutes. Released: March 20.
With John Lund (Lance Horton), Brian Donlevy (Charles Quantrill), Audrey Totter (Kate McCoy Quantrill), Joan Leslie (Sally Maris), Ben Cooper (Jesse James), James Brown (Frank James), Nina Varela (Delilah Courtney), Ellen Corby, Fern Hall (townswomen), Minerva Urecal (Mrs Stuart), Jim Davis (Cole Younger), Reed Hadley (Bitter-root Bill Maris), Ann Savage (Glenda), Virginia Christine (Jenny), Marilyn Lindsay (Rose), Nacho Galindo (John Pablo), Richard Simmons (captain), Gordon Jones (sergeant), Frank Ferguson (barman), Post Park (stage driver), Tom McDonough (one of Quantrill's men), Ted Ryan (soldier), Richard Crane (lieutenant), Carl Pitti (Bourreau), Joe Yrigoyen (guard), Jimmie Hawkins (tramp), James Kirkwood (old man), Paul Livermore (Bill

Anderson), Hal Baylor (Zeb).
A city girl inherits a saloon in a town controlled by a gun moll. *See pp.* 12, 151–153, *152, 153.*

1953: SWEETHEARTS ON PARADE (Republic).
Director-associate producer: Allan Dwan. Writer: Houston Branch. Photography (in Trucolor): Reggie Lanning. Art director: James Sullivan. Set decorators: John McCarthy, Jr., James Redd. Costumes: Adele Palmer. Music: Robert Armbruster. Choreography: Nick Castle. Special effects: Howard and Theodore Lydecker. Editor: Fred Allen. 90 minutes. Released: July 15.
With Ray Middleton (Cam Ellerby), Lucille Norman (Kathleen Townsend), Eileen Christy (Sylvia Townsend), Bill Shirley (Bill Gamble), Estelita (Lolita Lamont), Clinton Sundberg (Dr Harold Wayne), Harry Carey, Jr. (Jim Riley), Irving Bacon (Sheriff Doolittle), Leon Tyler (Tommy Wayne), Marjorie Wood (dressmaker), Mara Corday (Belle), Ann McCrea (Flo), Tex Terry (Zebe), Emory Parnell (mayor), Muriel Lawrence (teacher).
Period musical-romance about a music teacher whose ex-husband returns to town as the head of a carnival show. *See pp.* 12, *152, 153.*

1954: FLIGHT NURSE (Republic).
Director: Allan Dwan. Producer: Herbert J. Yates. Writer: Alan LeMay. Photography: Reggie Lanning. Art director: James Sullivan. Set decorators: John McCarthy, Jr., Charles Thompson. Costumes: Adele Palmer. Music: Victor Young. Songs, 'The Nurse's Prayer', by Edith A. Ayne, 'Gimme My Shute' ('Blue Tail Fly') and 'Mushi-Mushi', lyrics by Dwan. Special effects: Ellis F. Thackery, Howard and Theodore Lydecker. Editor: Fred Allen. 90 minutes. Released: March 1.
With Joan Leslie (Lt. Polly Davis), Forrest Tucker (Captain Bill Eaton), Arthur Franz (Captain Mike Barns), Jeff Donnell (Lt. Ann Phillips), Ben Cooper (Pfc. Marvin Judd), James Holden (Sgt. Franz Swan), Kristine Miller (Lt. Kit Ramsey), Maria Palmer (Captain Martha Ackerman), Richard Simmons (Lt. Tommy Metcalf), James Brown (pilot), Hal Baylor (Sgt. Jimmy Case), Thomas Browne Henry (officer), Morris Ankrum (officer), Gene Collins (wounded soldier), Harry Lauter (soldier), Sumner Williams (psycho).
An Air Force Flight Nurse renounces her love in order to stay on duty in Korea. *Dwan's last film for Republic. See pp.* 11, *155.*

1954: SILVER LODE (RKO Radio).
Director: Allan Dwan. Producer: Benedict Bogeaus. Executive producer: Leon Chool;uck. Writer: Karen De

Wolfe. Photography (in Technicolor): John Alton. Art director: Van Nest Polglase. Set decorator: Charles Thompson. Costumes: Gwen Wakeling. Music: Louis Forbes. Editor: James Leicester. 80 minutes. Released: June.

With John Payne (Dan Ballard), Dan Duryea (Ned McCarthy), Lizabeth Scott (Rose Evans), Dolores Moran (Dolly), Emile Meyer (Sheriff Wooley), Harry Carey, Jr. (Johnson), Morris Ankrum (Zachery Evans), John Hudson (Michael 'Mitch' Evans), Robert Warwick (Judge Cranston), Stuart Whitman (Wickers), Alan Hale, Jr. (Kirk), Frank Sully (Paul Herbert), Paul Birch (Reverend Field), Florence Auer (Mrs Elmwood), Roy Gordon (Dr Elmwood), Edgar Barrier (Taylor), John Dierkes, Myron Healey.

Accused of murder on his wedding day, a Westerner becomes the object of a manhunt as he tries to clear himself. *The first of ten films Dwan made with producer Ben Bogeaus. See pp. 13, 154–157, 154, 156.*

1954: PASSION (RKO Radio).

Director: Allan Dwan. Producer: Benedict Bogeaus. Scenarists: Joseph Leytes, Beatrice A. Dresher, Howard Estabrook, from story by Leytes, Dresher and Miguel Padilla. Photography: John Alton. Art director: Van Nest Polglase. Set decorator: John Sturtevant. Costumes: Gwen Wakeling. Music: Louis Forbes. Editor: Carlos Lodato. 84 minutes. Released: October 6.

With Cornel Wilde (Juan Obregon), Yvonne De Carlo (Rosa Melo/Tonya Melo), Rodolfo Acosta (Salvador Sandro), Raymond Burr (Captain Rodriguez), Lon Chaney, Jr. (Castro), John Qualen (Gaspar Melo), Anthony Caruso (Sgt. Munoz), Frank De Kova (Martinez), Peter Coe (Colfre), John Dierkes (Escobar), Richard Hale (Don Domingo), Rozene Kemper (Senora Melo), Rosa Turich (Mrs Carrisa), Stuart Whitman (vaquero), James Kirkwood (Don Rosendo), Robert Warwick (money lender), Belle Mitchell, Alex Montoya, Zon Murray.

In California's pioneer days, a young vaquero seeks revenge against the men who murdered his family and stole their land. *See pp. 157, 157.*

1954: CATTLE QUEEN OF MONTANA (RKO Radio).

Director: Allan Dwan. Producer: Benedict Bogeaus. Scenarists: Robert Blees, Howard Estabrook, from story by Thomas Blackburn. Photography (in Technicolor): John Alton. Art director: Van Nest Polglase. Set decorator: John Sturtevant. Costumes: Gwen Wakeling. Music: Louis Forbes. Editor: Carlos Lodato. Exterior locations at Glacier National Park, Montana. 88 minutes. Released: November 18.

With Barbara Stanwyck (Sierra Nevada Jones), Ronald Reagan (Farrell), Gene Evans (Tom McCord), Lance Fuller (Colorados), Anthony Caruso (Nachakos), Jack Elam (Yost), Yvette Dugay (Starfire), Morris Ankrum (J. I. 'Pop' Jones), Chubby Johnson (Nat), Myron Healey (Hank), Rodd Redwing (Powhani), Paul Birch (Colonel Carrington), Byron K. Foulger (Land Office employee), Burt Mustin (Dan), Roy Gordon.

After a man is killed for his lands, his daughter fights to hold the property. *See pp. 12, 157–158, 158.*

1955: IT'S ALWAYS SUNDAY (Hal Roach Studios; episode for the *Screen Director's Playhouse* television series).

Director: Allan Dwan. Scenarist: D. D. Beauchamp, from story by Jesse Goldstein, Frank Fox. Photography: Ed DuPar. Art director: William Ferrari. Editor: Bert Jordan. 29 minutes. First broadcast: March 28.

With Dennis O'Keefe (Reverend Parker), Sheldon Leonard (George), Fay Wray (Mary Parker), Chick Chandler (Eddie), Grant Withers (William Brackett, Sr.), Eilene Janssen (Nancy Parker), Robert Easton (Stanley Moran), Terry Rangno (Danny Parker), Diane Jergens (Sue Stradler), Jimmy Hayes (Bill Brackett, Jr.).

Mayhem results when a minister good-heartedly loans his friend's car to two men he's never seen before. *The first of two films Dwan directed for television. See p. 162.*

1955: ESCAPE TO BURMA (RKO Radio).

Director: Allan Dwan. Producer: Benedict Bogeaus. Scenarists: Talbot Jennings, Hobart Donevan, from story, 'Bow Tamely to Me', by Kenneth Perkins. Photography (in Superscope and Technicolor): John Alton. Art director: Van Nest Polglase. Set decorator: Fay Babcock. Costumes: Gwen Wakeling, Lucille Sothern. Music: Louis Forbes. Special effects: Lee Zavitz. Editor: James Leicester. 87 minutes. Released: April 9.

With Robert Ryan (Jim Brecan), Barbara Stanwyck (Gwen Moore), David Farrar (Cardigan), Murvyn Vye (Mekash), Robert Warwick (Sawbwa), Reginald Denny (commissioner), Lisa Montell (Andora), Peter Coe (guard captain), Anthony Numkena (Kasha), Alex Montoya (Dacoit), Robert Cabal (Kumat), Lal Chand Mehra (Pookan), William Benegal Raw (young horn player), John Mansfield (sergeant), Gavin Muir (astrologer), Pete Kooy, Bob Corby, Little Babe, Tessie, Marg, Mary, Judy (elephants), Neil (chimpanzee), Roger (leopard).

On a Burma plantation, an English girl faces native superstition and the danger of a 'wanted' stranger. *Dwan's first wide-screen film. See pp. 12, 159.*

1955: PEARL OF THE SOUTH PACIFIC (RKO Radio).
Director: Allan Dwan. Producer: Benedict Bogeaus. Scenarists: Jesse Lasky, Jr., Talbot Jennings, Richard Landau, from story by Ann Hunger. Photography (in Superscope and Technicolor): John Alton. Art director: Van Nest Polglase. Music: Louis Forbes. Editor: James Leicester. Exteriors filmed in Tahiti and at Malibu Beach. 85 minutes. Released: July 4.
With Virginia Mayo (Rita Delaine), Dennis Morgan (Dan Merrill), David Farrar (Bully Hayes), Murvyn Vye (Halemano), Lance Fuller (George), Basil Ruysdael (Michael), Lisa Montell (Momu).

Greedy for pearls, three adventurers destroy a peaceful South Sea island. *See pp. 158–160, 159.*

1955: TENNESSEE'S PARTNER (RKO Radio).
Director: Allan Dwan. Producer: Benedict Bogeaus. Scenarists: Dwan, Milton Krims, D. D. Beauchamp, Graham Baker, Teddy Sherman, from story by Bret Harte. Photography (in Superscope and Technicolor): John Alton. Art director: Van Nest Polglase. Set decorator: Alfred Spencer. Costumes: Gwen Wakeling. Music: Louis Forbes; song, 'Heart of Gold', lyrics by Dave Franklin. Editor: James Leicester. 87 minutes. Released: September 21.
With John Payne (Tennessee), Rhonda Fleming (Elizabeth 'Duchess' Farnham), Ronald Reagan (Cowpoke), Coleen Gray (Goldie Slater), Anthony Caruso (Turner), Leo Gordon (sheriff), Myron Healey (Reynolds), Morris Ankrum (Judge), Chubby Johnson (Grubstake McNiven), Joe Devlin (Prendergast), John Mansfield (Clifford), Angie Dickinson.

A gambling queen, a gambler and an innocent cowpoke are all involved in a shooting and a double-cross. *Dwan's favourite among his films for Bogeaus and RKO. See pp. 13, 160–162, 160, 161.*

1956: SLIGHTLY SCARLET (RKO Radio).
Director: Allan Dwan. Producer: Benedict Bogeaus. Scenarist: Robert Blees, from novel, 'Love's Lovely Counterfeit', by James M. Cain. Photography (in Superscope and Technicolor): John Alton. Art director: Van Nest Polglase. Set decorator: Alfred Spencer. Costumes: Norma Koch, Arlene Dahl (for her strip costume). Music: Louis Forbes. Editor: James Leicester. 99 minutes. Released: February 8.
With John Payne (Ben Grace), Rhonda Fleming (June Lyons), Arlene Dahl (Dorothy Lyons), Ted De Corsia (Sol Caspar), Kent Taylor (Frank Jansen), Lance Fuller (Gauss), Ellen Corby (Martha), Buddy Baer (Lenhardt), Myron Healey (Williams), Frank Gerstle (Dave Dietz), Roy Gordon (Norman Marlowe), Thayer Roberts (Ames), Gloria Victor (Marlowe's secretary), George E. Stone (gangster).

An ambitious gang leader tries to take over the city government by double-crossing a pal. *See pp. 12–13, 163–164, 162–164.*

1956: HOLD BACK THE NIGHT (Allied Artists).
Director: Allan Dwan. Producer: Hayes Goetz. Scenarists: John C. Higgins, Walter Doniger, from novel by Pat Frank. Photography: Ellsworth Fredericks. Art director: Hilyard Brown. Set decorator: Joseph Kish. Music: Hans J. Salter. Editor: Robert S. Eisen. 75 minutes. Released: July 29.
With John Payne (Sam MacKenzie), Mona Freeman (Anne Franklin), Peter Graves (Lt. Lee Couzens), Chuck Connors (Sgt. Eklund), Audrey Dalton (Kitty), Bob Nichols (Beany Smith), John Wilder (Tinker), Stanley Chah (Kato), Nick Blair (Papiro), Nelson Leigh (Roomey), John Craven (MacKay), Robert Easton Burke (Ackerman).

During the Korean War, a Marine Captain tells his men the story behind an unopened bottle of Scotch he always carries with him. *See pp. 12, 162.*

1956: HIGH AIR (Hal Roach Studios; episode for the *Screen Director's Playhouse* television series).
Director: Allan Dwan. Scenarist: A. I. Bezzerides, from story by Borden Chase. Photography: Jack MacKenzie. Art director: William Ferrari. Set decorator: Rudy Butler. 29 minutes. First broadcast: September.
With William Bendix (Joe Redman), Dennis Hopper (Steve Redman), John Alderson ('Swede'), Leo Gordon (Tom Martin), Hal Taylor (man with bends), William Doty, Don Kennedy, Mike Ragan, John Mitchum, Duane Thorson (sandhoggers).

An underwater construction worker is believed lost in a cave-in beneath the Hudson River.

1957: THE RIVER'S EDGE (20th Century-Fox).
Director: Allan Dwan. Producer: Benedict Bogeaus. Scenarists: Harold Jacob Smith, James Leicester, from story, 'The Highest Mountain', by Smith. Photography (in CinemaScope and DeLuxe Color): Harold Lipstein. Art director: Van Nest Polglase. Costumes: Gwen Wakeling. Music: Louis Forbes. Song, 'The River's Edge', by Leicester, Bobby Troup, sung by Bob Winn. Special effects: Lee Zavitz. Editor: Leicester. Exteriors filmed in Mexico at Ameca-Ameca, Lake Tehuantepec, Gorge of the Gods, Sleeping Lady Mountain. 87 minutes. Released: April.
With Ray Milland (Nardo Denning), Anthony Quinn (Ben Cameron), Debra Paget (Meg Cameron), Harry Carey, Jr. (Chet), Chubby Johnson (Pop Whiskers), Byron K. Foulger (Barry), Tom McKee (customs officer), Frank Gerstle (Harry Castleton, customs officer).

Trying to cross the Mexican border with stolen money,

an unscrupulous con man enlists the help of an innocent rancher who is married to a former girlfriend. *See pp.* 13, 164, *165.*

1957: THE RESTLESS BREED
(Alperson Productions-20th Century-Fox).
Director: Allan Dwan. Producer: Edward L. Alperson. Executive producer: Richard Einfield. Writer: Steve Fisher. Photography (in Widevision and Eastmancolor): John W. Boyle. Art director: Ernest Fegte. Set decorator: Howard Bristol. Music: Edward L. Alperson, Jr.; songs, 'Angelita', 'Never Alone', with lyrics by Dick Hughes, Richard Stapley. Choreography: Miriam Nelson. Special effects: Jack Cosgrove. Editor: Merrill G. White. 81 minutes. Released: May.
With Scott Brady (Mitch Baker), Anne Bancroft (Angelita), Jay C. Flippen (Marshal Steve Evans), Jim Davis (Ed Newton), Leo Gordon (Cherokee), Rhys Williams (Reverend Simmons), Myron Healey (Sheriff Mike Williams), Scott Marlowe (James Allan), Eddy C. Waller (Caeser), Harry Cheshire (Mayor Johnson), Gerald Milton (Jim Daly, barman), Dennis King, Jr. (receptionist), James Flavin (federal agent), Billy Miller (Ogna), Marilyn Winston (Banee), Evelyn Rudie (Kehta), Clegg Hoyt (Spud), Marty Cariosa (Tohna), Joe Devlin (Morton), Fred Graham.

In a small Western town, the son of a secret service agent seeks to avenge his father's murder. *See pp.* 12, 164–166.

1958: ENCHANTED ISLAND (RKO Radio-Warner Bros.).
Director: Allan Dwan. Producer: Benedict Bogeaus. Scenarists: James Leicester, Harold Jacob Smith, from the novel, 'Typee', by Herman Melville. Photography (in Technicolor): George Stahl. Art director: Hal Wilson Cox. Music: Raul Lavista. Special effects: Albert M. Simpson. Editor: Albert E. Valenzuela. Filmed in Mexico. 87 minutes. Released: November.
With Dana Andrews (Abner Bedford), Jane Powell (Fayaway), Don Dubbins (Tom), Frederick Ledebur (Mehevi), Ted De Corsia (Captain Vange), Arthur Shields (Jimmy Dooley), Less Hellman (Mrs Moore), Francisco Reiguera (sorcerer), Carlos Leon (fisherman), Augustin Fernandez (Kory-Kory), Eddie Saenz, Dale Van Sickle, Paul Stader.

Period adventure-romance in which the men from an American whaling ship clash with headhunters on a South Sea island. *See pp.* 12, 166, *166.*

1959: *Will You Marry Me?* (unrealised project).
Comedy, owned by Bogeaus and set in Rhode Island, from which Dwan fashioned a screenplay; the producer could not get it financed.

1960: *The Bridge of San Luis Rey* (Unrealised project).
Dwan helped Bogeaus prepare a re-make of the Thornton Wilder novel Bogeaus had produced in 1944. Abandoned when Dwan discovered Bogeaus didn't own the property any longer.

1960: *The Glass Wall* (unrealised project).
A drama about insanity which Dwan also prepared for Bogeaus, with the same results as *Will You Marry Me?*

1961: MOST DANGEROUS MAN ALIVE
(Columbia).
Director: Allan Dwan. Producer: Benedict Bogeaus. Scenarists: James Leicester, Phillip Rock, from 'The Steel Monster' by Rock, Michael Pate. Photography: Carl Carvahal. Costumes: Gwen Wakeling. Music: Louis Forbes. Editor: Carlos Lodato. Filmed entirely in Mexico. 82 minutes. Released: June.
With Ron Randall (Eddie Candell), Debra Paget (Linda Marlow), Elaine Stewart (Carla Angelo), Anthony Caruso (Andy Damon), Gregg Palmer (Lt. Fisher), Morris Ankrum (Captain Davis), Tudor Owen (Dr Meeker), Steve Mitchell (Devola), Joel Donte (Franscetti), Jay Novello (policeman).

An ex-convict survives a cobalt bomb explosion, but discovers his body is turning to steel. *Shot and completed independently in 1958, the film was sold to Columbia, which did not release it until three years later. See p. 167.*

1967: *Marine!* (unrealised project).
A film adaptation by Harry Brown of the biography of General 'Chesty' Puller and his Korean campaign, to have been directed by Dwan for Warner Bros. Abandoned when Jack Warner sold the studio. *See p. 167.*